Table of Contents

Dedication

This book is dedicated to my wonderful wife, Addie, who lived all of these stories with me. She is the love of my life and one of the greatest missionaries that God has ever called. To our children, Guy (Rusty), Greg, Candy, and Tim I dedicate these stories for their loving support and sharing their Mom and Dad with the people of Perú.

Acknowledgements

THE AMAZON CALL takes us on a journey to the majestic rain forest of the Amazon. We meet the people who taught us a lot about ourselves. The Aguarunas became a part of our family and we of theirs. We have been blest by a loving family, church, and so many friends who prayed, supported, and encouraged us along the way. Many Work and Witness teams helped change our world forever.

I am indebted to Ellen Bustle for proofreading these stories. She was a great encouragement to me, even though she was enduring cancer treatments. She and her husband, Louie Bustle, have been incredible supporters of our missionary endeavors.

My thanks go to Rick Guilfoil and Dust Jacket Publishing for putting this project together. They have spent countless hours in preparing this book for publication.

I trust that these stories will glorify the Lord Jesus who gave us the call, supplied our needs, protected us, and built His church just like He said He would.

– *Larry Garman*

Foreword

No one has given of themselves more than Larry and Addie Garman, making sacrifices beyond most missionaries. When we worked in South America, we referred to them as the 'real' missionaries. I have been on the river with them at the end of nowhere. It would be a challenge to move your family there and live without many conveniences. When they first went there, they found only a piece of ground and a couple of buildings. They stayed and lived among a people, loving them into the Kingdom!

The Garmans are lay people who answered the call of God to go where few would go and spend a lifetime. It was the call of God that held them steady. They would drive their car to the end of the road, get into a boat, and ride for hours to their home. They would stay for several months at a time before going back for supplies.

Dr. Garman did his medical training as a chiropractor and had a private practice for two years before going to the field. He also graduated from the Biola School of Missionary Medicine with special studies in Tropical Medicine, Pharmacology, and Dentistry, working an additional time with an oral surgeon. He became the expert in the area on snakebite treatments. The Nazarene Clinic that Dr. Garman established was fully recognized as a Public Health Clinic in Perú and was registered with the government. To achieve this status was no small feat.

"Doc" trained many of the Bible School students to be nurses as well as pastors so that they could treat diseases and dispense medicines. Each day while they were at the Bible Institute, the students had a class in public health, and those who had the aptitude would be trained further in afternoon clinic times. This is an excellent example of evangelism and compassionate ministries working hand in hand.

This book is a compilation of short stories. You will read moving stories of thrill, danger, and the power of God in this book that will make it hard to put down. The Holy Spirit will grip your heart as you experience the Garman's passion and burden for lost people. If you have been one of the fortunate ones, you have heard some of these personally from Larry…either in a church service setting or sitting in his living room in the jungle. He did have a habit of stopping the story at a tense part and saying it was time to go to bed. Then he would turn the generator off and leave us in the dark. Our children would beg for the ending of the story. It would be finished the next night…or maybe never.

Dr. Louie E. Bustle
Retired Director of Global Mission
Church of the Nazarene

A Tribute To
Dr. And Mrs. Larry Garman

The sheer magnitude of being God-called missionaries to people in a remote, dangerous jungle area has been, historically, the most daunting of all callings! To such a region – the jungle of the Amazon – and its people, the Lord of the Harvest summoned Larry and Addie Garman in 1964. Here they faithfully and effectively served for 45 years.

This humble couple has written one of the most remarkable and inspirational mission stories of the modern era. Few people have made such a Christ-difference in the lives of so many, particularly in a primitive culture deeply embedded in nature worship, superstition, and witchcraft. It was not easy. They went with a poignant sense of divine urging, but also with the normal human trepidations, especially with their young children. The early years were testing times with meager visible results. Slowly, the Spirit began to move and ultimately a spiritual movement was ignited. It spread like wildfire throughout the villages up and down the mighty Marañon River. Conversions to Christ numbered in the thousands with most of them becoming members of the Church of the Nazarene. In recent years the Aguarunas themselves have been passionately evangelizing other tribes throughout Amazonia.

The secret to the success of this couple may be stated simply: enabled by the Spirit, they enfleshed the life of Jesus among the people of the jungle. One of my cherished friends spent some time with the Garmans in their jungle home. He later said to me, "To travel with Larry up and down the river and watch him interact with the people in the villages was the nearest thing to Jesus-in-the-flesh that I have seen in my lifetime." Such holy living opened the hearts of the Aguarunas to the liberating gospel message that gloriously transformed their lives.

In this book, the Garmans share personal stories from their long years of service to our Lord and His people of Amazonia. It is great reading! Along with chuckles and tears, it will bring new excitement and challenge to the reader about our denominational mission to "Make Christlike disciples in the nations."

Dr. Jim L. Bond
General Superintendent Emeritus
Church of the Nazarene

Whatever It Takes

Looking out through the clinic window, I noticed the dugout canoe rapidly approaching our small port on the Kusu River. I watched as the man placed his paddle aside and leaped from the frail craft, plunging a long round cane pole into the soft mud. He tied the canoe to the pole with a stout thick vine that held it steady. Then he gently lifted a young child from the floor of the canoe and hurriedly climbed the hill. Concern from the floor of the canoe was etched heavily on his bronzed complexion. Excitedly, he informed me of his son's condition: severe abdominal distress, loss of appetite, and fatigue.

Upon examination, diagnosis was made of intestinal parasitical infestation, with accompanying low-grade anemia. I prescribed medication and explained to the father the course of treatment. I was about to dismiss them from the clinic, when the father spoke in very sad tones. "I am afraid," he stated, "that my son will die, because a year ago we lost a son with a similar condition." I noticed the pained look in his eyes and tried to console and reassure him that his son would be fine.

"Give him the medication and bring him back in a day or two," I repeated. I watched as they descended the hill and entered their dugout canoe to begin their journey home. My heart was saddened for this man's loss and also the seeming lack of faith in my diagnosis. I turned my attention back to the work at hand in our clinic, hoping that the day would come when the Indians completely trusted me. It had been a long battle for me, knowing that their fears and superstitions often overrode our better judgment.

Once more I looked toward the river, and what I saw startled me. Quickly I turned to my helper, Moisés, for an explanation. The dugout canoe was not heading upriver towards the village where they lived, but was moving rapidly up the Kusu River in the opposite direction from their home. Moisés, searching for words, explained to me that they were going to the home of the witchdoctor for treatment of the young boy.

"But they have the medicine and I told the father that his son will be okay," I stammered. He countered with the fact that many came to the clinic and then went to the witchdoctor.

My heart was heavy and I thought to myself, 'What can we do to help them understand?' In desperation I said to Moisés, "I would like to visit the witchdoctor tonight, is that possible?"

Moisés answered, "Yes, but we will have to go after dark, for the witchdoctor only works at night. During the day he takes toe` (baikua, a hallucinating drug), to have good visions from the spirit world to heal his patients. I will be back later to take you to Chimpa's hut this evening," Moisés said, as he turned towards home, leaving me with my thoughts.

It was a beautiful afternoon as the children and I bathed in the river and then went to the house for supper. We had settled in that evening, relaxing in our tiny living room, enjoying the family, but when I looked out through the screened window, I saw a light bobbing up and down approaching our home.

It was Moisés, and he called out to me, "Doctoroooooo," throwing his voice like the Indians do when calling someone to meet them. "I am ready to go to Chimpa's hut," he called.

'Oh, no, he remembered', I thought to myself, looking out into a very dark jungle night. We exchanged greetings and then I said to Moisés, "Let's go another night, after all they do not know we are coming and they might be offended by our unannounced intrusion."

He responded by saying, "The boat is ready and there will be no problem going unannounced to the witchdoctor's hut deep in the forest."

Reluctantly I said goodbye to my wife and children and followed Moisés to the port with my flashlight in hand. We began paddling upstream along the river's edge where the current was the weakest. Looking back over my shoulder, I could see the lights of our little house situated in the middle of this huge expanse of jungle isolated by time and distance. In the background, the old diesel motor droned on, providing electricity for this lighthouse in the middle of nowhere. I was leaving the comfortable and familiar to enter the unknown, and fear tugged at my heart.

A few more strokes of the paddles took us around a bend in the river, and all of a sudden we were engulfed by an inky blackness. A very faint moon tried desperately to break through the heavy clouds overhead, casting eerie shadows on the water. I could no longer see the lights of home, or hear the monotonous sounds of the diesel generator that provided a certain sense of security. I only heard the splashing of our paddles and the gentle lapping of water on the sides of the boat.

Slowly we moved along upriver, the quietness broken only by the sounds of the rain forest at night. Animal sounds could be heard in the canopy as predators roamed, searching for their prey.

I was absorbed by the steady sound of paddles dipping into the water and the mechanical motion of our boat gliding along with no resistance. My mind was racing with vivid imaginations of what lay before us this night. The air was still and humid as I cradled the paddle in my arms before stroking the water again. Moisés broke the silence and, pointing toward the shore up ahead, stated, "There is the port of Chimpa, the witchdoctor. Look at all the dugout canoes tied along the bank. Yes, there are many people here tonight for this encounter with the shaman."

Our boat smoothly nudged its way into the nest of canoes and came to a gentle stop at the edge of the mud bank. Moisés stepped out onto the shore and began tying the rope to a small tree at the edge of the river. I stepped ashore with my flashlight focusing on a small muddy trail that led from the port to the hut of Chimpa some distance away. "Let's go," he said, and led the way along the tiny path that would soon take us to our destination.

Surrounded by darkness and gripped with fear, I said to Moisés, "Maybe we shouldn't go unannounced, they might resent our visit. Let's go home."

"No," he replied, "We don't have far to walk." He took off, leaving me by myself in the still of night. Not wanting to be left behind, I quickly followed his fleeting shadow, my flashlight doing 360-degree circles to make sure there were no snakes on the trail. The path was very muddy and overgrown, with low vines reaching out for my face, neck, and upper body, rapidly getting my attention. Rounding a sharp bend in the trail I could hear the chant of the witchdoctor in the dark distance. "Wi jai, jai, jai, jai, wika senchi."

The adrenalin coursed through my veins, the hair stood straight up on the back of my neck and arms and I wondered, 'What am I doing out here?'

Again I pleaded with Moisés to turn back, but he only said, "We are almost there and I will call out to them to announce our arrival." On we trudged through the forest, as the chanting was drawing closer and becoming louder. Up ahead I could see the faint outline of a thatched roof hut under a very pale moon that desperately tried to break through the heavy clouds. Shafts of orange yellowish light penetrated through the bamboo poles forming the walls of this hut set back deep in the forest.

Moisés stopped and called to the occupants of the home. "Yatsaju Chimpa, pujamek?" *(Friend Chimpa, are you there?)* I tensed there in the darkness, uncertain of our presence in this environment of spiritual warfare. 'How would we be received?' I pondered. I felt very alone and isolated from my comfort zone.

My thoughts were interrupted by the reply from within the hut. "Eh eh, yatsuju pujajai, yaitpu" *(Yes, I'm here, who's there)*? Moisés explained that it was the doctor.

"Okay, friend, come in and sit down." We entered the hut, ducking through the doorway of upright poles tilted at a slight angle to allow us entrance. Once inside, my eyes adjusted to the dim light provided by the glowing embers of a three-logged fire on the floor near the distant wall, and a wick lamp giving off a smoky orange yellowish light.

Surveying my surroundings, I noticed the young boy I had treated earlier in the day, lying on a thin bamboo mat in the middle of the room. His frail body was motionless, eyes transfixed and nearly hypnotic as one witchdoctor, sitting on a small hand carved stool, made sucking sounds on the boy's abdomen. Another witchdoctor was chanting loudly, encouraging the one treating the boy. A grandfather of the child was off to one side, preparing tobacco leaves over the coals of the fire and shouting encouraging words to the witchdoctor who was bent over the boy.

Scattered around the hut were concerned family members whose faces I could barely make out in the semi-darkness. The silence was broken by a terrifying cry from the witchdoctor, lifting his mouth from the boy's abdomen. His long back hair shot back over his shoulders, while jerking his head to one side with a painful agonizing expression on his face. He immediately spit onto the dirt floor, exercising the belief that he had extracted the disease that was causing the boy's infirmity.

The grandfather was waiting for this dramatic moment, and he quickly brought the tobacco leaves from the fire and handed them to the witchdoctor who then purified his mouth with tobacco smoke so that he would not be contaminated with the same mysterious disease.

I marveled at the powerful impact this dramatic scene had on the family members. There was the immense feeling of relief and the knowledge that the boy would be delivered from this sickness. I was deeply aware of the tremendous impact that witchcraft held over their lives.

With a heavy heart, we excused ourselves that night after telling each one our goodbyes. We walked in silence back down the trail to the boat. The night was seemingly darker yet and my mind was weighed down by thoughts of the incredible chains of witchcraft that had bound a people for centuries.

The trip home was one that immersed me in loneliness and sadness as I thought about Jesus sending us to help bring them from darkness to light, and from the power of Satan to God.

Our boat rounded the last bend in that serpentine river, and in the distance I could see the lights of our home and hear again the throbbing of the old diesel motor breaking the eternal sounds of the rain forest.

I struggled with deep-seated emotions that night, wishing for the possibility of erasing the depressing scenes of the witchdoctor's hut and escaping into the confines of our comfortable home with my family, thus blotting out the memory of the last few hours.

As I glided into the port, my mind took me back a few years and across a long trail that had led me to a very important landmark in my missionary career.

High on a steep hill, overlooking the great Marañon River below, I found the graveside of a famous pioneer missionary, Esther Carson Winans, who in 1928 laid down her life for these people. I read the inscription on her headstone, "Though she be dead, yet she speaks." I remembered kneeling that day and committing my life and service to the Lord.

Esther came to Perú in 1917, later married Roger Winans, and together they made the two-week trip by mules across the mountains to the remote, sleepy little village of Pomara, where they began work among the Aguaruna Indians. Her body had been racked by bouts of malaria, and after giving birth to a baby girl, she slipped away to be with Jesus. Just before her death, she said some very prophetic words. "It looks as though we have come to sow, so that those who come later might reap." She died, never seeing the harvest, and now it was up to others.

Before our boat struck the shore, I said a prayer. "Lord, I want you to know that whatever it costs, we are willing to pay the price if you will bring these precious people to yourself." God honored that commitment and began to build His church as He said He would. To God be the glory, for great things He has done.

Crisis

His cold black eyes darted from me to the intravenous tubing that hung loosely from a bottle of plasma that was attached to a nail on the wall of our small clinic located in the middle of the rain forest. This was his first experience inside a clinical facility, and his first encounter with someone of my skin color.

Long black hair, cut in bangs across the forehead, floated smoothly over his broad shoulders. Blue-circled tattoo markings were etched over the prominent cheekbones of his bronzed face. The facial features were strong, but portrayed fear and uncertainty. His clothes betrayed the fact that he lived deep in the jungle, as they were threadbare and patched. Strong large feet, calloused by time and endless trails, caught my attention as I glanced at the thin, frail lady lying on my examining table next to where he stood, motionless.

Earlier that morning they had arrived at the door of our clinic. Approaching the clinic, I saw the two men hovering over a bamboo stretcher, anxiously awaiting my arrival. When I began examining his wife, he informed me that they had come from a great distance. He pointed to the low-lying hills that gently arose from different heights past the village of Kusu in the distance.

They had forged streams and walked numerous hours, finally arriving at our Nazarene clinic. I looked toward the distant fog-shrouded hills knowing the heroic sacrifice they had made, carrying the loved one over steep, muddy, rocky trails, seeking help for her precarious condition.

For a long moment my thoughts took me back to a Sunday evening in another setting, worlds apart from the jungle I now called home. Addie and I were called to be missionaries. She was called at the age of twelve, and I was called while I was a student in college. We had made plans and had governed our lives to that end. I thought we would probably be sent to Africa someday. I was finishing up two years in private practice, and we were anxiously awaiting an appointment to missionary service. It seemed as though our Mission board had forgotten all about us, and the wait continued.

It was a beautiful Sunday evening as we anticipated hearing yet another missionary share his stories of spreading the Gospel around the world. He was from Perú, South America. He immediately captured my imagination as he told about a group of Indigenous South Americans living deep in the Amazon Rain Forest. He had made a trip to help another missionary clear ground for the beginning of a new mission station. He spoke of their physical suffering and need of medical attention.

As he spoke my spirit came alive and I wept like a baby. I knew God was calling me to these people of the rain forest. When the service ended, I excitedly took a reluctant Addie down to meet him and tell him that God was calling me to these needy people.

Addie didn't share my excitement because she had intense fears of rivers, snakes, spiders, and things that creep, crawl, bite, and sting. Besides, we had three small children to think about and the jungle didn't seem to her the appropriate place to take them. She faked a weak smile as we introduced ourselves to the missionary.

I was bubbling over as I told him of our preparation and that I felt God would have us go to that place. He informed us that he had been in our mission headquarters a couple of weeks earlier and that they had mentioned to him that there was a young couple in California that they were thinking of sending there. That service took place in the College Avenue Church of the Nazarene in Whittier, California, and the rest is history.

His motioning hand snapped me back to reality as he pointed to his wife lying on a bamboo woven mat with poles tied on either side by stout thin vines. I looked into the sunken dark eyes of a dying woman of perhaps thirty years of age. Her bones protruded through dehydrated skin. Her thin lips were parched and her face was expressionless, as if all hope had dissipated. Her skin was as pale as death and her emaciated form called out for help.

I was told that she had hemorrhaged for nine days. She was so weak that she could not lift her head off of the mat. Her vital signs were desperately failing, and her life hung by a thread.

It was nearly two weeks after that Sunday evening service that a very important life-changing letter arrived in the mail. With trembling hands I opened it, calling to Addie at the same time. It read. 'Dear Dr. and Mrs. Larry Garman: The Department of Foreign Missions is desirous to know if you would be interested in a rural assignment. If so, we would like for you both to meet with the Department in January 1964.' I was so excited that I wanted to shout. A rural assignment…I was raised in rural Ohio. What they called rural must have come from another dictionary.

She needs a transfusion, I thought to myself, but remembered that all I had on hand was plasma. The decision was made, bottle hung, and IV tubing attached. I held the 20-gauge needle in my hand while preparing the vein for insertion. I was ready to plunge the needle into the vein when his authoritative voice broke the deadly silence. Pointing to the needle, tubing, and plasma bottle, he asked, "Won't this kill her?" Right away I was reminded of their belief system. If a witchdoctor treats a patient and that patient dies, he is held accountable, accused of bad witchcraft and killed in cold blood. At that moment I knew what was running through his mind.

He had never seen the inside of a clinic, known a doctor, or ever viewed a hypodermic needle and all that goes with it. To him this was all very mysterious and bordering on witchcraft. She will probably die anyway, whether I treat her or not, I reasoned to myself. I debated for a long moment, while my thoughts raced ahead of me. What would become of Addie and our three young children if I were violently killed?

Time was approaching for us to fly back to Kansas City to have our interview with the mission board. Addie had been struggling since that letter arrived. She thought, 'I just can't take these three small children to such a forgotten, isolated, and dangerous place as the Amazon.' Her struggles were intense and the battle raged within.

At that time she was teaching a fifth grade Sunday school class of girls at our church. Saturday evening arrived and she was so burdened with this terrifying decision as she opened her lesson to prepare for her class the next day. She was struggling within her soul when she finally found the lesson for her class. It was entitled, "The story of Roger and Esther Carson Winans in the jungle of Perú." With tears streaming down her cheeks, she asked me to pray with her. The Lord's peace and assurance came and Addie said, 'Yes,' to the jungle of northern Perú. There came the times when she took each child and said, "Lord, here is Rusty, he is Yours, I take my hands off." She placed Greg, Candy, and later Tim on the altar as well. His grace has been sufficient.

I said a short prayer and was keenly aware of the great risk I was taking as the needle broke the skin, penetrated the vein, and was soon locked into place with tape. I looked into his terrified eyes as I cautiously opened the valve and plasma rushed through the tubing. As a young missionary doctor, I wondered if this would be the beginning or end of our missionary career.

On this dramatic stage of life, two cultures and belief systems met head on, and I wondered what the outcome would be. The plasma bottle ran dry as two men stood anxiously by to note any change in the patient's condition, each with his own thoughts. The man with long hair had been taught the customs of his people around the glowing embers of a small log fire. These customs had been ingrained in him from early childhood. He was taught that death does not come from natural causes, but from bewitchment, and therefore revenge killing is in order. The other man thought of someone who sacrificially gave us His life so that through His death, we might have life. After all, Jesus had said, "*I am sending you to open their eyes so that they turn from darkness to light and from the power of Satan to God… (Acts 26:17b-18 KJV)."*

At first there was a small stirring. Then she opened her eyes and asked for water. Her husband quickly responded with intense love as he placed a cool drink to those parched lips that consumed the life-giving liquid. The eyes of both men met for a brief moment and faint smiles were exchanged as two miracles took place: the miracle of God restoring life through his healing touch, and the miracle of two cultures merging together for a common good.

It wasn't long before she was up and around and on the road to complete recovery. I had prayed with them every night in the clinic and knew that God was working in their lives. The day finally came for her to be discharged from the clinic. We exchanged goodbyes, and I watched them head down to the river and get into the dugout canoe that would take them back to the trail, and then to their home deep in the forest. As the canoe rounded a bend in the river, and they disappeared into that green expanse of jungle, I stood alone on the bank reflecting on my calling to the Amazon.

Thanks be to God for the successful mergence of two cultures under the anointing of the Holy Spirit. His grace is sufficient. The question was answered, and it was the beginning of the young missionary's career.

The Amazon Call

The Brown Stuff

"Boys, how would you like to go with dad up the Kusu River by canoe to visit the village of Chingmai?"

Rusty, seven years old, and his five-year-old brother, Greg, were excited and responded, "Yes, Dad, when are we going?"

We each told Addie goodbye and made our way down the two steep hills leading to our port where the twenty-foot-long sleek canoe was gently bobbing up and down in the clear waters of the Kusu stream. Canoe voyages were a favorite pastime of the children and they looked for every opportunity to paddle in the quiet waters in front of our home deep in the jungle. This small river emptied its contents into the larger, fast rolling Marañon River that gobbled up the Kusu in view of our house.

The Marañon River begins in the high Andes Mountains in Perú. Along its course it picks up many smaller rivers as its volume grows. It is filled with silt, washed down from the hillsides, causing it to take on a brown dirt color, especially after torrential rains. When the clear waters of the Kusu meet up with the silt-laden Marañon, the color takes on a coffee with cream effect that our children all called the brown stuff. The brown stuff is a swirling, turbulent mass of water--very frightening to the inexperienced.

I will never forget the day long ago when Máximo from the village of Listra left his canoe tied up at our port, and then took the trail to Chipe one half hour away. Rusty and Greg were playing with several Indian children when they spotted the canoe hugging the bank with a nice hand-carved paddle lying on the floor, begging to be used. The boys meandered down to where the innocent canoe was gently swaying back and forth in the water sending out an invitation to four little boys who took the invitation very seriously.

Máximo wouldn't be back from Chipe until later and, after all, they were just going to borrow it for a little while and then leave it right where it was tied. They took turns paddling up stream, rocking the canoe back and forth wildly, and splashing each other with cool water. The boys were having a great time with Máximo's canoe, giggling and laughing as they dove from the wobbly sides into the warm waters and swam back to repeat the process over and over.

Lying on the bottom of the canoe, resting from their antics, the four boys did not realize that their frail craft was slowly drifting toward the dreaded mysterious brown stuff. The brown stuff was legendary to our children. It represented all that was mysterious and unknown in the river, like piranhas, alligators, anacondas and all kind of nasty things lurking and waiting, ready to gobble up little unsuspecting kids.

We had inherited a pair of water skis and decided that we would try them out on the smaller calm river. Since none of us had ever water skied or really been around someone that had, the stage was set for some hilarious moments. We didn't have a speedboat, but that didn't stop us. We cranked up the thirty-three horsepower outboard motor on our large cargo boat to see if we could get up enough speed to ski. I went first, and our boat lumbered down the river, dragging me along in its wake, allowing me to drink enough water to float a battleship. After several tries, I managed to finally stagger up on wobbly legs, only to be thrown forward on my belly. Not smart or quick enough to let go of the rope handle, I would be dragged in that compromising position until the sheer drag of water caused me to let go.

At last it was the boys' turn to try their hand at drinking river water. They, being much lighter, got to their wobbly feet quicker than I did, amidst shouted instructions from dad and cheers from mom, for their short-lived moment of glory before they, too, tasted the river from their back side.

It wasn't long, though, until they mastered the art of hanging on for dear life. The local people came from their huts and gardens to see these crazy people walk on water amid the shouts of "Watch out, the alligators will get you!" One day I was pulling the boys very close to the brown stuff when I heard over the roar of the motor their screaming voices begging me not to go through that unknown and mysterious part of the river, threatening to let go if I did.

Suddenly one of the four boys looked up from the security of the drifting canoe and realized that they were headed directly for the brown stuff. All four boys bolted upright, surveyed the situation, and as one they all bailed out of the canoe, and stood on a small sandbar in the middle of the river that was threatening to sweep them into the dreaded brown stuff. I heard their desperate cries for help, cries that could have awakened the dead.

I ran to the bank overlooking the river in time to see that beautiful hand carved canoe being swept over the rapids and rocks, caught in the heavy cross currents, carried swiftly through the brown stuff and on downriver, never to be seen again. There stood four boys pleading for help as I raced to the edge of the river. I called for them to swim to shore with all their might, but to no avail. They were not budging from their little sandbar for fear that they would be carried into the forbidden brown stuff. I coaxed and reassured them that they could make it and that I would help them if they couldn't get to shore. They looked again at the swirling menacing brown stuff and begged me to come after them. Finally, I entered the river and helped them to the safety of dry land.

Later that afternoon, Máximo came back from Chipe on his way home. Not finding his canoe, he came to our home, inquiring as to its whereabouts. Sheepishly Rusty and Greg related the story of how they saw the runaway canoe disappear into the brown stuff. Máximo was very kind and only charged me S/.500.00 Peruvian soles for the lost canoe, and thus lived on forever the legend of the brown stuff.

Addie and our daughter Candy waved to us as our canoe pulled away from the bank heading upstream to the village of Chingmai. My experience in paddling a canoe could have been compressed into probably less than one half hour, but, after all, the Kusu River was calm and posed no threat to novices like us.

Rusty, being the oldest, sat in the bow of the little canoe, with Greg in the middle, and I sat on the carved seat in the back, propelling the craft with a lovely hardwood paddle. All went well as we rounded bend after bend of this small river flowing through the middle of our evergreen paradise. The sun was high overhead when we passed the port of Chimpa, the witchdoctor, and the thatched roof hut of Kunchiwai. The gardens on either bank were beautiful with bananas ripening under a tropical sky.

At long last we came to the boulder-lined rapids about one fourth mile below the village. Skillfully we pulled and pushed the little canoe through the weakest part of the rapids as we had seen the Indians do on so many occasions. Once above the rapids, we congratulated each other on our accomplishment and took our positions in the canoe for the last leg of our journey to the village. We were making good time when all of a sudden the current became swifter and I struggled to keep the canoe pointing upriver.

Rounding the bend, we were met by a very strong current coming across the rocks, pushing us backward downriver away from the village that now was just across the river from our position. I tried to keep the canoe steady, but the force of the heavy current threatened to turn us sideways and send us back downstream. I shouted to Rusty, "Son, grab those overhanging branches and keep the canoe pointing upriver."

He reached up, wrapping his arms tightly around the branches to steady the bow, when the current struck the side of the canoe shoving us back downstream, yanking him from the canoe. He was clinging to the branches with his feet dragging in the ferocious river, screaming for help. I looked up and saw him hanging on for dear life. Our canoe swung around under the unrelenting pressure of water carrying us back downstream. I shouted, "Rusty, hang on, don't let go!"

Desperately I tried to get to shore so that I could rescue him from falling into the river. The canoe swung around downstream about twenty yards from where he was hanging and screaming. Scrambling to the rocks, I manage to get the canoe to shore, but in the process, I dropped the paddle in the swift current. I stood there, turning my gaze from the fleeting paddle to Rusty, tenaciously clinging to the branches and yelling at the top of his lungs.

"Greg," I said, "jump out onto the rocks and hold the canoe and don't let go." Bravely, five-year-old Greg held onto the rocking canoe as I went slipping and sliding across the rocks to get Rusty before we would be dragged into the river. Rusty's cry for help soon turned in another direction. Hanging there, he saw that I was not making much headway, so he began calling for Segundo, a bilingual schoolteacher who lived in the village. Miraculously Segundo heard his cries for help from a distance and came running to the river. He untied his canoe and paddled skillfully to where Rusty was hanging and managed to retrieve him just before he fell into the raging waters.

Soon we were on our way back home after catching up to the drifting paddle. Rounding the last bend in the river, we could see the brown stuff in the distance and it didn't seen so intimidating now that we were safely home.

The Amazon Call

"Fingers"

"Doctor, what do you people eat that looks like fingers?" The question came from my Indian friend, Moisés.

"Fingers?" I replied in disbelief. "What are you talking about?"

"The rumor has spread like wildfire in the village that you have a tribe of people in your homeland whose fingers you cultivate by cutting them off and that they grow new ones. The fingers are then canned and sent around the world for consumption." Moisés' information was a puzzle to me.

Our home in the jungle has very large windows covered with screen but no glass, as it is very hot in the tropics. When we first arrived, the Indians came daily, looking in our windows to see how these new missionaries lived. They came from three different villages. We had a constant stream of people looking in at nearly every window all day long. We didn't have television, but the Aguarunas did. We were it. Channel Two was the bedroom, Channel Four the living room, and Channel Eight the kitchen. The favorite channel for the women was Channel Eight as they would stack up large rocks below the kitchen window. One lady would stand, clinging onto the windowsill, observing every move Addie made in preparing meals. She would relate all that Addie was doing to the ladies standing below her on the ground. "She is opening a can, pouring the contents into a pot, and placing it on a table that throws out fire," she would relay to those anxiously awaiting her running commentary.

Indian women cook on three logs, placed strategically at different angles on the dirt floor of their hut, so a stove was a new contraption to them. So many things that Addie did in the preparation of food was very mysterious and bordered on witchcraft from the ladies' limited worldview.

One day, a lady was observing Addie open a can and extract something that startled her beyond belief. Panic was written all over her face as she jumped from the rocks, her eyes dilated and the word 'fingers' tumbled from trembling lips as she ran off into the jungle with others following her. Crossing several streams and never looking back, they soon arrived at the village out of breath, gesturing wildly, and relating to everyone what had been witnessed in our kitchen.

'Fingers,' we mused, what could they have seen that looked like fingers? Addie went to her meager storehouse to try and solve this mystery. We would have to purchase many of our food items out on the coast of Perú and truck them in over the great Andes Mountains to the Marañon River. Then we would load them on the large wooden cargo boat for transportation downriver to our home deep in the forest. Addie would have a detailed list of needed supplies to last up to eight months.

One time we forgot to buy salt, and there was none to be had in the jungle. The Indians in our area would go way downriver once a year to a well known salt stream, boil the water in a metal container, and then collect the rock salt crystals as residue. This brownish rock salt would be loaded into woven baskets and taken by canoe back to the village for domestic use. Unfortunately they had run out of salt and had none to share with us at that time.

A few days later a pilot from the Summer Institute of Linguistics landed his pontoon plane on the Kusu River right below our house. He just stopped in to visit for a few minutes on his way back to his base. Upon leaving, he asked Addie if we needed anything. She asked if he might have a little salt on board his plane. "As a matter of fact," he replied, "I do have a small container of salt in the plane." He gave us all that he had and it got us through until more could be purchased.

Looking over her supply of canned food, Addie exclaimed, "Here it is!" She held up a tall can containing long slender wieners. The mystery was solved!

Powdered Milk

He arrived at the door of our home that beautiful warm afternoon and handed Addie a paper that he had just written. I had asked the students of the Bible Institute to give me their testimonies for future reference. Upon leaving his hand written testimony he stated, "I want to tell you personally what it says."

This young man, about twenty-one years of age, began sharing that many years ago in the village of Kusu lived a family by the name of Chuintam. He went on to say that the young mother, wife of Alejandro Chuintam, gave birth to a baby boy and that the mother suffered greatly after the delivery with a post partum infection and was near death's door.

Kusu is a village located on the banks of the river with the same name. Our mission station shared the corner of the Kusu River where it emptied into the larger Marañon River, about three miles down stream. Many from the village came on Sunday morning by canoe and trail to attend Sunday School and the preaching service, until the day arrived that a church was finally erected in their village. Alejandro didn't care about church or spiritual things and seldom darkened the door of that little church. However, his wife was very faithful, but now lay dying in her hut. Alejandro set out in his dugout canoe seeking help for his wife. He went to the Nazarene clinic and told of his wife's serious condition. He said that the missionary doctor gave him medicine to combat the infection and the young mother's life was miraculously spared. The mother slowly recuperated and at long last was back on her feet, but her milk had dried up and the little boy was suffering from malnutrition.

They made a drink of starchy yuca water to give to the young child, but, lacking protein, the baby was literally starving. The child was listless and cried constantly. His eyes were dull, his hair was falling out and all hope was lost. Day by day the desperate mother pleaded with God to help her baby.

Again the father made the long trip to the mission station seeking help for his son. He asked the missionary wife if she had any milk she could spare, as there was no milk in the village.

Indian babies are nursed until two to three years of age, because milk is not available in the village. If it were available, it would be very expensive and not really an option. Usually when twins are born, one is given to a grandmother to nurse and care for, which means the child lingers for a short while before the inevitable happens.

Children who are born with severe physical challenges don't survive because of the lack of special services and facilities to support parents in an economically depressed part of the world. Unfortunately the jungle is usually a place where 'survival of the fittest' holds true.

Soon a bag of powdered milk was placed in his hands along with a baby bottle and instructions for its preparation. Several days later he was back asking if there was more milk. This took place several times over a space of months and then he appeared no more.

Years passed and the missionaries moved their mission station twenty-five miles away and all contact was lost with the people in Kusu.

Addie stood there that day, fascinated by this young man's story. He then broke the silence. With tears streaming down his face, he told her that he was that baby of long ago. He said, "My mother has told me this story over and over again while I was growing up."

Addie was speechless and emotionally moved upon realizing that such a small investment of powdered milk in the life of a dying baby would produce such startling results in a grateful family. The young man graduated from our Bible Institute, and then took the pastorate of a local church for a year. Later he went to the Seminary on the coast of Perú where he received a more advanced degree. Today he and his wife pastor the church in the village of Numpatkaim.

Isn't it wonderful how a daily compassionate ministry pays incredible dividends?

Lost Dog

"Hoo, hoo, hooo-" the quiet, dark and serene night was shattered by this mysterious sound coming from deep within the rain forest. I gave my wife a puzzled look as we both stared through the screened window into the black night. Before we could respond, the sound was repeated again. Silence followed and only the normal sounds of the night greeted our ears. Then, again from another direction came this mysterious sound that faded in the distance. Sleep came with much difficulty that night as those sounds repeated themselves over and over again in our minds.

The next morning I anxiously sought out our helper and asked him if he had heard those mystifying sounds of the night before. He grinned and told me that a lady from the nearby village was searching and calling for her lost dog. I had been challenged to find Bible stories that our people could relate to. The story of Noah and the Ark was difficult for them because the only means of water transportation was a dugout canoe or a small cargo boat that was nothing more than a canoe with sides on it.

As a new missionary, I was eager to communicate the concept of Jesus being the Lamb of God, the Good Shepherd, and tell those wonderful parables of the lost sheep and the ninety and nine, without realizing that they had never seen a sheep and had no idea of a sacrificial lamb. That destroyed about one-half of my New Testament. I was struggling to find an equivalent concept to communicate biblical truths. I turned to Moisés (my helper) and said, "Tell me about the lost dog."

He began by reminding me of the times on Sunday morning when I had observed the ladies carrying small pups in the front of their dresses as if they were babies, and noticed how they chewed food and placed it into the pups' mouths. These pups will grow and be trained to hunt. If you have a good hunting dog, you will have meat on the table. So, dogs are prized animals. The caring for pups is the work of the women. They care for the dogs until they are old enough to be trained to hunt.

The dog will be tied to a bamboo bed with a short vine around his neck. At night the dog will curl up close to the dying embers of a three-logged fire in the middle of the hut. Occasionally the vine would break and the frisky pup will explore the jungle while the couple is not at home.

When they arrive home after working in the gardens and find the broken vine lying on the floor and no sign of the dog, the husband will look at his wife and she knows that she had better hit the trail. She will light a small wick lamp from the still glowing embers and set off to search for the lost dog. The lamp gives off a faint smoky orange-yellowish glare that will allow you to barely see one foot in front of the other. She will risk her life to find the pup as she crosses streams and follows small thin-cut trails deep into the rain forest. She will stop in a small clearing, calling for the lost dog. "Hoo, hoo, hoooo."

She will continue searching and calling and listening in clearing after clearing until she finally finds the cold, shivering pup cowering behind the safety of a fallen tree. She probably will not treat the lost pup like Jesus did the lost sheep. She will beat him half to death, tie a stout vine around his neck and literally drag him back across the trails until she reaches home where everyone rejoices because the lost dog has been found.

Now we have our story and a new link of communicating the gospel. It's incredible how the Lord uses our feeble attempts to proclaim the Good News by opening the doors of understanding. The Holy Spirit is faithful in enabling us to share the story of Christ using a different cultural context.

Anniversary Dinner

"Doctor, we want to invite you and your wife to a special meal tomorrow at noon in the dining hall of the Bible Institute." The students heard that we had a wedding anniversary coming and they wanted to help us celebrate. This was unusual because they didn't celebrate special days. Birthdays were not celebrated, since the older people had no idea as to their age or even when they were born.

When we first arrived in the rain forest our people did not keep birth records since they did not have a written language yet. The Linguists were just translating their language and starting bilingual schools for the children that went up to the second grade.

I remember the day when one of the prominent schoolteachers from the village of Kusu brought one of his students to the clinic for treatment. After examining the child, I asked his age in order to measure the dosage of medicine to treat his ailment. The teacher immediately told the child to open his mouth. With one hand on the boy's head and the other holding his chin downward, he proceeded to count his teeth and then told me that the boy was ten years old.

Wedding anniversaries were not celebrated. No one knew when they had been married as no register was kept. Also, some had more than one wife. It was hard enough to keep up with multiple wives, let alone know when you married them.

We were surprised when they announced their desire to prepare a meal in our honor. How excited, elated, and grateful we were for this gesture, because they had never done anything like this before. Two of the students that were known for their hunting skills set out that afternoon, destination deep into the rain forest. We bathed in the river that afternoon, finished supper, and were relaxing in our small home deep in the jungle when we heard a commotion outside.

There was a bright moon that unforgettable evening as I stepped out into the front yard and saw the two hunters returning from a successful hunt. Both wore only the typical hunting trunks. They were grinning as they walked passed me and saying, "Tomorrow we will have lunch together."

I noticed the large open-weave basket hanging from one man's back with a large vine strap tied to it and draped over his arms and shoulders. My eyes passed from him to the basket, which was filled with green banana leaves wrapped around some red meat, dripping blood out the bottom. The other student carried the old rusty shotgun that had provided many meals for our students throughout the years. Soon they disappeared into the night and I stood alone, wondering what wild animal had they killed.

The sun rose on another beautiful, tropical day in the rain forest. Parrots flew noisily overhead. I could feel the intense heat on my back as I climbed the steep hill leading to the Bible Institute. About half way up, I turned to look out over the emerald green forest that stretched out before me with the serpentine river winding its way through that vast expanse of jungle. To my left I watched the smaller Kusu River meander down from the small mountain range in the distance, emptying its contents into the larger river.

From my vantage point I saw our small soccer field, surrounded by banana plants with their long broad leaves glistening in the sunlight, caught my attention for a long moment. On that field we had shared a lot of joy and special memories of playing against the nearby villages. The sun was hanging high overhead and its potent rays caused us to squint as we looked up and slowly made our way to the top where the dining hall was located. Our clothes were saturated with perspiration as we walked into the small dirt-floored building.

Once again we had conquered those three hundred and twenty-five steps to the top of this hill that overlooked the great valley below. There were tables with backless benches lining the walls, and students were in formation, ready to pass by the large cooking pots that were placed on the floor before them. Upon entering the dining hall, the students ushered us as special guests to the front of the line. We stood there with spoons and bowls in our hands while Tuya, the cook, removed the lids from one pot after another.

The first two pots were full of boiled yuca and bananas. The third pot was brimming with a bubbly soup that contained the wild game killed the night before. Tuya stood over that pot with a big grin on his face. I noticed his large bare feet, thick and toughened by countless and endless trails. He wore short pants that betrayed legs that were extremely bowed.

Tuya was a wonderful likable man who exemplified Christ. Two of his sons had graduated from the Bible Institute, and he and his wife were faithful members of the church in the village of Chipe where he traveled from daily to cook.

He held a large wooden spoon in his hand that he used to stir the hot contents of this large pot of soup. Addie and I glanced intently into that pot, wondering what meat we would be eating. Floating up through the grayish broth we spied a large dark round object that bobbed up and down, and then rolled over. We stared into the large open eyes of a monkey. The tongue was hanging out of its mouth, and the ears were still attached. Some of the facial hair had not been completely singed off. Tuya shoved the head to one side of the pot where it bounced off the metal wall, sank to the bottom, and then floated back to the top where it rolled over. Again we looked into those dark lifeless eyes.

I thought that Addie would pass out as Tuya fished around for her piece of meat. He continued to stir and finally trapped a lower leg bone with feet and toes intact that he lovingly plopped into Addie's bowl. He fished around until up floated an arm bone with hand, fingers and hair still attached to the knuckles, that he dropped into my bowl. At this point Addie and I were a little green at the gills.

I was glad that we knew something about their culture as we watched that head bob up and down in the soup. Only he who kills the animal gets the head, thank the Lord. It was an unforgettable meal because Addie had the good fortune of sitting right across the table from the hunter. She tried not to look at him, but she couldn't help herself. Occasionally she would look up and see him holding that monkey's head like a piece of watermelon, munching on the soft meat around the cheeks and tearing the tender meat from the lips and face with broth dripping from a chin that produced a satisfied grin.

We have had many anniversaries since, but none as memorable. What does monkey taste like? It resembles dark turkey meat. If it's a young monkey, the meat is tender and very tasty, but if it's an old monkey it's stringy and tough.

Happy Anniversary!

Ants Alive

"...the day of the Lord comes as a thief in the night." ~ I Thes. 5:2b

Subconsciously I was twisting, turning, and scratching my body all in one motion as that burning, itching feeling aroused me from a deep sleep. It was about two a.m., and darkness engulfed our bedroom while my hands mechanically clawed at my skin. It must be a nightmare, I thought, as sleep laden eyes struggled to open. Fingers automatically dug into the scalp and then methodically moved from neck to shoulders and arms.

The itching, burning sensation was unbearable as I reached for the flashlight that stood on its end beside our bed. *(In the jungle there is no electricity after 10:00 p.m. because the generator has been shut down for the night.)*

Arms flailing, I managed to knock the flashlight over and it rolled under the bed out of the reach of my grasping hand. Half in and half out of the bed, my hand desperately searched and finally retrieved the runaway object. Frantically, I turned the flashlight on and my sleep-dazed eyes sprung to life, while my free hand rapidly followed the itching from head to arms and legs.

The beam of light shone on our pillows and bed sheets as glazed eyes fixed upon a moving mass of black. Still clawing at my body from head to toe, I sprang to the floor brushing tenacious little black objects from my skin. They clung to my feet and climbed up my legs as I danced across the floor shaking them off and yelling to Addie at the same time.

"ANTS!" She shouted, jumping desperately from the bed scratching and shining her light all in one motion. We ran to the doorway and focused our light on the bed and wall behind it. The pillowcases and sheets were covered with thousands of black ants. The bed and wall behind it were a symphony of movement in black as we were being invaded by tens of thousands of flesh eating ants. Some might call the upper Amazon where we live one giant anthill. There are so many species of ants, from the tiny red fire ants to the large two-inch long army ants, each with their own nasty stings.

This encroaching horde began fanning out in every direction, crawling into every crack and crevice of the room, flushing out their victims. Cockroaches flew from the walls and ceiling to the floor and ran for their lives, looking for some exit from that punishing world of pain. As they ran, hundreds of ants clung to their bodies, injecting them with minute amounts of formic acid until they stopped dead in their tracks and were devoured before our very eyes, leaving only pieces of wings and legs spread out across the floor. We were fully awake now, watching this advancing army. These ants come periodically unannounced, looking for insects to feast on. They drive the people from their huts and then scour the homes from roof to floor. They don't disturb the food supply since they are only interested in insects.

I noticed a large black object jumping across the floor, trying to escape through the defense of this moving army. It was a huge spider and each jump became shorter as hundreds of ants encased its body, finally bringing it to a stop by sheer weight. In a matter of moments the spider was consumed. We stepped back out of the way of their path and projected our light around the room. Coming out of the open closet ran a large black scorpion, tail up and stinger flexed as innumerable ants climbed its frame and brought it to a screeching halt and it was eaten within a few seconds.

We let them have the room and moved to the living room, while they completely cleaned every room. When they reached the living room, we jumped over their trail and headed for the bedroom, where we found no trace of ants, but evidence of their vanished presence in the form of legs and wings from their victims.

As quickly as they came, they disappeared and left, but we didn't sleep the rest of the night. They taught me one important lesson: to be prepared for we know not when they might come again.

"A Little Child Shall Lead Them"

My attention was drawn to the screened window of our small clinic deep in the Amazon. Like a magnet, the beauties of the rain forest drew me to gulp in the splendor of a perfect day. The rays of sunlight glimmered from the evergreen emerald sea of trees and plants. They shone as if recently painted with a transparent sheen. The birds were conversely chattering, while tree locust emitted their high-pitched squeal that sounded like active high-tension wires along a major highway in the United States. I was absorbed by the absolute tranquility of our surroundings.

The silence was ruptured by the desperate cries of a woman's voice. I looked toward the river, but my gaze was met by the huge tree that stood like a lone sentinel at the corner of the Kusu River where it dumped its clean peaceful water into the muddy turbulent Marañon River. I saw the unmistakable meeting of the waters as the darker larger river gobbled the clean water up. Yet I saw no sign of human activity. Then, again, the desperate cries for help reached my ears. Again I focused my attention on the large tree, and at that moment a long dugout canoe rounded the corner and glided into the calm waters of our port.

A man jumped from the canoe, and with one motion plunged a long twelve-foot cane pole into the soft mud bank to which he tied a stout vine that was attached to his sleek craft. He then lifted a large child from the bottom of the canoe and hurriedly climbed the steep muddy bank that led toward the clinic. The next sound I heard was that of the death cry. A woman was rapidly following the man up the hill, beating her chest, pulling at her hair, and crying, "My son is dying, my son is dying." When they neared the clinic, I opened the door, ushered them inside, and instructed the man to place the child upon the examination table. It was then that I looked into the face of Walter, his son. I recognized Santos and Rosa from the village of Chipe, just upriver from the mission station.

I first met Walter when he was about ten years old. Addie decided to reach out to the children from the villages of Chipe, Kusu, and Listra, and thus announced the very first Vacation Bible School. They came across the trails and by canoe, arriving early in the morning on the announced day. As new missionaries we were so excited to see the small dirt-floored church overflowing with happy, but very shy children. Addie taught them songs, then a story about Jesus followed by handcrafts. She had made copies of Bible scenes on the old spirit duplicator machine we had inherited. Crayons were handed out, but no one moved. They had never seen a crayon before and didn't know what to do. Addie instructed them to color the pictures as they thought they should look.

The children knelt on the dirt floor with their papers neatly lying on the backless benches, and begin to color the pictures. Walking around, giving encouragement, we noticed one boy's work in particular. His painting was absolutely beautiful. The colors blended perfectly and remained within the lines. "What is your name?" we asked him.

"Walter," he replied. His pants were well worn and high up on his legs, and his shoeless feet made them look even higher. He was slender and tall but very shy. The older children helped their brothers and sisters color their papers, and all of them enjoyed the activity immensely. A few adults came with their children to see what VBS was all about. It wasn't long until they also were kneeling down on the dirt floor coloring right along with the kids. Class was over and happy children, protecting their papers with their lives, made their way home by trail and river.

The next day they came way before the appointed time and brought more of their friends. A large group of adults came also, as word reached eager ears.

I glanced down at the young boy lying before me on the examination table. His mother was softly crying in the background as Santos told me of his son's condition. My eyes swept over the pale body and immediately focused on his shirt pocket. There inside was a little blue pocket-sized New Testament. The week of VBS was one that would ever live on in our memory. Addie had told the children the first day about a prize they could receive for perfect attendance and memory work. During the week there was an altar call and many children came to pray and ask Jesus into their hearts.

Walter was one of those who accepted Jesus as his Savior. His memory work was flawless and attendance perfect, thus he earned a brand new pocket-sized New Testament. His paintings were incredible, considering his age and background. They hung from the long pole that held up the thatched leaf roof of his home. Each picture was pinned to the pole with a long slender twelve-inch dart from his father's blowgun. They were there for all to see, adorning the hut with brilliant colors.

His back was arching, chin fixed, immobile, and definitely in pain. His low groans elicited more uncontrolled crying from his mother. Looking into the concerned, saddened face of his father Santos, I asked, "What has happened to your son?" I knew both Santos and Rosa well. They cared nothing for spiritual things and seldom attended church. Walter had virtually been on his own, seeking spiritual guidance from others. On some occasions, when visiting the church in Chipe, we could hear the drums beating and the high pitched laughter of those drunken from the intoxicating effects of the masticated masato drink. In that group were Santos and Rosa, while their twelve-year-old son was singing choruses and listening to the Bible stories from Lucho Asangkay, pastor of the village church.

Two years had passed since Walter's conversion, and he was now twelve, and on the brink of death. Santos informed me that nine days earlier Walter had been running through the jungle barefooted and had stepped on a sharp bamboo shoot that penetrated deep into the soft flesh of his foot. Walter washed the deep gash with river water and said nothing to his parents of the accident. Several days later they noticed him limping and inquired as to what had happened. They observed his refusal to eat, and brought him to the clinic since his condition was worsening. Upon examination I observed a terribly inflamed, festered sore on his foot. His jaw was fixated, speech was difficult, and there was a pronounced hyperextension of his back. Diagnosis was made and the parents were informed that their firstborn son, their pride and joy, was dying from advanced tetanus.

I explained to them the nature of the disease, and that we did not have the tetanus antitoxin on hand, and even if we did it would probably be to no avail. Rosa was desperately crying now and begged me to help her son. Her grief and despair broke my heart, and a feeling of utter helplessness flooded my being. I wanted to help in someway, so I offered to send them upriver to the Peruvian army camp where there was a doctor in attendance.

I watched our boat disappear around the corner as I said a prayer for this precious boy whom we had come to love deeply. That afternoon our motorist arrived, informing me that he left them at the army camp where the road into the jungle ended. In our family prayers that night, our saddened hearts prayed for a miracle.

The next day we were up bright and early preparing to take our children to the coast and send them to the jungle school where they would be away from us for four and a half months. The trip would take up to four days of travel, three of those by road and one by air. We were sad, knowing that in a few days we would say goodbye to our children for those long months. Addie packed a lunch and off we went.

It was a beautiful sunny day and our long dugout canoe boat plowed slowly upriver fighting the heavy current. Hours passed and in the middle of the afternoon as we rounded yet another curve in the torturous serpentine river, we noticed that someone was frantically waving to us from the shore. Nearing the shoreline I could see the gardens of yuca and bananas in the background on the low-slung hills that rose gently to meet a blue sky. It was Santos waving and calling to us. Our boat struck the mud bank, and Santos who had been crying, said, "Walter is dead."

I jumped from the boat with Addie following, and I asked, "Where is he?" He replied by pointing up a thin cut trail that led past the gardens, and stated that he was with his mother in an abandoned hut on yonder hill. We followed the grief stricken father through the garden area and finally came to a small hut that the Indians use when cultivating and harvesting their crops. We entered through the narrow doorway and saw Walter's body lying on a small table. Rosa desperately clung to Addie, crying incessantly. Looking into the peaceful face of our Sunday school boy, I asked, "When did he die?"

"Yesterday the army doctor gave the same diagnosis, and that he didn't have any medicine that would help. He told us to take our son home. I borrowed a canoe and we left from upriver today."

Rosa was crying as she kneeled in the front of the canoe. She would call out to every person she saw standing on the bank of the river, "My son is dying, my son is dying."

"I was steering the canoe," he continued, encompassed by sadness, "when Walter spoke to us from where he was lying on a bamboo mat in the middle of the canoe. His words were pronounced with great difficulty since his lower jaw was nearly locked." My wife stopped crying and I laid my paddle across the canoe giving him our fullest attention.

"Dad, Mom," he said, "Don't cry for me, because I am going to be with Jesus. Dad, you know that sometimes we go to bed hungry, because there's not enough to eat, but in Heaven I'll never be hungry again. At night when it's cool, we don't have enough blankets to cover us, but I'll never be cold again." Twelve years old, I thought to myself, and what a testimony! "Dad, when I die," and he motioned to his shirt pocket, "please take my New Testament and place it over my heart, because I want to meet Jesus with His Word on my heart." Walter closed his eyes and went to his eternal reward where he will never be hungry, cold, or sick again.

I stood on holy ground that day in the presence of the Lord. I turned my attention to this grieving father and mother. I spoke to Santos and Rosa, but words were hard to come by. Finally I asked them, "Would you like to see your son again someday?"

"Oh, more than anything," they responded.

"Do you know where Walter is right now?" I asked.

"Yes, he's with Jesus in Heaven."

"That's right," I replied, "And if you give your hearts to Jesus, one day you will be with your son again."

That day, in a little abandoned hut on a jungle hillside in a remote part of the Amazon, two people gave their hearts and lives to Christ. Walter was buried with his pocket New Testament over his heart.

Santos later became treasurer of the Amazon district for the church. Last year Rosa went to be with her son, Walter. I am so glad God called me to be a missionary.

Santos, Father of Walter (on left)

Amazon Animal Capers

If it crawls, walks, runs, flies, licks, bites, or stings, our children have probably had it as a pet.

There was sheik Shelia the Ocelot who ate more meat than our son could buy. Perry the Parrot pecked with one end and messed up the house with the other.

Snoopy Buttons (Raccoon family) opened a flour sack and white washed the inside of our house. Then came Rocky the Fox that vomited tuna fish in the back seat of our Suburban on a long family trip.

How about Fluffy's great air adventure? Our daughter's cat got loose and ran through the aisle and under every seat of the airplane at 20,000 feet.

Could we ever forget Speedy the Boa Constrictor brought home from boarding school on a pontoon airplane adorning our daughter's neck, and later our Christmas tree?

Next came Skippy, the small rodent that looked like a miniature Kangaroo, hiding peanuts under the rug (crunch) and in the bed (lump).

Life became very interesting when Rocky, the snapping little finger-eating Caiman (alligator), came to live with us. Our boys caught him on an alligator hunting expedition fresh out of the waters of the Amazon. His life was one of extremes. Soon after his capture we left for furlough to the United States, taking Rocky with us.

Leaving the warm tropical jungle we traveled to the high cold elevations of the Andes Mountains where Rocky became almost rigid and frozen during the night. The children put the frozen, lifeless, stiff Caiman in a bathtub of warm water, where he miraculously came back to life, only to then travel by plane to Los Angeles and customs. "You can't bring an alligator into the United States," we were told.

Our son, Greg, started to dump the now feisty, snapping, tired-of-traveling Caiman onto the counter saying, "I want to keep my cage."

The customs official, backing up and startled asked, "You say it's a Caiman?"

"Yes," replied our son.

"Oh, you can bring Caimans in to the United States," he stammered. Greg, elated and relieved, boxed up his pet and off we went to our rented house, where Rocky was tied up in the backyard. Unaware of the intense summer sun and its effects, Greg found his baked Caiman that afternoon and buried him in his adopted land. Our children learned that extremes can be devastatingly dangerous.

River Baby

"Doctor, Pastor Tomás from San Pablo wants to see you outside. He says it is an emergency." I was enjoying the beautiful and spontaneous singing to the playing of guitars that Sunday night in our church on the New Horizons mission station. Immediately I walked to the back of the church and went outside, wondering what emergency could have brought Pastor Tomás all the way from San Pablo on this dark cloudy night.

The night was damp with a slight chill in the air as I approached Tomás, standing in the shadows off to the side of the church. He greeted me and extended his hand in friendship. It was cold and clammy to the touch. He was a dear friend and one of our first students in the Bible Institute years ago. His eyes displayed fatigue and concern. His clothing was wet and he shivered slightly as he spoke rapidly, informing me that they had just arrived from the village.

"My wife is in a canoe down at the port and desperately needs your help. We have been on the river all afternoon and into the night." I looked at the darkness all around me and realized the great risk and sacrifice they had made to bring his wife to the mission station. They had traveled through some of the roughest and most dangerous areas in the river after darkness had fallen across the jungle. "My wife has been in hard labor all day and the baby won't come, please help her," he pleaded.

"Can you bring her to the clinic?" I asked.

"No," he replied, "she's in too much pain to be moved." Hurriedly I made my way to the clinic about one-fourth of a mile from the church. Gravel crunched under my feet and my flashlight poked through the darkness that engulfed me, while my mind raced ahead thinking of the challenges of yet another difficult birth. This was not the first time I had been asked to assist in a complicated delivery under very unusual circumstances.

Arriving at the clinic, I immediately began preparing the medical kit that had accompanied me on numerous emergency calls of every description. The kit was a large, metal, waterproof ammunition case from the Korean War. Methodically I packed it with what I hoped would be the necessary supplies and headed for the port. The clinic was located on a high hill overlooking the Marañon River. The port was at the bottom of this hill on a steep, slippery trail. The trail was difficult to traverse during daylight hours, but at night it could be treacherous. Carefully we picked our way down, planting one foot on solid ground before lifting the other.

Different medical scenarios played images on my mind. Would this be a breech delivery? How many hours has she been in labor? Is she fully dilated and is there hemorrhaging? After several excruciating minutes we finally reached the lower level and hurried across the small clearing to the port.

In the darkness I could see the dugout canoe with its shallow wooden sides built of planks bobbing up and down in the backwater. There was a small sixteen horsepower Briggs and Stratton motor bolted to a board nailed across the back of the tiny boat with a ten-foot long shaft and a little two-bladed insignificant propeller attached to it. I shuddered to think that they had braved the river in this most delicate craft.

In the middle of the canoe, a small makeshift roof of bamboo poles and thatched leaves were tied together with thin vines to help protect the expectant mother from the raw elements of nature. Approaching the canoe, I heard the excited voice of one of its occupants. She had delivered the baby, but the afterbirth was yet to come. Carefully I stepped into the round bottom of the canoe. It wobbled back and forth unsteadily. I knelt on the wet floor in front of the patient. After a quick gloved examination, checking vital signs, and monitoring the baby, I gave the mother the reassurance that all was well. A few minutes later, the contraction came and the placenta was expelled. I examined the afterbirth with my flashlight and then gave the mother an injection. After thanking my helper, I stood to my feet and stepped ashore, marveling once again at the scene before me. The little canoe was swaying softly, the mother was resting comfortably and the baby was sound asleep. I stood there that night absolutely amazed at the bravery of these resilient people of the rain forest.

I climbed the steep hill that led from this incredible scene to the familiar sights of the clinic. It had been a long day and I felt very tired as I walked back to the church. The service was just about to end when I slid onto a bench and wondered what surprises tomorrow would bring.

The Amazon Call

God's Warrior

A light breeze brought damp humid air coursing through the bamboo walls of numerous huts in the village of Chipe that unforgettable night. Dark ominous clouds were gathering in the sky with the hint of rain on the way.

Children unconsciously pulled on ragged blankets to cover their near naked bodies as they huddled closer together for warmth on split bamboo beds. Skinny hunting dogs were asleep, lying next to the dying embers of a three-logged cooking fire in the middle of the hut, with stout vines tied around their necks, anchoring them to the closest bed.

The damp mud floor was littered with cooking pots from the evening meal of boiled manioc and green bananas. The only movement was that of innumerable cockroaches busily searching for tidbits of leftover food.

Terrifying screams piercing the midnight air broke the silence. Men sprang from their beds clutching shotguns and spears and silently moved toward the doorway. Women leaped from their sleeping quarters carrying small wick lamps that they lit from the dying embers of the cooking fire. Cautiously they made their way outside as chaos broke loose in the village. Little children came running from their beds, crying and clinging to their mothers' legs. Immediately the barking of dogs could be heard from numerous huts.

Holding their weapons in readiness, the warriors surrounded the perimeter of the village, poised with their backs to the river, facing the forest. They knew that a full-scale revenge raid was about to take place. A few months previously they had participated along with two other villages in a revenge killing raid in the village of Kanga two days away across the trail. They were aware

43

that their turn had come. You could see the smoky yellowish-orange light of the lamps that the women were holding aloft around the village. The men were aware that any minute warriors would spring forth from the forest, war cries would ring out across the jungle, and fighting would begin. They kicked at the barking dogs to silence them, and told the children to hush as they listened for sounds of raiding warriors. Their trained ears were greeted by silence and the eerie sounds of a tropical night.

Then again came those piercing screams, but not from the forest. They came from the direction of the river. As of one, every man turned and faced the river. Slowly they moved toward the river peering out into the inky blackness. "There," they shouted, as the voices of three men were heard frantically calling for help.

"Save us, we can't get to the shore, we have lost our paddles and our canoe is heading for the rapids and whirlpools of Hankichak." Their voices trailed off in the distance, fading into the dark night.

The three men had crossed the river early that afternoon to participate in a masato beer party. Late that night, in a drunken stupor, they tried to return to the main village when their canoe was struck broadside by a huge wave. Thinking that they were going to capsize, they dropped their paddles in fear and clung desperately to the sides of the weaving bobbing canoe screaming for help, knowing that fifteen minutes downriver a watery grave awaited them. They could not get to shore and their canoe was caught in the heavy current and drifting quickly towards the rapids.

The women were crying and pleading with the men to go after the runaway canoe. They held their smoky yellowish-orange dim lamps aloft, but only the shadowy faces of crying children and concerned men were etched out of the darkness. No one responded to the desperate pleas that night. Again the women begged the men to save them, but they responded that it was too risky. "We do not have sufficient light and no motorized craft. They are on their own, because we too would be drawn into the whirlpools and all would be lost."

Women and children were running up and down along the riverbank, crying, when out of the shadows emerged a lone figure that hopeless night. His long black hair bobbed up and down on bare strong shoulders and he carried a large paddle in his hands. He wore only the hunting trunks typical of the men when they are out fishing or hunting at night. His feet were bare, thick, and calloused from endless trails. He strode through the group of men and every eye fastened on his face as he disappeared down the bank and into the darkness.

Coming to the river's edge, he untied the thick vine that held his long dugout canoe securely to the stout cane pole driven deeply into the sandy soil near the water's edge. The canoe was black and barely visible since it blended into the intense darkness. It was swaying back and forth in the cross currents along the river's edge, straining at the vine that held it steady. He had hand carved the long twenty-foot canoe from a fallen tree deep in the rain forest.

He walked to the back of the canoe and sat upon the hand carved seat, dipping his paddle into the water. Standing nearby was a young man looking out into the darkness for some sign of the runaway craft carrying the three helpless men. The older man commanded the young man to grab a paddle and accompany him, to which he did automatically. Obeying that authoritative voice, he shoved the canoe into deeper water and jumped into the bow, taking a kneeling position there. The older man, with long deep strokes, moved the canoe out onto the treacherous river that night, crisscrossing the heavy currents back and forth, searching for the runaway craft.

Long excruciating moments passed as their canoe picked up speed and was now moving rapidly toward the rapids and whirlpools of Hankichak. The young man in the bow was terrified, his eyes dilated, looking in every direction for some sign of the runaway, but his gaze was met only by the engulfing blackness that surrounded them. He wondered why he had obeyed that authoritative voice, but it was too late now as the frail craft was streaking downstream in the dead of night. Water splashed up from the side of the canoe, striking their near-naked bodies, chilling them to the bone. They could hardly make out the tree line on the distant shore as dark ominous clouds swirled overhead.

The older man was exhausted, arms aching, perspiration dripping from his tired body and every muscle screaming for rest, but on he continued with deep powerful broad strokes of his paddle. Rounding the next bend in the river, the young man stiffened and bolted upright in the canoe. In the distance they could hear the deafening roar of the water crashing upon the rocks at the beginning of the rapids.

"Lucho, turn the canoe aside and save us," the young man shouted above the din of noise. His hands clung desperately to the sides of the canoe that rocked back and forth in the clutches of the powerful cross currents. They could feel the river drawing them closer to the brink of disaster. Lucho responded by thrusting his paddle once again into the raging river, propelling it further toward the great rapids.

Time was of the essence as the canoe darted through the night picking up speed in the strong cross currents leading to the opening of the rapids. "Look," shouted the young man above the roar of the water, "Over there!" He pointed wildly to a dark object swaying in the rough current. It was the hapless craft bobbing up and down, drifting nearer to the rapids. A few minutes earlier he had laid his paddle hopelessly aside while clutching desperately to the sides of the canoe when it swayed from side to side in the heaving water. Now he frantically grabbed the paddle and with renewed energized excitement, paddled with all his strength.

The man in the stern, with new determination, called upon his reserves of strength to bite the water once more with deep powerful strokes. His well-conditioned muscles responded to the Herculean task of overtaking the runaway before they entered through the gateway to the rapids and whirlpools below.

Who was this man who was risking his life to save three drunken men from a watery grave? His name is Lucho Asangkay from the village of Chipe. As a young man he lived many miles up the Marañon River near the village of Yama Yakat. He came from a family of revenge killers. After one raid of retaliation, his family fled from the upriver area and established themselves downstream, founding the village of Chipe. Of all his brothers, Lucho was the most notorious for his exploits as a fighter and fierce warrior. His name was a household word all over the upper Amazon, since he had killed many men in tribal raids. He drank and fought with the best of them and was always victorious.

It was Sunday morning in the mission church, located on the banks of the Kusu River where it joins the great and mighty Marañon. A large crowd from the villages of Chipe, Kusu, and Listra filled the small church to overflowing. I looked out over the congregation that memorable day, observing the colorful people seated before me on those backless benches. There was Kunchiwai with his shotgun propped up by his side. His long black hair, cut with bangs across the forehead, hung loosely over his bare shoulders and round blue-tinted tattoo markings stood out on his high prominent cheekbones. Standing to the side of the church was Yaun from the village of Kusu. Attached to his ears hung earrings made of lovely feathers, and on his head rested a large beautifully bright colored crown of red and yellow Parrot feathers. His feet were bare and portrayed strength from walking a thousand trails.

In the back of the church, just outside, stood Chimpa, the local witchdoctor, observing the service. He wore the typical itipak (man's skirt) cinched around his waist with a thin vine knotted over the abdomen. The itipak is made on a handloom from local thread and dyed from vegetable extracts. He was bare-chested and leaned on the four-foot-high railing wall of the open church building. He made an impressive sight. His dark eyes took in every aspect of the service and his countenance was one of importance. On one ear hung a huge old safety pin and the other exposed a large hole bare of adornments.

The women sat on one side of the church with their children nestled between their legs and the men occupied the other side. An old skinny hunting dog slowly walked from the back of the church all the way to the front and promptly lay down on the dirt floor just in front of the small crude altar. He fell fast asleep as small flies buzzed his infected eyes.

We had been praying for weeks that these precious people would recognize their need and come to the altar seeking God. We were struggling with cultural concepts that made confession a very difficult challenge. They had never been a conquered or dominated people. They were proud warriors and fiercely independent. In their culture you do not forgive your enemies, you just kill them. Kneeling at the altar and confessing was a foreign concept.

This unforgettable Sunday, at the end of the sermon I gave an altar call and it was evident that God the Holy Spirit was speaking to hearts. Only the sound of rustling leaves from a light breeze could be heard that morning years ago. In the silence that ensued, a man from the men's section of the church made his way to the altar. He was a young strong warrior and you could feel a deep sense of awe flood the congregation.

Lucho Asangkay knelt at the altar and began to pray. The men couldn't believe their eyes, not Lucho of all people, why he had never bent his knee to anyone. Only his sobbing and rocking back and forth while holding onto the altar broke the deafening silence. His tears splashed from the altar onto the dirt floor and that morning long ago, Lucho Asangkay was transformed into a new creature in Jesus Christ.

For two years Lucho taught a men's Sunday school class out under the trees on the Kusu mission station. The results were rewarding as men from other villages came into direct contact with God's warrior. At this point Lucho decided that his village must have a church and he set out to build one. Timbers were carried in on his shoulders and those of two other men. One of the first village churches became a reality. He began holding services and preaching the best he knew how. In the village a small bi-lingual school had been started that went to the fourth or fifth grade. He sat in the classes with the children to learn how to read and write.

On occasion, I would walk the trail from the mission to the village of Chipe to visit the church on Sunday mornings. The trail led past Lucho's house and there he would be pouring over the scripture in broken sentences, reading out loud, unaware that he was being observed. My heart leaped for joy as I saw this man grow in grace and knowledge.

From a distance one could hear the singing as a few men, women and children lifted their voices in praise to their Creator. Their sound was a pleasing contrast to the monotonous beating of drums and high-pitched laughter coming from a drunken crowd just a few yards away in a nearby hut.

Time drifted on and something happened in the village of Chipe. "There goes God," some would shout out as Lucho passed by on the trail. Those who feared and respected him now reviled and mocked him, for he no longer joined in the drinking and fighting of days gone by. They persecuted him unmercifully. He was tempted to drink and fight, but God wonderfully held him steady. Life in the village became more and more difficult for God's preacher, until that fateful night on the river.

A few seconds passed and their canoe came alongside the runaway and the three men rolled into the larger canoe, lying on the bottom, shivering in the cool damp tropical night. The two men dug their paddles into the murky wet blackness, pulling deep strokes one after another, struggling with the heavy current. Their muscles burned and sweat poured from every pore of their tired bodies. The deafening sound of water crashing against the huge boulders at the opening of the rapids caused them to struggle on with every ounce of energy left in their exhausted arms. With their last waning bit of strength, they broke the strong current that was propelling their craft toward the rocks below and moved into the backwater that allowed them to reach the distant shore and safety from the raging river.

Three drunken men staggered onto the small beach, relieved that their nightmare was over. They couldn't believe that they had been spared a watery grave that night. Slowly the two men walked the canoe along the bank, pulling it way back upstream toward the village. On into the night they worked, passing bend after bend in this serpentine river. Finally they came around the last bend in the river and could see the yellowish-orange glow of numerous wick lamps. They could hear the loud crying of many women, the cry of death. They were chanting and crying that five men had drowned in the river this night.

On past the village they walked until they came to the spot in the river where they could paddle across the fast rolling river. Five men entered the canoe for the difficult crossing. Lucho and the young man skillfully maneuvered their craft through the night to the other side. As the canoe emerged out of the inky blackness, a cheer arose as three now somewhat sober men stepped from the canoe into the arms of their overjoyed families. Crying turned to laughter and sorrow to joy on the banks of the river that memorable night.

A hush ran through the crowd of people lining the bank when Lucho stepped from the canoe and walked past them on the way to his hut. Not a word was exchanged, and he disappeared into the darkness. The men of Chipe would never be the same, because that night it was not a message they heard, but one they saw, and it changed the history of the Aguarunas forever.

Revival broke out and many of those men followed in the footsteps of Lucho. God had found a man, a man willing to risk it all and put his life on the line to save three drunken men from certain disaster. Village after village invited Lucho Asangkay to visit them and present the claims of Christ. He traveled to distant villages proclaiming the Good News to a people hungry for change.

"God's Warrior" - on left Lucho Asangkay on right Jorge Wampatsag (DS - Amazon District)

Today, forty-four years later, his name is still a household word in the upper Amazon; not for drinking, fighting or revenge war raids, but for the untold number of people he has personally won to his Lord. He's an old man now, bent with age, but vibrant and unwavering in his love for the Master.

The beautiful aspect of missions is that there is always "The rest of the story." It's generational, ongoing, and non-ending, because we elect to continually support the Great Commission.

Now for the rest of the story. Years later on a Monday morning, the director of the Bible Institute asked me to substitute for one of the absent teachers. I walked into the class of the first year students beginning their three-year preparation to become pastors. I did not know any of these students, so I asked them to stand one by one, give me their names, and tell me which village they were from. The excitement mounted as students gave their names and told of their home villages. I was overwhelmed when three men mentioned that they were from the Morona River and it had taken them many days of travel to reach our mission station. They were Huambisa Indians from a neighboring tribe and had been evangelized by the Aguarunas. Next, a young man about twenty years old said, "My name is Sejekam and I am from the village of Chipe downriver."

We had lived our first sixteen years on the backside of Chipe and I had treated nearly everyone at one time or another in the clinic before moving our mission station twenty-five miles upriver many years before. The name Sejekam rang a bell and so I asked him, "Who is your father?" He stated that his father was Hector Sejekam. "You are Hector's son!" I said in amazement.

"Yes," he repeated, "do you know my father?"

'Do I know your father,' I thought to myself. He never cared for things spiritual and seldom darkened the door of the church. "How is your father?" I asked.

"You haven't heard," he responded. "My dad gave his heart to the Lord sometime back and is now serving on the church board in the village of Chipe."

"Your dad got saved and is on the church board?" I said almost in disbelief.

"Yes," he countered, "and that is the reason I am here preparing for ministry."

My mind went back to a dark, foreboding night in the village of Chipe many years before. Hector Sejekam was one of the three drunken men in a runaway canoe headed for destruction in a raging river. God had a plan that night and He found a man to fulfill it.

To God be the glory, for great things He has done.

"Look to the Ant, You Sluggard..."

Proverbs 6:6

Looking across our beautiful front yard which faced the slow moving waters of the Kusu stream and the soft rolling hills in the distance covered with the evergreen beauty of the rain forest beneath a cloudless blue sky, I spotted an ugly brownish-black six-inch-wide trail zigzagging through our well manicured lawn. Curiously I approached the spot and was astonished to see thousands of one-fourth-inch-long brown ants going in both directions as fast as their six little legs could carry them. It reminded me of the Los Angeles Freeway at 5:00 p.m. on Fridays, except those ants coming from the direction of the river were carrying triangular shaped pieces of green leaves with the point extending skyward on their backs, while those rushing toward the river were leafless.

Dumbfounded, I watched them for a long time, standing there in our front yard, learning lessons of nature. In their haste, an occasional ant trying to pass another would veer out of his lane and run headlong into opposing traffic. His cargo was then dislodged, fell to the ground, and was trampled on by hundreds of tiny feet in the space of seconds.

I observed that they had two choices in regards to the fallen leaf. One was to try and retrieve it without getting trampled on, or leave it on the trail, turn around in traffic causing a little bumping and head disappointingly back to get another piece of leaf. I saw many leaves on the ground, so evidently the latter was the better choice.

I looked in both directions, but their trail disappeared around trees and fallen logs. Instinctively I followed those ants running at top speed toward the river. Their trail led around a fallen tree, and then, about thirty yards away, took me to a beautiful fifty-foot tall tree whose leaves gracefully waved under a gentle breeze. The trail stopped at the foot of this lovely giant, and my eyes fastened on two lanes of traffic running the length of the tree. One lane was packed with ants climbing to the tallest part of the tree, going to the farthest branch and cutting out a small triangular piece of leaf with their powerful scissor-like jaws from the most distant leaf. The descending lane consisted of thousands of ants carrying their cargo back down the tree, appearing to me like miniature sailboats as they connected with their freeway and were soon out of sight.

I decided to follow them and find out where they were going and why. Their trail led me on a twisting turning journey nearly sixty yards away to a spot on the hillside behind our home. Once there I observed a large volcano shaped mound of fine loose reddish dirt with ants coming and going from its mouth. I was fascinated with the size of the area around this mound of dirt, since it was quite large and a beehive of activity. Climbing back down the hill, following their trail to our front yard. I was amazed how much of our lawn they had destroyed. I determined then and there to rid our yard of their presence. After all, they were destroying a beautiful tree. They can find another tree away from our lovely lawn, I thought.

I have done a study on these ants, commonly known as the leaf cutters. Their dedication, work ethic, and division of labor for a common cause are absolutely admirable. Beneath that volcano shaped mound of dirt is a nest of extensive and multiple tunnels that may run underground to a length of ten to twenty feet. In the nest lives the queen mother, about the size of a newborn mouse. She lays hundreds of thousands of small white eggs that soon hatch, filling the nest with willing workers.

"Go to the ant, you sluggard; Consider her ways and be wise, which having no guide, overseer, or ruler, provides her supplies in the summer, and gathers her food in the harvest" (Proverbs 6:6-8 NKJV)

These ants work diligently at the task of providing food for their great numbers. The leaves, carried into the nest, line the walls of these cavernous tunnels. The dampness of the tunnels and moisture from the leaves cause a fungus to grow on them, which is, in turn, the food they eat.

The division of labor is as follows: A group of ants called the scouts are sent out to find a tree that will provide a good supply of leaves. Once a tree is found they begin surveying and laying out a trail from tree to nest, trying to cover the shortest distance possible. They cut every blade of grass, remove every small twig and leave the ground barren and seemingly lifeless all along this new trail.

Next, they lay a scent on the trail that will be picked up by the leaf cutters, leading them from the nest to the tree. Back at the nest, guarding the entrance to the tunnels, are the soldier ants. They stand guard against predators like large insects that try to gain entrance to eat the succulent white eggs laid by the queen. When one of these intruders invades the nest, the soldier ants attack them with their razor-like jaws, cutting them to shreds.

Further inside the nest are the workers whose job is to receive the cut leaves and carry them deep inside to line the walls of the tunnels.

The stage is set, all is ready, and the leaf cutters begin their march to the tree. It's amazing to me how these tiny one-fourth-inch-long ants stand at the base of a giant tree, look upward, and say to themselves, 'Tree, you have had it, we are going to strip you bare.' The audacity of these seemingly impotent creatures to tackle a job of this enormity is beyond belief. They actually believe they can do it and so they set out to work.

If we could proportionately compare these one-fourth-inch-long ants to a man it would be something like this: the man would be six feet tall, able to carry eight hundred pounds on his back, and run at speeds of fifteen miles an hour all day long. They are a marvel of creation.

That day long ago I formulated a plan. I took a five-gallon can of gasoline and a book of matches with me to the front yard. I poured a small amount of gasoline along a ten-foot section of their trail. I then lit a match, saw flames leap across the barren ground, and watched ants pop, fry, and sizzle. This will discourage them, I thought, picking up the can of gas and turning to make my way back to the fuel house.

I glanced at the scorched trail once more, only to see a confused little ant shake his head to clear his senses, and then stand on wobbly legs. I couldn't believe my eyes as he picked up the scent, heading again to the tree, with hundreds of others joining him.

Frustrated, but not defeated, I took another course of action. Following their trail I made my way up the hillside to the volcano shaped nest, where five gallons of gas was poured into the hole. I then made a thin trail of gas some distance from the hole. Grinning to myself, I lit a match and the explosion that followed was heard halfway around the mission station, creating a minor earthquake in Northern Perú.

When the smoke cleared, the view was incredible. The hole was blown to smithereens and then the entire jungle grew silent. With the empty gas can in one hand and matches in the other, I congratulated myself on this new hard-fought victory. Taking three steps down the hill I glanced about once more, looking over my shoulder, gloating about my success, when my attention was instantly focused on a slight movement and flickering of dirt where the mouth of the nest had been located.

All of a sudden up popped a small round head, followed by two little legs clawing at the dirt in great desperation as if to escape this tomb of death. Next appeared two more legs and then two more, as finally an entire body lay prostrate on the ground. Fascinated, I watched as this little ant stood on all six wobbly legs, shaking his head and then turn toward the trail gathering speed as he went, heading straight for the tree.

He was followed by thousands of companions as soon as the hole was open again for normal traffic. I stood there in disbelief, but learned a great lesson that day. Determination, tenacity, and everyone working for a common cause can bring the victory.

There are many analogies that could be brought into play here, but the one I know most about is our missionary enterprise worldwide. From our local church and district NMI activities around the world a common bond holds us together. Prayer, fasting, links, alabaster, compassionate ministry, radio, work and witness, reading books, World Evangelism Fund and all the other nitty-gritty things we do, many of which might seem small and insignificant, lend themselves to one purpose, and that is bringing people, worldwide, to Jesus.

NOTE:
By the way, several days later I looked upon that tree which had been vibrant in color with her green leaves glistening under a bright tropical sun, only to see her branches bare with not a leaf in sight. It looked as if winter had set in and her empty limbs were another reminder to me to stick tenaciously to the task of bringing people into the Kingdom.

Christian leaf cutters, stay at the job. We will win the world for Christ!

Lost on the Trail

My Indian helper came to me one day stating that we needed to build a cookhouse on the end of the clinic so that the patients' families would have a place to prepare food for their sick loved ones. "We do not have funds to purchase the sheets of metal for a roof," I explained.

"No problem," he said. "We can build the framework with poles cut from the jungle, and then bring in the long yarina leaves to weave on the lattice poles with thin vines to make a good roof that will withstand high winds and heavy rains."

"Great idea," I responded, "but where can we obtain the yarina leaves?"

"Tomorrow I will take two workers upriver and we will cut them from the forest in the high country," he answered.

I was a new, young, energetic missionary at the time with a great desire to learn everything about their culture that I could. "Moisés, I would like to go with you tomorrow to help with this project."

He paused, looked serious, and said, "No, you wouldn't be able to keep up with us on the trail."

His words hit me like cold water. 'I will show you what I am made of,' I thought to myself, and so countered with, "Yes, I can."

"Are you sure?" he replied.

"I will be ready in the morning. What time are we going?" I asked.

"7:00 A.M.," came the reply.

"Ayu, Kashin Wainyami" (Okay, see you tomorrow), I said and left for home. The next morning after breakfast I told Addie that I would be gone upriver most of the day and thus made preparations for the trip. I put on a long sleeved shirt to keep the bugs off, and high boots to walk in the mud and defend myself from any snake we might accidentally encounter. I was ready and climbed into our long dugout canoe boat for the trip ahead of us.

We struggled upriver against the heavy current, rounding bend after bend on the twisting, muddy torrent of the Marañon River. About forty-five minutes later we headed for shore in an area unfamiliar to me. As our boat glided into the mud bank lined with dense jungle I noticed that there was no trail and the undergrowth was so thick you could hardly see through it. "Moisés," I asked, "where is the trail?"

"It's a little used hunting trail," he replied, and I stood dumbfounded watching all three machete-wielding men spring up onto the bank after securely tying up the boat to a nearby tree. They were all barefooted and wore only hunting trunks with no shirt. They paused, looking back at me as I clumsily stumbled out of the boat onto the shore, standing in dense undergrowth.

"This way," they said, and were off in a flash, swinging their machetes viciously at stubborn plants covering what had been at one time used as a hunting trail. I followed a few yards behind them trying to keep up the best I could. The morning air was stifling and humid, and birds flew off in every direction to escape these intruders.

The old hunting trail was narrow and covered with low hanging vines that they hurriedly cut as they sprinted along. They, being shorter of stature, left hanging vines at about my chin height, which allowed more than one of these to get a choke hold on me, causing me to stop and free my neck from its death grip. The trail became steeper and steeper as we climbed higher and further into the jungle. Perspiration was dripping from my now saturated clothing. My feet were hot and my legs were tired from running uphill in heavy boots, slipping and sliding along the narrow trail. The men's tough conditioned feet carried them swiftly through the jungle as I plodded along getting further behind. Every muscle in my body cried out for relief from this unrelenting torture I was enduring all in the name of proving to them how tough I was.

They had never traveled in cars and their strong muscled legs carried them like deer through the forest. Stopping to get my breath for the umpteenth time, I noticed that they too had stopped and were swinging their machetes at something on the side of the trail. Soon my weary legs took me to a small clearing where they had already cut a number of Yarina leaves and were rolling them into a long bundle. I paused, wiping perspiration from my forehead and hiking up my pants that were eternally being pulled down by sweat-drenched boots. Oh, how tired I was on that unforgettable day long ago in the rain forest of Perú.

I watched as they cut the Yarina leaves from a clump of leaves growing seemingly right out of the ground. Each clump had about twelve long leaves. The Yarina has a stout stem in the middle and thin two-foot individual leaves grow out from two sides and each stem is about ten feet long. They cut ten stem leaves off, leaving two on the clump to regrow. These leaves are rolled into a tight bundle and tied with long round vines. Each bundle weighs approximately thirty pounds and is about ten feet long. They quickly made two bundles and informed me that they were going into the high country to look for more leaves. High country, I thought. I was exhausted now, and had no desire to further torture my tired body. They hesitated, waiting for me to join them. Right away I formulated a plan of action.

With renewed confidence and looking at my watch (they had no watches), I told them that I would take these two bundles of leaves to the boat and return for more. "You go on to the high country, and bring the bundles to this central receiving and distribution center while I make trips back and forth loading the boat." Good plan I thought to myself. This will be a wonderful lesson for the men on organization and administrative skills.

Why, we will do this job in half the time and I won't have to kill myself doing it. I can take these bundles to the boat and come back up the hill at my own pace. As Moisés turned to go he asked, "Can you find the boat?"

'What a dumb question,' I thought, and said, "Sure, no problem."

They took off, fleet of foot, and disappeared into the forest. I stood for a long moment congratulating myself on a well-laid-out plan. I proceeded to place one long bundle over my shoulder and the other cradled under my free arm, and turned to go downhill to the boat. I was making good time threading my way down the thin cut trail, when the bundle on my shoulder got tangled up in a hanging vine that spun me around, throwing me to the ground. I picked myself up, readjusted my load only to have it happen again.

As I sat on the damp soil looking skyward, I noticed just how thick the canopy of the rain forest is and that hardly any sunlight penetrated its entanglement. It was then that I noticed the intense burning sensation spreading all across my neck. It felt like someone had lit a thousand matches and pressed them to the skin on the back of my neck. The pain was excruciating as I reached and pulled off untold numbers of tiny red fire ants. In my haste to show the Indians that I was tough, they didn't have time to teach me the art of shaking the leaves vigorously before putting them on my shoulder. At long last the burning subsided somewhat and once again I got to my feet, brushing leaves and dirt from my tired body.

The trails in the rain forest are usually narrow and twisting with tree roots ready to trip the unwary. The ground covering is always damp and wet with decaying vegetation. Since the sun cannot penetrate the entanglement of trees, vines, and a myriad of jungle plants, the trails become very slippery and precarious, especially the steep slopes.

That day I spent more time on one part of my anatomy than I care to talk about. With my dignity somewhat recovered, I looked around to get my bearings and see what direction the trail to the river took. I then discovered that the trail had vanished, disappeared, and was nowhere to be found. Turning in every direction, I was greeted by the quietness of the jungle, but no trail. It seemed as though all life in the jungle had come to a quick stand still and there was only silence to greet my ears. At my feet lay two bundles of tied up leaves with thousands of little red ants running here and there. I shuddered at the thought of picking those up again. There I stood, tired, thirsty, covered with mud, clothes wringing wet with perspiration, alone, and scared to death. I was afraid to move from this tiny clearing, knowing that if I did, something would either bite or sting me. At that moment I had a real fear of snakes. I knew that the next step I took would probably lead me to one of them. I stood frozen in time, wondering what to do.

Then it came to me. I reached way back into my missionary training and did what any good Christian would do in that lost state. I screamed at the top of my lungs. I would have prayed had I thought about it, but I just wanted to hear and see another human being. My yelling was only greeted by silence.

Desperate now, I cupped my hands around my mouth like I had seen the Indians do and yelled in a falsetto voice. They can communicate for a long distance this way as their voices carry from clearing to clearing. I listened, but there was only silence. Again I called with a more controlled voice. My ears, hungry to hear another human sound, picked up a slight trailing falsetto voice deep in the forest. Again I listened, concentrating all of my energies in the direction of that slight sound I had heard. This time it was a little clearer and stronger. Faintly I heard, "Doctorooooooo," somewhere up the trail.

I made a new trail that day without a machete. Both feet never hit the ground at the same time. The adrenalin was flowing and I followed the sound of that voice. Panting and out of breath, I stopped in a small clearing to call again. My heart was racing wildly and my excitement was mounting at the thought of seeing another human. I called again and waited.

"Doctorooooooo," came the sound again, but much clearer and distinct. I relaxed a bit and took off on a dead run. Around the bend in the trail I could see the three men calmly cutting and tying up bundles of leaves. I stopped to get my breath, brush off the bigger chunks of dirt, straighten up my disheveled hair, and slowly strode into camp, like nothing had happened. They knew exactly what had happened, but asked no questions. That is the beautiful part of their culture; they never try to embarrass another person.

I told them that this idea of splitting up and working in two groups was not a good idea. We came out here together and we needed to stay and work together to get the job done. Moisés only smiled as he continued cutting leaves.

I learned a great lesson that day that has helped me across the years in challenging times. The Lord is only a prayer away and if we call on Him and listen we will hear His still small voice and we can follow it to safety.

P.S. My two bundles of leaves…I have no idea where they are. For all I cared they could have rotted in the jungle and they probably did.

Murphy's Law in the Amazon

Sunday dawned with a blue sky and fluffy white clouds lazily drifting overhead, advertising a perfectly beautiful day in the rain forest. Today I announced that we will be going with Miguel (an Indian bi-lingual teacher) to his village of San Pablo to encourage the new believers in establishing yet another young church.

Preparations had been made Saturday for the trip downriver. Addie baked most of the morning, preparing bread, cinnamon rolls and other goodies. Sleeping gear, mosquito nets, and other items were readied for the trip on Sunday. We would take the long dugout canoe so that all could go on this anticipated evangelistic adventure. The Garman family of six, Miguel, and two young men from our Nazarene colleges would be going right after the morning worship service and lunch.

Addie went to the kitchen to prepare breakfast while I went to take a quick shower. Usually we bathed every afternoon in the cool waters of the Kusu River. However, this Sunday morning I decided to shower in our bathroom. It was so small you could stick out your elbows and nearly touch the walls.

I will never forget our very first night in the jungle, settling into our small house in the rain forest. The sun disappeared in the western sky and night came quickly. With darkness came the bats flying in the house. The bats flew one way and Addie the other, screaming, "Kill it! Kill it!" Candy, our three year old was crying, following Addie, shouting "Mommy, Mommy, what is it?" That first night I killed fifteen bats in the house, knocking them out of the air with my broom as they came at me like dive bombers.

One of those bats flew into our small bathroom and I flew in right behind him, closing the door so that he could not escape. He flew up, down, and side to side nearly making me dizzy. I couldn't even swing the broom in those closed quarters, since the walls were so close together. I struggled to get the upper hand, but I didn't have built in radar. All at once I was on the defensive, throwing up my flailing arms, protecting my face and wondering why I had elected to be a hero. For some unknown reason that bat took a nosedive right into the toilet.

Immediately, I slammed the lid down and thought to myself, "Bat, you have had it, goodbye," and I flushed the toilet. I waited a long moment, until the rushing sound of water was over and lifted the lid triumphantly. To my surprise, he was hanging on to the edge of the bowl with two tiny feet and was dripping wet. He had that sad, terrified look on his face and couldn't believe what had just taken place in that swirling dark world.

Turning on the shower, I lathered up with soap and then, without warning, the water stopped. Covered with soap, I realized that all four water tanks had run dry. Our water supply came from two hundred and fifty gallon tanks that were on a hillside above the house. Water was gravity fed through a one-inch plastic pipe from the tanks to our home. To fill the tanks, we had to crank up the diesel generator, go to the river, and climb out onto a large raft made of empty fifty gallon sealed steel barrels that were tied together. There was a platform made from cane poles, nailed onto a wooden frame. On the platform sat our water pump with a three-foot plastic pipe that hung out over the raft and into the river. Throwing open the switch, the electric pump would pump water through a two-inch tube that snaked its way over the lawn and up a hill one hundred yards away to fill the tanks.

With soap stinging my eyes, I shouted to Addie that the tanks were dry and she needed to send one of the boys to pump water. I stood in the shower for what seemed like an eternity as soap began drying on my lathered body.

A few minutes later I heard one of the boys yelling back to his mother these dreaded words: "Mom, tell Dad that the pump isn't pumping water."

"Larry, the pump isn't pumping," Addie said.

"Addie, tell the boys to prime the pump with water."

More time passed and again the dreaded message was relayed to me, "Mom, tell Dad that the prime won't hold and the pump isn't working."

"Boys," Addie said, "bring up a bucket of water from the river, so that your dad can rinse off." At long last the bucket of water arrived and I dipped a cup into it to rinse off the dried soap. At this point, there is no water in the house, the pump won't work, and Murphy is working overtime. When I emerged from the bathroom Addie asked, "We aren't going to go downriver are we?"

I responded, "No problem, I'll fix the pump in a jiffy," and off to the river I went with tools in hand. Climbing onto the raft, I dismantled the water pump with perspiration dripping from every pore of my body. While I was working on the pump, Moisés, our boat driver, asked if he should take the long dugout canoe boat upriver to the village of Chipe to pick up the Indian women and children for Sunday school.

"Yes," I responded, and added, "we will take the long boat to San Pablo after the morning service." He soon returned with a load of people and informed me that the outboard motor wasn't working well. "I will work on it right after I finish fixing the pump," I told him.

At that moment Addie sent word that the kerosene stove wouldn't light. Kerosene stoves are notorious for breaking down when you are busy, tired, at night, or getting ready to go some place in a hurry. "Tell Mom that I will work on the stove right after church," and to myself added, 'after I work on the pump and the outboard motor.' Leaving both inoperable, I went to the house to clean up again, change clothes and go to church.

Entering the house, I took a quick look at the stove sitting there inoperable and, I'm sure, silently laughing at me. Again came that familiar voice, "Larry, I don't think we are supposed to go downriver today."

Once more I responded, "No problem, as soon as church is over, I will finish repairing the pump, outboard motor, and then tackle the stove." I added that I would have these jobs done in no time.

We went to church that beautiful sunny day and celebrated a wonderful service with Indians from three villages. After the church service, I changed clothes and began tackling my chores again. The raft rocked a little as Mom's messenger of good news jumped on board relaying the following message. "Dad, Mom wants to know how she can cook lunch without a stove."

"Tell Mom to use the primus," I replied. The primus is a one burner, small kerosene pressure stove that has to be pumped every few minutes to keep the flame burning. Addie painstakingly cooked one item at a time, which meant that the meal took a long time to prepare and no two dishes were hot at the same time.

Lunch was over and again Addie broached the subject of going downriver. "I don't think that we are supposed to go downriver today," she stated.

Calmly I responded, "No, as long as there is a way, we should explore it. We can take the speedboat downriver and tomorrow I will fix the outboard motor on the dugout boat."

Addie responded, "We can't all go in the speed boat, it's too small for nine people, sleeping gear, and food. No way."

"As long as there is a way we should try and go," I countered. At long last the boat was loaded with all the supplies and people. The load was so heavy that the boat sat low in the water. We were ready for a beautiful ride downriver when I realized that we had forgotten to bring the kerosene lamp. "Rusty, run to the house and bring the lamp." Soon he returned triumphantly with the lamp in tow. Addie, holding Tim on her lap, took the lamp and balanced it on one knee.

The twin outboard motors were started and we lumbered away from the quiet waters of our port on the calm Kusu River into the twisting, tumbling torrent of the larger and rougher Marañon River. The boat pitched and lurched in the heavy waves, causing kerosene to spill from the rocking lamp all over Addie's clothes. She screamed, "Larry, the kerosene is everywhere."

"Don't worry," I said, "We will take care of it, stay calm."

"Rusty, please check the motors to see if they are pumping water."

"Dad, one is pumping, the other is not."

"Larry," Addie yelled half crying, "What are you going to do?"

"Wait a few minutes and we will check the motors again," I countered.

The boat was rolling in the river making very little progress. "Dad, one is pumping but the other refuses to pump water," Rusty yelled from the back of the boat. Addie shouted above the noise of the motors and rushing water, empathically stating that we had better go back.

"Hang on," I said. "I will check on the motor." At that moment we crossed our own wake and water poured in over the side of the boat, drenching everybody and everything on board.

I turned to Miguel and told him that we've tried, but won't be able to go to San Pablo today. "Where shall we let you out?" I asked him.

"Drop me off at Lorenzo's hut just across the river," came the reply. Sitting low in the water and wet to the bone, we headed for shore. Approaching the shoreline, we hit a rock, breaking a shear pin on the one good motor. The boat sat helpless in the water and at the mercy of the river. One of the college students jumped into the river pulling the boat to safety, and looking skyward said, "That's enough, Lord, that's enough, we are going back."

Finally, after dark, we made it back to our port and home. Addie had a terrible headache and everyone else was tired, hungry, and wet. After unloading the boat, Addie said, "I need a cup of hot coffee." She looked at the inoperative stove and then remembered the small primus. She pumped up the pressure, opened the valve, lit a match and held it to the burner, but there was no response, no flame, so now even the primus stove wouldn't light. "Oh, no," she exclaimed, "nothing works."

I quickly went to our storage area, retrieving a can of canned heat (solidified alcohol). A match was struck, the alcohol flamed up and a cup of coffee was soon in the hands of a tired missionary wife.

Finally at 11:30 p.m. on that unforgettable Sunday, I had the kerosene stove operable. By the way, the San Pablo church is doing very well.

THANKS A LOT MURPHY.

A Dark Night

"But Doctor, you must come! My aunt is terribly sick, and I am afraid that she is going to die!"

It was a beautiful day with a bright blue sky, and fluffy white clouds floating overhead, as I looked upon the panoramic view afforded me through the screened window of the clinic that morning long ago. The turbulent waters of the Marañon River stretched out like a large bluish-green ribbon flowing between rolling green velvety hills disappearing into the tropical rain forest below the Kusu mission station.

Desperately the man tried to persuade me to accompany him back to his village at Nueva Vida way downriver where he claimed his aunt was very ill. He had come a long way to the Kusu clinic in search of medical help. He had hoped that I would immediately journey with him to treat the sick aunt. I questioned him at length about the sick aunt, because I had made other trips on the spur of the moment, one in a rainstorm and another in the dead of night, risking my life only to find the patients quite well.

We call the Aguarunas happy pessimists because of their near fatalistic approach to sickness. They are a very happy people, but extremely negative and pessimistic about the mysterious nature of illness. One does not die from natural causes, but from witchcraft. The fears of the spirit world held our people in bondage, thus a negative outlook on life was ingrained in them since childhood.

Again he pleaded, "My aunt has severe abdominal pain and the women are already saying that she is going to die." Against my better judgment, I said that I would make the trip downriver to examine his aunt.

Instructions were given to Moisés, my helper, to prepare the speedboat with enough gasoline for the long trip to the village and back. I prepared my emergency medical kit with the needed supplies to treat most of the tropical maladies of the rain forest. It was now early afternoon, and the sun was shining brightly overhead as we prepared to depart for our trip downriver. Goodbyes were exchanged between Addie and me, and she asked, "What time will you be back?"

"I will be home before dark," I replied, as the three of us embarked in the little boat with Addie's words still ringing in my ears to be careful.

Leaving the calm clear waters of the Kusu River, the boat was met with the turbulent, dark muddy current of the Marañon River. It was immediately rocked to and fro before it began to plane on its course down the twisting larger river. The boat plunged forward moving rapidly downstream. To my right sat Moisés, and directly behind me sat the anxious and pensive man from Nueva Vida. With the wind in our faces and the wake to our back we headed for the great, large, intimidating pongo called Hanquichank. A pongo is a section of river filled with rapids, cross currents, and swirling whirlpools, waiting to destroy any unsuspecting object venturing into its dangerous waters. This pongo is so menacing because the river drops about three feet, crashes across huge boulders, makes a complete right angle turn, divides the water into two parts each moving in opposite directions, while cascading through the canyon walls lining each side of the river.

Rounding the next bend in the river we could see the white-capped waves and hear the roar of a raging river racing toward the great pongo. The upper Amazon drops twenty feet for every mile it travels. The lower Amazon drops only one half inch for every mile that it travels on its way to the Atlantic Ocean. We were on the upper Amazon.

Approaching the pongo, my hands mechanically gripped the steering wheel of our small speedboat as adrenalin raced through my veins. My eyes were dilated and focused on the incredible scene unfolding before me in this powerful force of nature. I was searching that vast stretch of water, looking for the precise entrance to this swirling inferno.

My thoughts were abruptly interrupted by the calm voice of Moisés. "Enter on the right," he said, "and break the rapids head on, skim the outer edge of the upper whirlpool, and bear hard to the right following the main channel leading on downriver." He knew this river like his hand, and I followed his instructions to a tee. We shot the rapids and navigated the lower end of the pongo while the waters raged all around our small craft. Cold water splashed across the sides of our boat sending an exhilarating thrill through our tense bodies on this beautiful sunny day. Downstream we plunged and finally hit the calmer waters leading us past the dangers of Hanquichank.

I was extremely glad that we navigated this treacherous part of the river during daylight hours. On downstream we threaded our course through lovely country. The plush vegetation on every side, glistening under a tropical sun, was almost overwhelming with beauty. Emerging from the many hillsides were the occasional smaller streams, surrendering their crystal clear bubbly waters into the dark Marañon that seemed to gobble them up before our very eyes.

We passed typical Indian villages with their thatched roof huts dotting the many jutted hillsides in the rolling mountainous rain forest. These rounded huts were beautiful as they adorned the blue sky, breaking the monotony of the eternal green of the jungle. It was a welcomed relief for our searching eyes, and took our minds momentarily from the constant slap of water against the hull of our little boat.

My thoughts were interrupted by Moisés' command, "Steer to the left," as we rounded another of the many torturous curves in the river. He pointed out the unseen obstacle to novice eyes. There on the right, hidden below the surface of the water, was a sandbar waiting to bring our boat and its occupants to a grinding jolting halt. With a skilled navigator like Moisés who knew the river like the palm of his hand sitting by my side, this obstacle was soon left in our wake and we were on our way further into the interior.

The sun was hot. How welcome was the cool air striking us in the face as our motor pushed us on toward the village of Nueva Vida. The humdrum and lull of the motor relaxed us a bit as we viewed the occasional Indian garden of cultivated plants dotting the nearby hillsides. The stillness of the leaves on the papaya plants and their yellowish-green fruit ripening under a beautiful sky reminded me of God's provision to His creation.

Again the silence was broken as Moisés said, "Be careful and stay wide to the right as there are partially submerged logs up ahead." These logs, I knew, could do extensive damage to a boat and even cause it to capsize if not carefully avoided. To the right we went and soon were clear of that hidden danger lurking under the surface of the water. Around the next bend the village came into view, and a few minutes later we arrived at the sandy beach port of Nueva Vida. Stepping from the boat, we were greeted by excited villagers who ushered us up the semi-steep trail past the gardens of yuca and bananas to the hut of the sick aunt. Greetings were exchanged with the many concerned adults before ducking through the narrow opening made from the five or six light softwood logs that made a semblance of a door, allowing us entrance to the hut. Once inside, my eyes adjusted to the surroundings and finally came to rest on the agonizing lady lying on a split bamboo bed in obvious pain.

The one-room dirt-floored hut showed very sparse furnishings. There were several beds around the walls of the home, indicating where the many members of the household slept. A young lady attended the cooking fire made of three logs with a pot of green cooking bananas that were boiling for future consumption.

A black skinny hunting dog bared his teeth, snarling and straining at the strong vine that held him *(fleas and all)* to the nearby bed, as I drew close to the center of the room. Crossing the room away from the smoke of the fire, I could see the blackened, soot-covered small woven basket tied to a beam directly over the cooking pot. In the basket was a dried-out, well-used banana leaf that contained the dark brown crystal rock salt used for seasoning their foods. The constant heat from the fire kept the salt dry and hard. On a rack made of pieces of bamboo tied together with thin stout vines, about two feet from the fire, hung pieces of deer meat being smoked and cured.

The ladies hurriedly placed a curtain around the sick loved one to ward off curious eyes and allow me to examine the patient in privacy. While I was waiting for them to hang the make-shift curtain of rags, blankets, and plastic strung across a long round vine which was tied to a long pole attached to a corner of the bed with the other end fastened to the support pole of the roof, my eyes took in the details of this home in the rain forest.

Hanging on the wall were bleached white skulls of many wild animals that the hunter husband of this household had killed over the past several months to provide meat on the table for his family. These well-dried skulls were trophies of his skill with the ancient of all weapons, the blowgun.

Immediately my eyes swept to a spot beside the upright beam supporting the roof to that familiar black, elongated tube which fired those poisonous darts silently through the quietness of the forest into the tender flesh of those unsuspecting animals. The blowgun was resting on its bone mouthpiece that was placed upon a piece of balsa wood. A wad of cotton was stuffed in either end to keep the wasps and insects from building their nests inside, thus rendering the gun inoperable. Beside the blowgun was a quiver filled with poisonous darts, ready for the next hunt.

"Docturo," the call came from behind the curtain, as the anxious husband beckoned me to examine his wife. Slipping to the edge of the bed and ducking behind the curtain, I was face to face with a very sick lady indeed. She clutched at her abdomen as agonizing groans fell from her dry parched lips. Examination revealed an acute abdomen, but her vital signs were strong. An injection was given to rebuke the pain, and I calmly stated that she needed to be interned in the clinic upriver.

A confab between the relatives took place as to the merits of sending her to the clinic as opposed to her staying and being treated here at home, probably by the witchdoctor. The discussion became very animated about the pros and cons of her going far away to that strange clinic on the Kusu River. Time was passing very rapidly as the afternoon wore on without a decision being made. I looked at my watch and insisted that a decision be made now, while there was still enough daylight to reach the mission station and clinic. The women began crying when the decision was made to take her to the clinic. They cried and stated that she should stay, because she would die upriver and they wouldn't be there to care for her. They always prefer to die at home.

Down the trail our long procession proceeded. Strong and willing arms gently carried the sick young mother on a bamboo stretcher toward the river. Finally we arrived at the sand beach where our boat was tied. She was tenderly placed on the floor of the speedboat directly behind my seat in a small open space. Goodbyes were said amid the confusion of high pitched wailing and last minute instructions to the husband who sat close to his wife in the back seat. He had packed a few articles of clothing, a machete, a blanket, a cooking pot, and some pieces of yuca into two large baskets. His eyes portrayed fear and anxiety over the decision made to head upriver. The engine roared to life and we waved our goodbyes to the large crowd standing and crying on the bank, as our boat pulled from shore and headed home.

The sun was sinking low and looming like a big ball of orange on the horizon as shadows crept across the water where the treetops blocked out her warm rays. I knew that we must hasten before darkness encroached upon the jungle, thus making travel extremely dangerous. The motor was accelerated and the boat struggled against the heavy current, pushing its way upstream. Silently we made headway, as the boat picked up speed and began to plane on top of the water. The hum of the motor and splashing of water across the hull was interrupted only by faint groaning sounds coming from the sick lady as she lay on the floor of the fast moving craft. I held onto the steering wheel with one hand while the other automatically reached back to check the pulse of our patient. At the same time, I was carefully maintaining our course on the river with both eyes riveted straight ahead to avoid the many obstacles in this fast moving current.

We were about ten minutes into our trip, when the husband began to cry, stating that his wife was dying. Immediately we were persuaded to turn around and return downstream to the village we had just left. As soon as our boat reached the sandy beach, everyone converged on the scene crying and wailing as news was shouted back and forth that she was dying. I quickly examined the patient, discovering that she was suffering from hyperventilation. The speed of the boat, of which she was unfamiliar, gave the impression of taking her breath away, thus creating anxiety and causing the patient to hyperventilate. Explanations were made and again we were off for the mission station. Darkness was engulfing the river as the sun dipped behind the trees, disappearing in the western sky.

To my immediate right sat Moisés, relaxed and settling back for the long ride home. Directly behind me and to the middle of the boat lay the sick mother, with her husband close by sitting in deep thought. All attention was now given to the river with its constant slapping against our small craft. Only the faintest outline of the trees could be seen as our boat sped along in the inky darkness of the Amazon. With one hand on the wheel and the other on the now normal pulsating wrist of my sleepy patient, I pondered the trip ahead through the rough obstacle-filled and unfamiliar waters that lay between the mission station and us.

My mind replayed the events of the afternoon and the trip downriver, through the dangerous often unseen obstacles in this the headwaters of the Amazon. I was jolted to attention, remembering the great pongo with its menacing whirlpools and rapids, and the submerged logs, sand beaches, and large boulders jutting out to nearly mid river. Reality struck with paralyzing force as I thought to myself, 'How can we pass these many obstacles in the dead of night?'

The adrenalin flowed, and my eyes were dilated to pick up any dark objects in the river. My heart raced and thumped against my chest as fear mounted. In an anxious voice, I called out to my guide Moisés, "Where are the submerged logs we passed on the way downstream earlier today?"

The calm reply was given, "We are still two bends in the river away from them."

"How far are we from the sand beaches and the boulders that we passed on the way downriver?"

"They are a long way in the distance yet, don't worry, I will tell you when we are near their position." Reassured by his words, I held a steady course to the middle of the river. The eerie sounds of the rolling river at night turned my thoughts to home and my wife and family who would be anxiously awaiting our arrival. Cool air stung my face as we raced along. 'Wouldn't a cup of hot chocolate taste good followed by a warm bath in the safety of our home?' I thought to myself.

Again my thoughts were interrupted by the command, "Turn to the right, the submerged logs are off to our left." To the right I cranked the steering wheel and almost instantly heard the terrifying rush of water as it banged over those jutting logs, half in and half out of the water. The boat cleared the logs and made for calmer water to the right.

'One obstacle down and three to go', I thought, while my heart was pounding rapidly from this harrowing experience. "How far to the sand beach?" I asked.

"We are a long way from it yet, maybe fifteen minutes upriver," he replied.

The sick lady was sound asleep as the injection I gave her back at the village was taking effect. Her husband was slumped forward in his seat in deep sleep. Moisés was relaxed and studying the river. I was tense, shoulders tight, and eyes peeled straight ahead searching for the middle of the river. "Bear to the right," Moisés said, as the sand beach swept out to our left about one hundred yards straight ahead. To the right we went and safely passed that unseen obstacle without any difficulty.

"The rocks are about five turns upriver." Moisés stated. "We will want to swing sharply to the left and follow the shore line about fifteen yards out," he said in a reassuring voice. The curves were counted one by one, and sure enough we heard the cross currents as the water bounced over the huge boulders, when we made our approach into the fifth turn. Assuredly Moisés coached me to hold a steady course to the left. Our boat lunged up and over the slight drop off and shot clear of the rocks, leaving the turbulent waves in our wake.

'One more to go,' I thought, only the great pongo of Huankichank stands between home and us. "Moisés, how far to the pongo?" I asked.

"In about ten minutes we should be at the lower end of the canyon wall where it divides into the two currents," he responded. I examined the pulse of my patient once more, only to find that she was a lot more relaxed than I was. I quickly reviewed the details of the pongo in my mind, as to how we would enter the lower end of the canyon and then traverse its narrow course through some of the most dangerous waters in the Amazon, especially at night. I was relieved just to know that Moisés was sitting by my side to guide me through this treacherous stretch of river. The motor drummed on into the dark jungle night. 'Lord, you know our circumstance. Please comfort my wife in this hour of wondering. How good it will feel to step on solid safe ground again,' I thought.

The noise was nearly deafening as we approached the pongo. Moisés sat straight up and I leaned forward, straining to see some familiar point of reference in this boiling inferno. My heart beat wildly, and tense hands gripped the steering wheel as we entered the lower opening of the pongo. I could feel the rocking of the boat as those strong tentacles of cross currents pulled heavily on this little insignificant craft.

"Ease the wheel to the left," Moisés commanded. "Steady, steady, bring it slowly to the right and hold that course." We could feel the boat climb up the trough created by the two currents coming in at different angles. The noise was unnerving, and water splashed over the top of our boat chilling us to the bone. Our small craft rocked and swayed from the incredible force of the crosscurrents. Up and up it climbed, until we crested the rapids that desperately tried to pull us into their death grip. It seemed like an eternity passed before our little craft broke through the last threatening wave and flew over the top to leave the pongo roaring to our right and directly behind us. "Full throttle ahead," was Moisés' last command. We powered our way to calm water and safety with a great sigh of relief. "Thank you, Lord, for helping us safely through the pongo this night," I said, and my hands released their death grip on the steering wheel.

Around the next turn in the river we saw the lights of home, a virtual lighthouse standing as a beacon in that vast, treacherous stretch of river. A few minutes later the little boat pulled into the quiet waters of the Kusu River and glided to a stop at the mud bank. 'Home at last,' I thought, as I breathed a silent prayer of thanks to the Lord for a safe trip and for Moisés, my wonderful friend and guide. A relieved wife welcomed us home that night.

The sick mother was taken to the clinic where intravenous fluids were given and her treatment was outlined for the next few days. Later she returned home, happy and well, to the village of Nueva Vida. Another crisis had passed, and the compassionate ministry of the church touched another life.

Spiritual Sequel to the Story of a Dark Night
Friends, you and I may pass through the deep waters of life on occasion, but we have a hope. There may be sandbars of doubt waiting to beach your journey to a jolting halt. There may be waves and cross currents of fear of the unknown causing you great despair, or submerged logs of sickness waiting to rip the bottom out of your faith. It could be the rapids and whirlpools of a hectic lifestyle that causes you much distress and anxiety, but you have a hope. As Moisés sat by my side that dark night, we have one "who sticks closer than a brother." He will guide us through the darkest night and will never leave us nor forsake us. One day, if we are faithful, we will see the lights of home, enter the haven of rest, and hear the words, "Well done, my faithful servant, enter into your rest."

The Amazon Call

My Most Unforgetable Character: Chimpa

We stepped from the long wooden cargo boat on the banks of the Kusu River, home of the mission station and new missionaries, the Garmans.

Many people came out of the forest to observe our every movement and see what we looked like. There stood Switch, a large stout barefooted man with long black hair hanging down over his shoulders. He wore a reddish itipak (man's skirt) around his waist, and flashed me a broad smile. That smile permitted me to observe those blackened stubs of teeth that had been ground down from years of chewing on bones and the use of a plant dye that had stained them permanently. Right away I knew we had a friend forever. Switch, his wife, and family lived just on the other side of the river on a small hill that rose above the corner of the Kusu and Marañon Rivers.

At first the people were wary of these pale-skinned newcomers, but little by little they warmed up to us and began chatting incessantly. We understood nothing they said. It all sounded very tonal and strange, but friendly. Little naked boys ran up and down the riverbank, jumping into the river and swimming back and forth, oblivious to our arrival.

The women stood in the background with little girls hanging onto their mom's legs for security. Small babies stuck their heads out over the top of the one-piece dress that was wrapped around the mother's body, and cinched in the middle with a stout vine. These babies soon drew their attention back to the task at hand and continued nursing.

As we carried our supplies from the boat to our new home deep in the rain forest, I spotted him standing off to one side. I couldn't take my eyes off of this man. His cold, dark but kind eyes followed our every movement as if he were intently studying these people who had come to live in this age-old land.

Glancing over my shoulder, I felt a strange fascination for this elderly Indian man. His bronzed face, etched with leathery lines of age spent under years of a bright tropical sun, displayed high prominent cheekbones that spoke to me of great inner strength. His hair was long and black, hanging down over his shoulders, cut in bangs across the forehead, and exposing ears with large slits in the lobes. One ear sported a big safety pin, while the other was unoccupied. He wore the itipak (man's skirt), tied at the waist with a thin vine. He had no shirt and was barefooted. Those feet were thick and heavily calloused from endless trails. They had never felt a pair of shoes and never would. The large toe on each foot was angled away from the rest of his toes, for they had been used as claws to climb many slippery hills and trails over his lifetime.

I learned that his name was Chimpa. In this culture people had only one name and sometimes the name came from nature, however he had two nicknames, "Captain Naaman," and both were from a Bible story about Naaman the leper who was Captain of the Syrian army. I am not sure how he obtained these names, but they were always used in an affectionate way. When we passed out oranges to those helping us unload the boat, Chimpa also extended his hand even though he hadn't carried one item to the house. Handing him the orange, I noticed his hands with those white patches of skin that stood out on his bronzed arms and hands. Perhaps the name Naaman came from this Bible story.

Chimpa would never come inside the church except to sit on the back row in Addie's Sunday School class with the women. One Sunday Addie was telling the story of Naaman the leper, and Chimpa listened with great interest. When she came to the part of Naaman dipping into the water, she counted; one, two, three, four, five, six times and emerging looking at his leprous hands with no result, silence filled the air with anticipation of the seventh time. Addie then showed a picture of Naaman emerging the seventh time with his hands clean and free of the leprous white patches. Perhaps Chimpa looked at his own blotched hands, and then exclaimed in a loud voice, "Waaaa," causing the women to turn, look at him and laugh out loud.

During the preaching service he always stood outside with his arms resting on the two by four railing. The church was enclosed with palm wood sides that were about three feet high, leaving the building open for coolness since it is very hot in the tropics. One Sunday I finished preaching and gave an altar call, but no one came forward. Again I repeated the invitation, but no response.

Chimpa stood in the back as usual listening to the young missionary fervently pleading with the people with no result. I again asked if anyone would like to come and pray, but silence filled the air for a long moment. In that quiet, reverent atmosphere, Chimpa thought he would help me out with the obvious, and blurted out loud, "No, there's no one." Snickers filled the church as men and women covered their mouths with their hands to keep from laughing out loud. Chimpa was not being irreverent; he just thought that I needed to know that no one was interested in praying that day.

He loved bread, and soon realized that Addie baked homemade rolls every Saturday. He would stand at the screen door looking in at the bread on the table, until the aroma was too much for him. He would open the door and walk into the house, eyeing the rolls, until Addie would give him one to eat.

His first wife was Yanwa, a feisty little lady who became one of Addie's first women converts. When Chimpa took another younger wife, she left him and went to live with her older children in the village of Chipe.

People came from all over the upper Amazon to be treated by Chimpa the witchdoctor. He was very popular and commanded a lot of respect as a powerful shaman. He would drink Ayawaska, a very powerful drink, made from the extract of a vine that produces a strong hallucinating effect, during the daylight hours, so that he would receive power from the spirit world to heal his patients at night.

We became great friends, and he would come to the clinic for treatment, and always held us in high esteem. When he took deathly ill, I went to his hut to visit him. He could no longer get up from his bed and the end was drawing near. I asked him if he would like Jesus to come into his heart and go to Heaven, but he politely told me no. I prayed that day with Chimpa and never saw him again, as death slipped into that hut and Chimpa departed from among us. As a young missionary, I then realized the paralyzing effect that witchcraft, superstitions and fears of the spirit world held over these wonderful people.

The Amazon Call

Yanwa

She was probably all of four-feet four-inches tall and dripping wet she might have weighed eighty pounds. She wore the one-piece dress wrapped around her body, tied over the right shoulder, and gathered at the waist with a stout thin vine. Yanwa never owned a pair of shoes and her tiny feet were calloused from a thousand trails. The large toes were separated from the others at nearly a forty-five degree angle, as they had been used like claws in climbing untold steep slippery jungle trails. Her hair was long and black with a hint of gray. It hung loosely over her shoulders that were stooped with age. Dark, fiery, but kind eyes lit up a face leathered with time from a blazing tropical sun. The hands were strong, supple, and rough from toiling in countless gardens through years without number. Everyone affectionately knew her as "Dukuwachi" (little grandmother).

Yanwa had been the wife of a very prominent witchdoctor by the name of Chimpa. When he came home sporting a new younger bride she left him and went to live with her grown married children in the village of Chipe. She became one of our dearest friends as time ebbed on in the rain forest. Her toothless smile, while clinging to my arm, would melt me right into my socks. Traveling from our house by boat, I would always search the high hill where she lived, because inevitably she would appear out of nowhere squinting into the sun, waving a thin hand our way. Occasionally we would cross paths on a mutual trail, where she would threaten me with her machete and I would mockingly threaten her with a club or boat paddle. Then we would both laugh and merrily go our separate ways. Her vivacious demeanor always brightened my day and made me feel like family.

Our first months in the jungle presented some very difficult cultural challenges. It was definitely a man's world and the women were relegated to a subservient status. Sunday morning in our small church on the hill overlooking the tranquil clear waters of the Kusu River was always a lesson in cross-cultural living. The men sat on the right side of the church while the women and children sat on the left. The church was nestled among the tall beautiful balsa trees that provided shade on hot tropical days. The sides were made of split palm about three feet high. There were no screens and the floor was of soft powdery dirt. The benches were backless with no padding, and the occasional turkey would jump up on the railing only to be chased off in no uncertain terms.

On many Sundays an old scrawny rib-protruding dog would meander up the aisle and plop down in a scooped out place in front of the altar and fall fast asleep, curled up in a ball with gnats buzzing his near blind eyes all throughout the service. Small naked boys wandered in and out of the church with sticks in their hands to pry open the lid of a trapdoor spider. Little girls sat with their mothers, wanting to be groomed. The ladies would examine their daughters' heads very meticulously. They would pull on a strand of hair, then pinch something between their fingers before placing it between their teeth. They would bite the little head louse and then spit it out. This was a social activity whenever a group of women got together and church was no exception.

In church services, I have seen puppy dogs and baby pigs carried in the front of the ladies' one-piece dresses. Some of the ladies wore many types of necklaces and armbands made from seeds, bones, teeth, and palm wood of every description. Blue round dotted tattoo marks stood out on the high prominent cheek bones of the women, and they sported a three inch piece of palm wood or bone shaft protruding from a hole in the lower lip.

The men on the other side of the church were quite picturesque. Some wore the itipak (man's skirt) cinched around the waist with a piece of vine. Most were barefoot and their meager clothing was well patched and threadbare. A crown of parrot feathers worn on the head was not unheard of, as well as an earring made of beetle wings or an old rusty safety pin.

Services were colorful and very animated because our people are spontaneous in their response to preaching. Since they were just learning to read and write, a lot of cultural hangovers were carried over into these services. Traditionally they had, throughout their history, been oral participators in any village meeting. Both men and women were accustomed to speaking out and exercising their right to be heard. Sometimes several people would speak out at the same time, creating organized chaos.

Yanwa came every Sunday and would sit in the women's section showing great interest in everything spiritual. Her personality was like a magnet, always drawing me to her side. Our conversations were very animated and usually drew a crowd that would be laughing and gesturing wildly. Religious services were new to the people, so Addie and I had to do almost everything at the beginning from teaching, leading the services, and preaching. Addie taught everyone in one large Sunday School class and I would preach.

After several months without any response at the altar, we prayed for a breakthrough. Occasionally a man would stand up and come down to the altar and we would get extremely excited, believing this to be the start of something great, but instead of kneeling he would look for his wife sitting in the women's section and tell her to get down there. She would make her way down the aisle, not knowing why, then stand next to her husband with a hand over her mouth, giggling. Addie would shift from one foot to the other hardly containing herself and groaning within her soul that this was not the way to come to the Lord just because someone ordered you to. Finally, two men were wonderfully saved, but then we had another long dry spell.

One day Addie came to the clinic expressing her concern about the church services. She said, "We aren't reaching the women. We have to do something different."

I said, "Well, I am open to suggestions."

She responded with, "Why don't I teach Sunday school to just the women in the church and you take the men out under the trees and teach them? We can teach our helper the flannelgraph stories and he can teach the lesson to the children in the chicken house."

At that time we didn't have any buildings other than the church. Beside it was the chicken house that had a roof over it. "Great idea," I responded, and so we worked hard to make it happen. It wasn't long until Addie was giving altar calls in her class and women were coming to Christ because they wanted to and felt the need to, not because someone ordered them to do it. The results were amazing. God was transforming the women.

One Sunday as Addie was walking to her class, God impressed upon her the need to teach one of them to participate in the class. Looking around the large class of women that Sunday, she decided to ask Yanwa to be the first woman to pray out loud publicly. "Dukuwachi (little grandmother), she said, pointing to Yanwa, "Would you open our class with prayer this morning?" Yanwa looked all around and behind her hoping to find another grandmother somewhere but there was no one else fitting that description.

Sheepishly she pointed to herself and asked, "You mean me?"

"Yes," Addie replied.

Yanwa gulped, took a deep breath, rolled her eyes with fear and said, "Ayu (ok)." Addie was elated, this would be a first and everyone bowed their heads and Yanwa began to pray. After a few moments of silence, Addie opened her eyes and looked at Yanwa. Her head was bowed, eyes closed, lips moving, but no audible words were coming forth.

At this point Addie became nervous, wondering how she would know when Yanwa was through praying. Should she keep watching her to tell when she was done or what should she do? Addie had been teaching the ladies to bow their heads and close their eyes when talking to the Lord, but what if they opened their eyes and caught Addie peeking, what would they think?

A lady who couldn't hear Yanwa and had moved over to the men's section spoke out and very loudly said, "Speak up, we can't hear you over here."

Yanwa stopped praying, lifted her head, opening her eyes and shouted in the lady's direction, "I'm praying to God and not to you," bowed her head and finished her prayer. Well, we were off and change did come to the jungle of northern Perú. Women began memorizing scripture even though they couldn't read. They would have someone read to them and they would commit it to memory.

It wasn't long until they began singing group specials and even duets and finally solos. I will never forget the first time in an organizational meeting of a new church that a woman was elected to the newly formed church board. They soon began teaching Sunday school classes and even leading the singing in many churches. A new day was dawning in the Amazon.

Yanwa passed on to her eternal reward many years ago, but left us with precious memories that continue to live. Thank you, Dukuwachi, for I will never be the same for having known you.

The Amazon Call

Nosebleed

Addie was preparing breakfast when the desperate calls for help penetrated the serenity of a new tropical day. The sounds came from the direction of the river. Immediately I looked out the screen window and saw a long, sleek, black canoe glide into our small port. From the canoe someone yelled that Garcia had a nosebleed. Turning to Addie I said, "Continue preparing breakfast and I will be back soon, because it's only a nosebleed." She looked out the window and wondered why they were carrying this man to the clinic if it was just a nosebleed.

Shortly after returning from the clinic, Addie asked, "How is Garcia and why were they carrying him for just a nosebleed?" I told her that he had hemorrhaged for three days, losing a lot of blood and was very weak, but that I had packed his nose and he should be fine.

Finishing breakfast and devotions I returned to the clinic to check on Garcia. Addie had water heating on the stove to wash the dishes and so had a few minutes free and decided to visit the clinic and Garcia. When she opened the door, she gasped and started to speak, for there was a large bowl filled with blood and the floor was covered with blood. Garcia's wife was holding his head as he vomited pure blood.

In a calm voice I said to her, "Act as if everything is normal, don't make a scene, and get out of here and go home." I didn't have to repeat that last phrase, because she turned and ran home, falling across her bed praying and crying to God to please touch Garcia, heal him and give us an opportunity to witness to him.

Addie is not a nurse, but she had to help me in the clinic during those first years until I could train nurses to help me. Sometimes I would end up with two patients at one time, the patient I was treating and Addie about to pass out on me.

I will never forget the day when a man came to the clinic begging me to go see his daughter who had severe head injuries and was in critical condition downriver close to the village of San Pablo. I prepared my portable medical kit while our motorist readied the boat for the long trip ahead. Leaving the port, I wondered what would await me downriver.

It was one of those picture perfect days in the upper Amazon as our boat glided along smoothly in the open water. The sky was blue and not a cloud was in sight as we rounded bend after bend in this constantly twisting river. Up ahead I could see the rapids and whirlpools of Huankichak, and the water was boiling as it banged into the large boulders at the opening of this monster water trap. Our boat rocked back and forth as the crosscurrents shook the very fiber of our wooden craft. Automatically my hands clutched the sides of the boat and water splashed in causing me to slide a little to the middle of the seat to keep dry.

Finally, our destination was in sight just around the next bend. In the distance we caught sight of a few huts on the left bank of the river. There were a few people lining the bank and watching as we stepped ashore and ascended the hill leading to the nearest hut. After exchanging greetings, we were followed by a group of men to the indicated hut where the woman was agonizing in great pain. Upon examination I found three long deep gash wounds of the scalp that penetrated to the bone.

I had been informed that her husband had slashed her head open with a large knife because he suspected her of adultery. The Aguarunas for generations considered adultery a very social evil and the custom was to hold the wife down as the husband slashed opened the scalp with either a large knife or machete. These wounds were slow to heal and many times severe infection would set in and cause complications. Her hair was matted with dried blood and she hadn't been able to bathe in the river for perhaps two or three days. Her eyes portrayed fear and acute mental anguish as she sat staring into space with a look of deep despondency and hopelessness written all over her countenance.

Her husband stood to one side contemplating the scene before him. He was quite elderly, frail, and somewhat confused. His wife was about nineteen years old, much younger than he. I was informed that his former wife had died and that through an arranged marriage he had taken this young lady as his wife. They had discovered that one of his sons had been living with her and thus she suffered the punishment.

Completing my examination, I determined that we would have to take her to our clinic upriver to properly cleanse and suture these deep wounds. The husband resisted and said that we could not take her from the village. He threatened to report me to the authorities. To make a long story short, we took her and some of her family upriver to the clinic where we began treatment.

Addie came over with a flashlight to help me cleanse the wounds. It was necessary to cut her hair and clean out the debris before suturing the scalp. The patient was groaning as I gave her local anesthesia and began to clean up the deep wounds. I was working intently when the light began moving from side to side and up and down away from my field of work. "Addie, hold the light still!" I pleaded, "I can't see to work."

When I looked up, Addie was swaying from side to side about to pass out, and the light was doing three hundred and sixty degree revolutions on the walls of the clinic. Finally I told her to go home and send one of the patient's family members in to help me finish the job at hand.

Sometime later I returned home and Addie asked me, "How's Garcia?"

"He has lost a lot of blood but the bleeding has stopped and I believe he is going to recover. He is very weak and will need a lot of care. We will have to monitor him closely and pray that in this weakened condition he will not succumb to any secondary infection," I replied.

The days drifted by and Garcia was responding to treatment, but remained very weak. We soon found out that he was the son of a very prominent witchdoctor who lived upriver near the village of

Shushui. One morning a canoe pulled into our port and a lot of commotion followed. We learned that his father had come to take Garcia home. Approaching the clinic, the old witchdoctor stated emphatically that he came to take his son home. I replied that his son was much improved, but still needed to remain under my care until he was completely out of danger. He said "No, I am taking him home now."

"You can't," I repeated, "because he needs further treatment and I can't release him yet."

Witchdoctors are very powerful people and exert tremendous leverage over the population. They take hallucinating drugs called Ayawaska, a powerful drug that produces visions from the spirit world. It is made from the extract of a vine. They take this drug during the daylight hours so that they will have the power to heal in the late hours of night. Finally the old man said, "I am taking my son home and I am doing it now."

We watched in sadness as Garcia was helped down the hill to the waiting canoe. As the canoe pulled away from our port and later disappeared around a bend in the river, a great heaviness swept over us. We had prayed every night in the clinic with Garcia and longed for his salvation. Now we had lost control and he was gone. We prayed for Garcia for many days, but as time passed and we lost all contact, he faded into our memory.

The clinic and Bible Institute demanded most of our attention and energy as the work was expanding into village after village. Part of this expansion was due to our clinical work at the village level. We would pack up dental equipment, medical supplies, and our family would head downriver in our large dugout canoe cargo boat.

We would stop in a village, talk to the headman, and offer clinical services to the people in exchange for an opportunity to share the Gospel. The needs were overwhelming and patients would line up for hours while we pulled teeth, gave injections, manipulated spines and counted out pills. There would be a church service in the morning and evening with clinic, swimming, eating, and bathing mixed in between. Addie and the children performed as nurse and medicine packagers. This process was repeated in many villages until a group was formed and a student procured for the Bible Institute.

It was the beginning of a new school year in the Bible Institute as men gathered together on the banks of the Kusu River to start their studies in preparation for ministry. They had come by raft, boat, and trail, leaving their families, gardens, and villages to serve the Lord. Sunday night came and all the new first year students lined up across the front of the church to give their name and tell where they were from. My heart was thrilled as I heard one student after another mention the village where we now had a new church and someone preparing for the pastoral ministry. Another man stood to give his name and I turned to Addie and asked her if she recognized him. She said, "No, who is he?"

"That is Garcia, the man with the nosebleed years ago," I responded. He had given his heart to the Lord and started a new church in the village of Shushui and then another one in the village of Wajuyat. There he stood that night, giving testimony to what God had done in his life and that he felt called to prepare for ministry.

The Amazon Call

94

Emergency

I sat shivering on a hand carved stool on the bottom of a dugout canoe that morning as we glided through the rough waters of the Kusu River under a torrential downpour. The sky had opened its floodgates and the rain pelted us on our way to the village of Chingamai. There was not a dry spot on my body as the rain found every possible entrance through my now saturated clothing.

Raising my head from its tucked-between-the-shoulders position, I glanced to look at the short stocky man standing in front of the canoe. His body was bare except for the small hunting trunks he was wearing. His legs were poised on the sloping sides of the canoe, balancing his weight evenly to keep from falling into the water as the frail craft rocked from side to side. Stout toes clung to the sides proving that he had done this a thousand times. He held a long twelve-foot cane pole in his hands that he drove into the riverbed right alongside the canoe. Pushing on that pole, he propelled the sleek craft along. When he ran the length of the pole, he lifted it from the water and then plunged it into the riverbed again, repeating this process over and over.

My eyes stung with the force of raindrops being carried by the wind. I observed the muddy banks on both sides of the river, and the occasional thatched-roof bamboo huts standing alone in small clearings under a dark foreboding sky. In all those huts the occupants were dry and gathered around the three-log cooking fires waiting patiently for the storm to pass. There was no movement in the trees along the bank, as all animal life had also sought shelter from the constant downpour.

He had come early that morning pleading with me to accompany him to the village because his wife was dying. She had given birth that morning and was hemorrhaging. His name was Pacora and he was a frequent visitor to the mission station, especially on Sundays. Pacora was an outstanding marksman with the ten-foot blowgun. Occasionally he wore the beautiful crown of feathers, obtained from the many birds living in the thick entangled canopy of the rain forest. They were birds that he had killed with this lethal weapon.

Pacora was well versed and steeped in all the customs of the Aguarunas. I remember the time he dug two latrines, one for himself and one for the rest of his family, after being convinced that a latrine indicated progress and was a good thing to do.

Then there was the Christmas that we received some clothing to give to the people as gifts. Among the items were six new trunks for the men. Our dilemma was how to divide these among at least a hundred men. I decided to have the men form a large semicircle just below the small hill upon which the clinic set. I was getting ready to toss all six trunks up into the air and let the men grab what they could as the clothing fell. Out of the crowd a voice cried out, "but I am shorter than all of these tall men, and I don't have a chance." It was Pacora, good-naturedly complaining. The trunks were tossed into the air, and arms were flailing in every direction for one of those coveted prizes. A moment later I surveyed the crowd and there, sporting a big grin, was Pacora (Zacchaeus among men), triumphantly waving his new trunks in victory. In all the commotion one pair had fallen to the ground, and Pacora, crawling on his hands and knees, latched onto it immediately.

Up ahead I caught a glimpse of the rapids with its roaring, foaming water crashing down over large, unmovable boulders. Automatically my hands clutched the sides of the canoe as it pitched from side to side, entering the lower trough at the foot of the rapids. Shielding my face with an uplifted hand, I observed Pacora leaping onto a large boulder, carrying the stout thick vine in his hands that was tied through a round hole in the sloping front of the dugout, holding on for dear life. He pulled the canoe slowly up the water trough as water splashed over the sides. He then jumped to another rock, pulling the canoe always upward through the forceful rushing current. I jumped onto the first large boulder and, grabbing the side of the canoe, I pushed as Pacora pulled. We struggled against the terrific rush of water, edging the canoe inch by inch through that boiling inferno until at long last we crowned the last rapid and entered into the calmer part of the river.

We both jumped back into the canoe, and Pacora quickly retrieved his long pole, plunging it again into the riverbed, propelling us along past the menacing rapids and on upriver. At long last, we reached the small port of the village of Chingamai. As our canoe glided into the mud bank, Pacora jumped to the sandy beach, jabbing his long pole deep into the sand and tying the dugout snugly to the anchored pole. I sat there dripping wet, observing my surroundings. There were several canoes tied up at the port, and all of them were half filled with water. Wading cautiously along the slick bottom of the canoe, I stepped ashore, only to be greeted by six inches of slimy, sticky mud. My feet were sopping wet as I slid along the trail toward the village.

Pacora led the way, passing hut after hut before we finally arrived at his hut. Methodically he removed several of the small upright balsa logs that formed the doorway and then, standing aside, he invited me in. Politely he brought me a small hand carved stool and motioned for me to sit down. It felt wonderful to be inside away from the relentless rain. I was chilled to the bone as water dripped onto the dirt floor from my drenched clothing.

Pacora invited me to the bedside of his wife. She was lying on a split bamboo bed. A small three-logged fire about five feet away provided some heat in the damp, humidity-filled home. Next to the mother's bed were two thin stout poles planted into the dirt floor supporting a small hammock with the newest addition of the family, fast asleep. Removing my instruments from a waterproof metal container, I examined Pacora's wife.

My conclusion was that the hemorrhage was contained, and only normal blood loss from afterbirth was present. Her vital signs were perfect and the patient complained only of a slight headache. At that point, she was in much better shape than I was, as cold wet clothing clung to my chilled body. Pacora flashed me a grateful grin as I handed him a few pills for the headache, and together we headed once again out into the rain for the long trip home.

The Amazon Call

Snakes Alive

We left our home one Friday afternoon to visit the village of Kubaim on the headwaters of the Cenepa River. Our dugout canoe boat was loaded with sleeping bags, mosquito nets, medical and dental supplies, and several tanks of gasoline for the long trip ahead of us.

We had never been to the headwaters of the Cenepa River before. Our excitement mounted as our boat left the tranquil, clear waters of the small Kusu River, and was greeted by the muddy, turbulent current of the great Marañon. Quickly our sturdy craft passed the narrow rapids and cross currents as it made its way downstream in the middle of the river.

Glancing back over our shoulders, we could see the beautiful little white house sitting on the corner of these two rivers. It was a haven of rest in this emerald green rain forest. There are no roads into this impenetrable part of the Amazon. You can only reach us by water. Next to the house stood the two little clinic buildings with their tin roofs glistening under a bright tropical sun. The sky was blue and cloudless this warm afternoon in the jungle of northern Perú.

I could hear the splash of water on the sides of the boat as its bow cut sharply through the heaving cross currents that rocked the craft gently back and forth. Occasional streams of spray shooting up from the sides of the boat refreshingly cooled our warm skin.

Past the rapids and whirlpools we sped along on our course downriver. Above the droning of the outboard motor we could hear the crashing of water across huge boulders in certain areas of the river, causing deep troughs and a bumpy ride. Automatically our hands clutched the wooden sides of the boat until once again we struck calmer water. It was a gorgeous day. Our hair was blowing in the wind and our eyes were consuming the breathtaking scenery surrounding us.

There was the occasional canoe bobbing up and down while its occupants gallantly struggled to propel their sleek craft against the relentless foe of fast moving water. Standing, barking in the bow of the canoe was the family's hunting dog, chasing away all intruders from his domain. He was so thin that you could nearly count his ribs at close range. His eyes were slightly clouded over from the scourge of gnats that constantly invaded his privacy. The canoe was laden with several stocks of green cooking bananas, and woven baskets mounded up with long dark brown yuca roots.

This family was returning to their home from a trip to the gardens. Nearby on a lonely knoll next to a small stream stood their bamboo-walled, thatched-roof hut. Little naked boys were playing soccer on a tiny sand beach not too far distant. Their ball was a well-worn hard round green tropical fruit. They returned our waves, standing there squinting into the bright sun.

Such a peaceful scene in this isolated, nearly forgotten part of the world caused us to reflect on our own lifestyle. Coming into view were the high cliffs of the Nueva Vida (new life) village, and around the bend was the mouth of the Cenepa River that emptied its contents into the larger Marañon.

Skirting the rough waters where the two rivers meet, we headed into the Cenepa. Her waters were clear and calm where we passed the village of Wawaim. This river is more narrow and shallow in parts now, as it winds its way through a low-slung mountain range. The sun was high overhead and one could feel its intensity as the day wore on.

Past the villages of Mamayakim, Tutino, San Antonio, Nuevo Kanam and Huampami we traveled as the hours drifted by. In the late afternoon we passed the Kanka River and headed into the homestretch toward our destination. Up ahead we noticed some rougher water as our boat was rocked by the strong cross currents and seemed to be climbing uphill. Addie excitedly yelled, "Larry, look, we are going up a waterfall!" I told her that was impossible to do in a boat.

She replied, "Look at the bank. See, the boat is going uphill." You could see the slight incline up ahead as the boat struggled against the heavy current that was indeed dropping from an upper level.

"This is called a pongo," one of the men shouted out above the noise of both the motor and river. A pongo is a designated stretch where there are severe crosscurrents, rapids, whirlpools and very rough water.

Our boat rocked back and forth, then crested the last wave and struck calm water leaving behind the pongo called "New Pongo." The local people, according to certain events that have taken place there across time, have named nearly every rough water area. Some have been named after animals, while others take the names of people who have drowned in that part of the river.

He told us that this pongo is extremely dangerous when the river is at flood stage. "However," he stated, "the river is low and 'New Pongo' poses no problem." Our boat rounded a bend in the river and again we felt the small craft swinging from side to side. Water splashed over the railing, indicating we were in another stretch of rough water.

Again, our guide told us that this is another pongo called Sajino. Sajino means wild pig, and evidently this pongo was named after this wild jumping animal. He then added, "It's only dangerous when the river is high, but since it's low water, we won't have any problem traversing its swirling waters." We were glad to see that he was right as our boat overcame the rocking and swaying leaving Sajino in its wake. The river was quite narrow at this point and the banks were lined with protruding rocks and the current was exceptionally strong. Long thin vines hung down from overhanging trees and afternoon shadows crept across the river, dancing on the waters before us.

Soon we entered another area of rough water and our boat again fought the strong rolling current that bounced from severe curves in the river. Again we were informed that this was also a pongo, and it is called Ronsoco.

Have you ever eaten Ronsoco? I remember the first time I partook of its delicious flesh. We were invited to eat with the students of our Bible Institute. I was served a bowl of soup and they told me that the meat was Ronsoco. I plunged my spoon into the bowl striking something hard below the surface. Lifting my spoon upward I noticed that it carried the lower jawbone of this animal with large stained black teeth still intact. This was my first exposure to the largest rodent in the world called Capybara. It is actually an l00-l20 pound flat-nosed rat.

We were told that this pongo is not navigable when the river is at high water, but it was low and we passed it quickly. We were soon approaching the village of Kubaim, our final destination. We saw beautiful, sleek black canoes tied at the port of Kubaim. People came to greet and meet us.

Since very few people traveled this isolated stream upriver, especially of our skin color, we were welcomed to the village by the headman, and then began unloading our equipment. As I was talking with him, our motorist came over to where Addie was standing and asked her, "Do you know were you are going to spend the night?"

Addie replied, "No, but wherever they allow me to spread out my bedroll and hang my mosquito net will be fine with me."

He said, "You are going to sleep in the snake house."

Addie threw him a startled glance and replied, "You're kidding aren't you?"

He grinned and said, "You'll see," and walked away.

About that time I called to Addie, "Honey, come, they are taking us to our sleeping quarters." Walking through the village, we approached a small thatched-roof, bamboo-walled hut, typical of all the huts in Kubaim. Nearing the hut we observed that there were seven large woven baskets tied on the side of the wall outside the hut. Addie surveyed the situation, noting that each basket was bulging at the bottom and tied at the top with a stout vine and that in each basket there was a large, live, poisonous snake.

These snakes had been collected to send to Lima to the Institute of Venomous Animals to be milked and the venom made into antivenom to be used in the treatment of snakebites. "Larry!" shouted Addie.

"Yes, I know," I replied. Turning to the headman I said, "My wife is a little nervous about sleeping in this hut with all the snakes on the wall."

"No problem," he said, and moved the baskets to another hut. Addie knew a lot about pit vipers of the Amazon, and was quite upset to share close quarters with poisonous snakes.

In our area, the people brought live poisonous snakes to me in baskets, which I would later transfer into boxes, storing them until we had a large number to be transferred to Lima. Sometimes we would carry the boxes in our boat upriver to where our car was located and then take them out to the coast in our Suburban Carryall.

Our clinic was the main treatment center for snakebites in the upper Amazon. Working with the Institute of Venomous Animals provided us with the three prevalent types of antivenom, so people came from great distances to be treated.

We learned a lot about the poisonous snakes of our region through association with the highest authority in Perú at the Venomous Animal Center. We learned that the pit vipers in our area do not lay eggs, but give live birth to as many as thirty-five baby snakes that are poisonous the moment they are born.

We stored the wooden boxes behind our clinic on top of fifty-five gallon steel drums until we were making a trip to the coast. Occasionally a snake would die and several days later we would smell the decaying remains, meaning that I would have to open the box, dispose of the snake and then wash out the box.

One day I was informed that there was a putrid odor coming from behind the clinic. Sure enough, as I examined the boxes I found one that was seeping a grayish liquid with a foul odor. I began to remove the screws that held the split top on as I had done on more than one occasion. Automatically I lifted the top and stared into the face of a large coiled pit viper, as little foot-long baby snakes began scurrying out of the box in every direction. My heart was racing wildly as I quickly clamped the top on again, realizing what a close call that had been. The oozing grayish liquid material with the foul smell was the afterbirth from the momma snake. Thereafter all lids were removed with great caution.

Addie knew all about these events and miracles of nature as we went to bed that night in the little hut in the village of Kubaim. Sleep did not come to her, as she wondered if any of those snakes were pregnant and about to give birth. Her prayer was, "Lord, please keep those baskets from breaking and don't let any of those snakes give birth tonight." She knew that if they delivered offspring during the night, they could crawl right through the open large weave of those baskets. She didn't sleep much that night in the village of Kubaim.

The next day was sunny and we had a wonderful time with the people. There was a service in the morning, and then clinic with a long line of patients waiting to be examined. I treated while Addie counted out pills. There were teeth to be pulled and injections to be given. After clinic we went visiting in the homes, bathed in the river, ate supper, and then had another great worship service.

When church was over we made our way back to our hut with flashlights in hand. The day had been hot and the evening was very still and extremely humid. Reaching our hut we noticed that something was different. There on the outside wall were the seven baskets hanging with their bottoms bulging from the weight of the huge poisonous snakes. We were told that the owner of the snakes didn't want them hanging on the other hut, so he moved them back to our hut.

Entering the doorway, shining our lights back and forth, the cockroaches scurried here and there to escape being seen. It had been a long, tiring, but rewarding day in the rain forest.

Addie laid awake most of the night praying that God would keep those baskets intact and that no snakes would escape.

Around midnight loud peals of thunder broke the silence and jagged streaks of lighting illuminated the sky, followed by a downpour that can only be experienced in the jungle. Thunder roared, and lighting cracked nearby casting its eerie shadows through that little hut, while rain pelted our thatched roof shelter. It rained unmercifully and now Addie's prayer switched from snakes to, "Lord, please don't let the river rise." On and on came the relentless rain, first on the heels of a driving wind and then that steady methodical beating of drops rolling from the leaf roof onto the already saturated earth, its rhythm lulling us back to sleep.

We were awakened after a fitful night's rest by the words, "Doctor, you can't go anywhere today, because the river has risen to flood stage." Quickly I dressed, rushed to the river and was greeted by a rolling, swelling tide of muddy, swirling waters that seemed out of control on their way downstream. The crashing of water over the rocks and the banging of its way around sharp bends in the river caused one to stand in awe of the fury and power of this force of nature.

At the port, men were frantically bailing water from their canoes. The canoes were tugging desperately at the vines that held them securely tied to long, wild cane poles planted deep into the riverbank. The port was a beehive of activity as men frantically and feverishly worked to save their frail crafts from being ripped away by the strong current that now was dashing madly downstream carrying trees, limbs, and logs on a desperate journey to nowhere.

Our boat was bobbing up and down, floating lightly in the water since our motorist had bucketed out all of the water. As the river grew and spread out, he had drawn the boat closer to shore where the backwater was calmer than the raging midstream.

The sun came out, driving the clouds away and it was another beautiful day in the Amazon, giving us the hope that the river would drop rapidly. "Doctor," the pastor called, "we want to prepare breakfast for you." While they prepared food, we began packing up our sleeping bags, mosquito nets, and equipment for the long ride home. We had to leave that day because Monday we were scheduled to travel from our home to the coast. We had commitments that couldn't wait. Finally the food was ready and we enjoyed a typical meal. Excusing myself I made a quick trip to the river, only to find that it was still raging and hadn't dropped at all.

We decided to hold a church service that turned into a long one with many people in attendance. Once more I took another look at the river, finding that it had not dropped an inch. "Doctor, would you mind treating a few patients?" A long line formed and we treated each one as the morning hours passed. Finally I announced that we would have to leave, now that the last patient had been treated.

We began packing our medical and dental supplies away and started the boat loading process. "Doctor, you can't go, the river hasn't dropped and the pongos are not navigable."

"We have to go," I insisted, as final preparations were being made for our departure. There were two lifejackets in the boat. Addie put one on, but a man grabbed the other one before I could get to it. People lined the bank in silence watching the boat bob up and down in the calm backwater, while the main part of the river was raging by. I stood up in the boat and offered a prayer for these wonderful people of Kubaim and also for our safety.

The 35 horsepower outboard motor was started and we said our goodbyes to these who had showed us such kindness. Addie waved and told the people lining the bank, "Thank you, we had a wonderful time and appreciate everything you did for us."

As our boat pulled away from the port the people in unison shouted back, "Goodbye, but you are not going to make it, you are going to drown."   What a wonderful send-off we had as their words echoed in our ears and our boat entered the fast rolling current on our journey home.

"Addie," I shouted above the roar of the motor, "Don't forget that when we go through the first pongo (Ronsoco) don't move, no matter how much water comes in over the sides and how wet we get."   Many lives have been lost on the headwaters of the Amazon as people try to stay dry when water pours over the sides of the boat. They panic and the ensuing shift of passengers to the dry side causes the boat to capsize.

Addie responded, "Yes, I know," clutching the side of the boat for dear life. Our dugout canoe picked up speed as our motorist skillfully dodged and avoided trees and limbs being whipped about in the racing torrent. Anticipating the three pongos we would have to navigate before we reached home, our eyes searched the river below for signs of the approaching pongo Ronsoco. There in the distance we could see the swirling water leading to the entrance to Ronsoco.

Addie was praying and holding on until her knuckles were white and fingers nearly numb. Our motorist swung the bow into the repercussive waves leading into the heart of the pongo. We held on as water poured in on the side drenching our cargo and us. The small craft rocked back and forth, but the motor propelled us past the cross currents to calmer water down below and Ronsoco had been safely navigated. One was down, two to go.

We breathed a sigh of relief and praised the Lord for helping us through the first obstacle. There was little time to rejoice because Sajino (wild pig) loomed in the distance. We could hear the roaring of the water pounding upon the rocks about one hundred yards below us and limbs and logs splashed lazily in our wake as we rapidly approached the entrance to its gateway.

Addie said a quick prayer and then we felt the cold spray strike us in the face as our boat was shaken and tossed in the violent clutches of Sajino. Almost as soon as it started, we were leaving the violent, short hold this pongo had on us. "Thank you, Jesus!" we uttered leaving behind the second of three dangerous obstacles in our pathway.

Our relief was short lived as our boat rounded yet another bend in the river and viewed the terrifying sight of "New Pongo." Addie shouted above the roar of the river and the incessant droning of the outboard motor, "Look, I can see the waterfall and it's boiling!" The waves were white-capped and the river, running at about 15 mph shoved, pushed, and spun every movable object within its grasp. Our motorist struggled valiantly with the boat trying to keep the bow crossing the waves at right angles. The current desperately tried to swamp our dugout with its twisting and churning in seemingly different directions at the same time.

Addie was now praying and watching with both eyes, consuming every detail of this treacherous encounter with nature. Terrified, we held on for the ride of our lives. The motor came out of the water, propeller spinning in the air as the boat smacked again and again on the rolling surface of this swelling tide.

Suddenly we had passed the worst of this pongo when our motor stopped unexpectedly. Shouts could be heard from one end of the boat to the other, "Grab any overhanging limbs, vines or branches and pull us to safety, but don't rock the boat. Be careful, quickly pull us to safety!"

What seemed like an eternity was only a minute or so before we finally came to rest in a safe backwater area away from the racing river that we had just barely escaped. We were grateful and thanked the Lord that our lives had been spared.

Our motorist was working on the motor, cleaning the fouled plugs when I told Addie that if our motor had stopped thirty seconds earlier, we would not be here now.

She looked at her watch and exclaimed, "Do you know what time it is?" It was about two o'clock in the afternoon. She continued, "It's eleven o'clock in Whittier, California." Our home church would be praying for us as they always did in Sunday services. We made it through with their prayers. The motor was soon operable and we were on our way, rejoicing in God's goodness and thanking Him for a praying church at home.

The Catalina

The commotion outside the screened window of our house was chaotic as throngs of Indians were gathering in the late afternoon hours, crying and talking excitedly. Addie and I were on the verge of tears ourselves after hearing of the tragic news.

A number of bi-lingual schoolteachers called on our home earlier that day, asking if I could communicate by our ham radio with Lima, the capitol city, or Yarinacocha (the Linguistic base), far away in the flat jungle on the Ucayali River. I said, "Yes, but our contact with Lima is early this evening."

The Aguarunas who are from the upper Amazon are fondly called happy pessimists since they are a very happy but extremely pessimistic people. All questions are asked in the negative and they expect a negative answer but desperately hope that the answer will be positive. They will see rows of worm medicine in the clinic pharmacy and ask, "You don't have worm medicine do you?"

"Yes, I do."

"You couldn't sell me any could you?"

"Yes, I can."

"You can't sell me two bottles can you?"

"Yes, I can."

For generations they have lived in a very negative world dominated by the spirits. Witchcraft, superstitions, and fears of the unknown spirit world have kept them shackled and enslaved to age-old customs.

I remember being awakened one dark night to the sounds of people approaching our home and calling my name. Through that fuzzy state of deep sleep, there echoed the singsong cry of approaching death.

We stirred and lay motionless until sleep dissipated from our fogged eyes, and our startled minds became alert, expecting the worst kind of news. "Doctor, please help us, my wife has been in hard labor for hours and now the baby is coming out the backside."

As he spoke, another lady was singing the death song, "She can't deliver the baby and she is going to die. The baby won't come out and she is going to die." By now we were wide-awake and my mind was racing with thoughts of what in the world is happening.

Grabbing my flashlight I headed for the clinic. It was so very dark and I wondered how they had managed to travel the dangerous, rough muddy river in a dugout canoe through this inky blackness. The night was cool and the humid laden air penetrated the very depths of my tired body.

Approaching the clinic I could see shadowy forms and hear the now soft crying of Job's comforter. Shining my light through the dark night I saw that it was Felipe from the village of Chipe, located upriver about thirty minutes from our mission station. He was excitedly explaining the condition of his wife as we placed her on the examining table. She was distraught and crying as the contractions were coming fast and furious. The moment was chaotic in that remote, isolated, forgotten part of the world.

A life and death process as old as man himself was taking place on this little-known dramatic stage of life. The panic-stricken husband watched intently while I examined his wife who was exhausted and nearly overcome by pain and fatigue. At the door of the clinic, Job's comforter was encouraging us with the death song.

Addie was busy helping with the flashlight, preparing water, and who knows what else, while I helped facilitate the complicated delivery of yet another Indian baby. Immediately the pessimistic death-laden atmosphere turned to one of rejoicing and deep gratitude on the part of a relieved father, tired mother, and a smiling Job's comforter as the newborn was crying and taking over where Job's comforter had left off.

We were stunned and in disbelief as the crowd continued to grow that afternoon after receiving the devastating news that Segundo Shimpukat brought earlier in the day. They came from the villages of Numpatkaim, Chipe, Chigamai, and Listra. Large and small clusters of people were talking, gesturing and spitting on the ground as they related the news that would change their lives forever. I went outside to try and console the incredible crowd that had gathered on the banks of the Kusu River where our home was located. I felt so hopeless and overwhelmed by their sorrow that it nearly consumed me.

During the months of January, February, and March, the bi-lingual schoolteachers from all the tribal areas of the upper Amazon go to the Summer Institute of Linguists base down in the low jungle where they receive special training to improve their teaching skills. They travel by an amphibian plane called the Catalina. The plane carries thirty-five people and sometimes flies under difficult climatic situations. When the teachers' course is finished, they return to a predetermined drop off place and are then ferried by dugout canoe boats to their respective villages. Several days ago Felipe and Segundo left in a large boat to receive the thirty-five teachers of our area and deliver them to their homes. They arrived at the prescribed meeting place to await the teachers' arrival. The indicated day came and passed with no signs of the Catalina or the teachers. Another day came and went with the same. On the third day they were talking with another man and wondering where they could be and what could have happened. That day was Sunday, and, while waiting, they saw a small plane fly overhead. They knew that the Linguists did not fly on Sunday unless it was an emergency, so they came to the conclusion that the Catalina had crashed and the small plane was out looking for the wreckage. Immediately they began their journey downriver notifying every village of the tragic plane accident, and the death of thirty-five teachers.

Canoes left the ports of every village nearby bringing crying mothers, wives, and concerned men to our Mission Station. They all knew that we had a ham radio and contact with the coast and outside world. Our contact was with missionary Bob Gray in Lima for seven o'clock that evening. The shadows of late afternoon encroached on the mission station as families of the deceased teachers waited for the time to pass. They desperately wanted details of the crash and any news of their loved ones.

The Indians are highly intelligent, but due to their isolation and unfamiliarity of a technical and scientific world, they struggle with the fears of the unknown.

When we moved to the Kusu as new missionaries, we sold kerosene to the villagers for their little wick lamps that were made from an old bottle or can that had a wick made from a piece of cloth stuffed down into the container. The lamps give off a smoky, yellowish-orange light that you can hardly see one foot in front of the other. These little lamps provide some semblance of light in their huts and also for church services. In the church they are placed on little pieces of lumber attached to the poles supporting the roof, strategically located in different areas of the church. We had noticed for several days that great numbers of people had been purchasing kerosene in every small container conceivable.

One weekday morning several men from the nearby village, dressed in their Sunday best, carrying their New Testaments and songbooks, arrived at the mission. Approaching them, I asked where they were going. They said that they were coming to the mission to sing and pray.

They were very troubled and sad because word had raced like wildfire through the village that there was going to be a three-day blackout of the sun and we would be immersed in total blackness.

We were informed that the people had been purchasing kerosene, storing in food supplies and stacking up firewood to live through this great darkness. Upon investigating, we found out that some of the bi-lingual schoolteachers had been informed and instructed about an eclipse of the sun that was soon to take place. The instruction included taking a piece of smoked glass and observing the actual eclipse by holding it to your eyes and watching this rare phenomenon. The teachers were to teach this to their students for the first time in perhaps the history of the tribe.

Being happy pessimists with limited knowledge of scientific phenomenon, the story spreading through the village was the following: there will be three days and nights of complete, terrifying darkness, and if you want to see where God lives, then look through a piece of smoked glass. Finally the day came and the whole village was in a state of shock and anticipation. The fifteen-minute eclipse came and went without the village hardly even realizing that it had happened.

"OA4TZ, OA4TZ, OA4TZ, calling ocean able 4 tired zebra. This is OA9G, ocean able 9 George standing by."

"OA9G, this is OA4TZ. Good evening, Doc, how is everything on the Kusu?"

At this point a multitude pressed close to the house, many looking in through the screened windows, but all hearing this life changing dialogue that would affect the lives of these precious, anxious people now listening and hanging onto every word. "Bob, would you please do us a favor?" I related to him the tragic news that we had received and that the concerned families were right outside our home desperately waiting for clarity. "Could you contact the Summer Institute of Linguistics for information?"

Larry on Ham Radio –"Our link to the outside world."

"OA9G, Doc, give me a few minutes to make a phone call, standby, OA4TZ." I informed the hushed crowd that missionary Bob Gray would be calling back in a few minutes.

It seemed like an eternity passed before the anticipated call finally came. I felt such compassion for these people who had become like family to us. Many of them had embraced the Lord, the church, and had shown much affection for us. They recognized the fact that we really did love and respect them without reservation.

"OA9G, OA9G, OA4TZ calling."

"OA4TZ, OA9G standing by."

"Doc, I called the Linguist house in Lima and they have communicated with their base in Yarinacocha deep in the jungle. The Catalina took a group of teachers to the low jungle and it got stuck in the mud on take off from the village. Tomorrow the teachers from your area will be arriving by road and should be home soon. All of them are healthy, safe and sound."

Outside our home that night, crying changed to cheering and laughing as mothers, fathers, wives, and families received the best news possible. "OA4TZ, OA9G here. Thanks, Bob, for your wonderful help, we are very grateful on this end. Have a great night, OA9G clear and off."

Amateur (Ham) radio has been our only link of communication with the outside world. Across the years so many dedicated ham radio operators have unselfishly served us in allowing us to talk with our children away in boarding school, our families and friends in the states, and our missionaries on the coast.

The Amazon Call

The Runaway

"Doctor, Doctor, the large boat is gone." His words echoed in my ears that beautiful morning, deep in the rain forest. I ran to the edge of the steep hill that looked out over the lush green tropical valley below, my eyes following the serpentine shape of the rising muddy torrent along the Marañon River, searching for some sign of the valued craft that provided our watery link with the outside world. My search was to no avail, as the boat had disappeared downstream, heading for the rapids and whirlpools of Hanquichank, one of the most dangerous areas in the entire upper Amazon.

Quickly my mind called to memory the events of the day before when the large dugout canoe with plank sides had been staked out on the island for repairs. It was a beautiful boat that had hauled our cargo for several years, but was now in need of caulking with tar as the seams had opened and water leaks were very evident.

The base of the craft was made from a large tree hewn out with painstaking effort. The Indians had selected a huge hardwood tree deep in the forest, and then began the tedious process of clearing away the underbrush and freeing the tree from numerous vines that entwined it with its neighbors.

Soon a platform scaffold of small poles, lashed together with pliable vines, was built so that the tree could be cut above the large flanged roots. Once the monster was on the ground, they began shaping it with an axe, making the basic outline of the canoe base. Several days of the muscle-burning and backbreaking work of swinging the axe transformed the huge log into the crude outline of a future canoe.

The nearly eleven-meter-long canoe is now ready to be fired. Dry leaves are placed in the concave open length and burned. The burning is carefully monitored and controlled while short poles are cut and wedged between the two sides, allowing them to be spread outwards to the desired pitch while the wood is hot and pliable. At this point the canoe is blackened from the burning process and everywhere you touch it, thick carbon covers your hands and clothes. After weeks of exposure to the elements and people, the carbon finally wears off.

The heavy canoe is now ready to be rolled from forest to river. Friends and family members are advised of the rolling day. The wife and female members of the owner's family begin preparing the local beer of masticated yuca that after three days of fermenting would provide the recompense for those rolling the base canoe out of the high forest to the river's edge.

The men hack out trails with machetes from the riverbank to the canoe. Round logs upon which to roll the heavy craft downhill are cut and placed under its massive weight. It is a festive, light-hearted occasion as the men secure a large stout vine on the bow of the canoe and begin shoving and pulling it downhill amid shouts of laughter and instructions. Hours pass by as perspiration-soaked bodies finally maneuver the burned log to the river's edge. Cheers of accomplishment ring out across the rain forest as the weary men head for the masato (beer) hut and a big two to three day drunken celebration.

The base canoe is then fitted with plank siding, caulked, painted, and transformed into a lovely cargo boat capable of carrying up to four tons of cargo. After purchasing the boat, it became our bus, truck, and main means of transportation. It was powered with a 40 horsepower outboard motor.

The boat had been tied to two long cane poles jabbed into the sand next to the island directly to the side of our house that overlooked the Marañon River. Last night torrential rains came, bringing a flood of water that ripped the two poles from their anchor and floated the boat that was laden down with two tons of water.

"Roger, Canicio, Mariano," I called to the Bible School teacher and students to help me pursue the lost craft. Together we ran down the 325 steps that led through the banana plants, past the radio tower to the lower landing. Rapidly we prepared a smaller boat and took an extra outboard motor to bring back the runaway. Two six-gallon gas tanks were hurriedly loaded on board, the boat was launched from its moorings, and our crew of four headed downstream in hot pursuit.

We left the quiet tranquil waters of the Kusu River in our wake as the long boat rocked and swayed when meeting the light chocolate-colored turbulent currents of the mighty Marañon River. We sped downstream with all attention and energy concentrating on the rapidly rising waters all around us. Logs and debris of all description had been pulled into the raging waters from cut down garden plots along the sloping sides of the river. Care was taken to avoid these dangerous obstacles that could break a shear pin on the tail of the motor, thus rendering the craft unmanageable and at the unforgiving mercy of the menacing waters.

We maneuvered the craft around the many curves, attempting to stay within the inner part of the curve close to shore and thus avoid the now mounting chaotic swirling logs on their mad dash downstream. All eyes strained, searching the river for some trace of the runaway, knowing that with every passing second we were coming closer to the inevitable thundering roar of Hanquichank, the great rapid area. Rounding yet another bend in the river, the rapids became visible in the distance. Hearts beat a little faster as the distant white caps broke and crashed over the huge boulders on the right side of the river.

"There!" someone shouted. All eyes turned simultaneously to see the runaway not more than fifty yards from the rapids, bobbing up and down in a small area of backwater. At any moment it could hit the main force of current and continue its devastating course through the rapids. Instructions were given and the crew made its approach to the bow of the runaway to drag the trailing rope from the water and tie it securely to our craft. Then we would try to pull it to shore and safety. Once on shore, we would bail the water from the runaway, attach the spare motor, and begin our journey back to the mission station.

The boat was now in tow and moving closer to shore when silence struck and our outboard motor shut down with a jolt. A second rope had slidden off the runaway's side, unnoticed, and had firmly entangled itself around the propeller of our motor.

I quickly reached into my pocket to retrieve my Swiss army knife to cut away the entangled mass, when the runaway, now caught in the open current and half full of water, began its swift descent to the rapids, pulling our lead boat and crew towards the whirlpools. Mariano and Canicio, standing in the bow of our boat, saw what was happening and jumped onto the large boulders and safety, straining to hold the lead boat's rope against the over-powering weight of the half submerged runaway tied with a death grip to our now motionless propeller. I continued searching my pockets for the always-present knife, but to no avail. Suddenly I realized that upon changing pants that morning, the transfer hadn't been made.

Desperately I tried to undo the knotted mess wrapped around the propeller but it was too tight. Mariano and Canicio held on the rope for dear life, but the enormous weight of the two boats was too much. The rope was wrenched from their straining arms as both boats now headed for the rapids and whirlpools below.

One quick glance told us that we were headed for disaster and only seconds remained before the boats would be spun around and gobbled up in the vortex of the menacing whirlpool that waited to draw us into its powerful clutches.

A quick prayer was offered and Roger and I each grabbed a gas tank to help us keep afloat and then the frightening spinning began. Incredible cold water gripped its victims as logs swirling around threatened to crush our defenseless bodies now moving toward the middle of the first whirlpool. Disoriented and drawn deeply into the spinning vortex, I defended my head from crushing blows of downward spiraling logs by gripping the empty buoyant gas tank and holding it tightly overhead. An eternity seemed to pass as we gasped for air after being erupted from the depths of this muddy, swirling tyrant, only to be drawn into the grip of a second lesser whirlpool.

Huanquichank is a phenomenon of nature. The river, on its downward trek, crashes into a sheer rock-walled mountain, carving out a large, deep rounded hole measuring some one hundred yards side to side. The crashing of water into the wall creates two large whirlpools and divides the waters into two parts. Half of the water makes a 90 degree right turn and heads downriver, while the other greater half forms a long backwater area that circles around the hole back up alongside the river's edge to a point where it then swings out to the main rapids and into the whirlpools again and continues to repeat the process, especially when the river level is rising, as was the case this day.

Cold and shivering, I was caught in the unforgiving hold of this watery monster. It tossed and spun my helpless body in such contortions that I lost all sense of direction before being vomited to the surface again. Frightened, I surveyed the seemingly hopeless situation as I surfaced from the death grip of the second whirlpool. Our bodies were being carried by the strong current into the backwater where we were actually forced upriver and dumped again into the rapids, repeating the whirlpool experience. It was one big merry-go-round that wouldn't stop to let us off.

I was swimming wildly against the current, but to no avail. I paused to rest and saw Roger latch onto a floating log. He straddled the log by lying on it and then used his hands as paddles, trying to break the powerful grip of the backwater, when he was sent spinning into the whirlpool. The log was wrenched from his hands and he swam desperately to stay afloat. Another log drifted by, upon which he hitched another ride, but this time kicking and paddling with all his might, he was just barely able to break the stranglehold the backwater held on him and reached the rocks where he exhaustedly pulled himself to safety.

I braced myself for my second ride into the rapids and whirlpools. The spinning and churning began all over again before I was spit up into the backwater preparing for yet another ride on the merry-go-round. My arms ached and weighed a water logged ton as I desperately struggled to stay afloat. My body was tired and bruised, but still I stubbornly clung to the empty gas can for buoyancy.

Before I knew what was happening, I was swiftly caught in the powerful grip of the strong current carrying me quickly to the rapids. Looking over my shoulder, I noticed a small dugout boat slowly moving upriver and heading for the distant beach. Just before entering the rapids for the third time, I saw people jumping from the small craft and unloading wild cane poles onto the beach. Over the rapids I went and disappeared into the first whirlpool. The Indians standing on the beach stared at the horrifying scene developing before their own eyes. Their cries could be heard along the beach as they knew the missionary was going to drown, because they had never witnessed anyone survive from the clutches of Hanquichank. I clung to the gas tank with waning strength and finally surfaced after what seem like an eternity in the bosom of the river, only to disappear into the second whirlpool.

Gasping for air, I emerged from that swirling hungry river only to again become the victim of the ferocious backwater that sped its prey on its way. At that precise moment I saw the small boat inch its way to my position at the far edge of the whirlpool in the heaving backwater. The motorist kept the boat at just the right angle without being pulled into the heavy current and the waiting whirlpool. His helper, leaning way over the side of the boat, grabbed my arms and began pulling me on board. I tried vainly to pull myself into the boat but my arms were rubbery and my strength was all but gone. The man continued pulling until I tumbled into the boat and lay prostrate on the bottom of the dugout. The motorist accelerated the motor breaking the force of backwater and sped to the far side of the river and the safety of the sand beach. Those two men risked their lives to save me from a watery grave.

Sequence - The motorist who risked his life to save mine from Hanquichank was Manuel Katan from the village of Chipe, thirty minutes upriver from our home deep in the forest. Six months after this incident, he was carrying several sacks of rice upriver when his dugout boat was drawn into the great whirlpool of Duship. His boat capsized and he struggled valiantly to escape, but drowned in the menacing pressure of that relentless swirl. This accident took place about twenty miles upriver from Hanquichank. I helped search the river looking for his body but with no success. Nine days later on a Sunday morning came the news that his badly decomposed body had been spotted in the backwater of Hanquichank.

I ferried the family members in our long boat and helped retrieve his corpse from the very spot where my own life had been spared and rescued by this man. It indeed was a day of reflecting about God's providential care and yet mourning the loss of a valued friend.

Pocket Knife

Our boat turned off of the turbulent Marañon River onto the calm clear waters of the Cenepa River that bright, sunny Friday afternoon. Alfredo, a student in the Bible Institute had asked me earlier in the week to visit his home village of Huampami to encourage the believers in their fledging church.

Our small aluminum speedboat churned up a large wake behind us. The wake spread evenly to both sides of the river as dugout canoes bobbed up and down from the powerful waves it had created. Rounding a long sweeping bend in the river, the village of Wawaim came into view. Beautiful symmetrical thatched roof huts lined the high bank on the West side of the river.

Little naked bronze-skinned boys, laughing and running along the beach, jumped into the soft warm waters of the Cenepa, swimming toward our speeding boat. At the river's edge, a group of women were washing the brown, thin, bark-like skin from mounds of yuca that had just recently been cultivated in their gardens beyond the huts on the many dotted hillsides in the distance. They were chatting and visiting with one another after a long day in the gardens. It was a peaceful scene that was soon left in our wake as we rounded yet another sharp bend in this twisting, serpentine river that led us past sand beaches, rock formations, and partially submerged logs that provided an obstacle course to navigate. I shifted my weight from one tired part of my anatomy to try and find relief from the hard aluminum backless seat upon which I was perched. Occasionally I pulled my cap down tightly to keep the wind from blowing it off into the water. The outboard motor droned on, breaking the silence of the monotony of curve after endless curve on this hot tropical day. I drug my hand through the water and then splashed my face with its cool, refreshing effect.

Just below the village of Tutino, Alfredo asked if we could stop and pick up his wife and children to take them to Huampami, as they had been visiting her mother in Tutino. Before our boat came to a complete stop on the beach, children and dogs swarmed us. The dogs were running up and down the beach barking incessantly at our boat, trying desperately to drive us away.

Soon Alfredo came walking back from a nearby hut with his family in tow. Mother-in-law had a large woven basket strapped to her forehead and hanging from stooped shoulders, for it was filled with yuca, bananas, a cooking pot, and a long machete. His wife carried a similar basket with a blanket or two and some well patched items of clothing. She was nine months pregnant and looked about to burst as she waddled up to the boat. I jumped up and helped her with the basket as she struggled to climb into the boat. His young daughter sported another smaller basket of eating utensils, and a tiny pup in the front of her dress. Alfredo brought up the rear carrying his well-worn rusted shotgun with a skinny, rib-showing dog in tow. All managed to find their places in the boat and now we were off on our final leg of the journey.

Past the villages of Tutino, Nuevo Kanam, and San Antonio, our now-loaded craft lumbered along as the sun was dropping in the western sky. Finally our destination was in sight. Up ahead the village of Huampami popped up out of nowhere. The familiar scene of huts lining the bank, with numerous canoes gently swinging in the backwater, and numbers of people bathing in the tranquil waters of the Cenepa, caused me to reflect on the serenity of this isolated village in the middle of the Amazon.

Hand waves were exchanged as our boat pulled into the mud bank where many canoes were tied. Excited greetings were formally exchanged and eager hands clutched our belongings, leading us up the steep hill toward the home of Alfredo. I was delighted to relinquish that hard seat and stretch my legs after those weary hours of travel. His hut was very small, so they carried my belongings to the cookhouse connected to the main house.

Checking out my surroundings, I found it was typical of the many huts I had slept and eaten in. Three logs lying at different angles on the dirt floor provided the fire upon which they cooked. Nearby the hunting dog was tied with a stout vine around his neck and anchored to a post of the hut close to the three-logged fireplace. At night he would move close to the dying embers for warmth when the air was cool and damp.

Clay and aluminum pots were stacked neatly upside down on a raised platform made of wild cane poles tied together with thin supple vines. A few white bleached-out skulls of animals lined one section of the bamboo wall, proving the skill of Alfredo as a hunter. Hanging from a roof beam was a basket of peanuts waiting to be planted. Peanuts are planted twice a year during the months of June and September after the rains and floods have subsided since peanuts produce better in sandy soil close to the river.

On another shelf, clay bowls awaited a meal of chicken soup with boiled yuca. Above the log fireplace hung a small blackened, soot covered woven basket attached to a beam supporting the thatched leaf roof. Inside the basket wrapped in blackened banana leaves was hard crystal rock salt used to season the food. Usually when soup is served, you drop a piece of rock salt into your bowl, stirring it around until your soup is salty enough. You then drop it into the next person's bowl who then stirs, tastes, and stirs some more until it is just right.

Opposite the three logs, attached to the far wall was a split cane pole bed where I would spend the night. Women began stirring about in the kitchen, first killing a chicken, plucking its feathers and cutting it up into numerous small pieces. The three logs were shoved together at different angles, providing a natural platform for the cooking pot. Dry twigs were placed in the middle of the opening left from the three logs. A torch made of dry banana leaves was lit from a neighbor's fire and brought into our hut where the twigs were soon glowing with red-hot fire. A small, feathered fan was swung rapidly back and forth until the ends of the logs caught fire. Black wisps of smoke poured forth and blackened the roof leaves overhead. The lady fanning the fire turned her head from the stinging in her eyes as tears gently rolled down her weathered cheeks. Soon the flames leaped around the pot perched on the three logs and the water began to boil.

Turning my back on the rising smoke, I began preparing my sleeping quarters for the next two nights. Mosquito netting was secured completely around my air mattress and sleeping bag to ward off the vampire bats at night. We were famished and the soup and yuca never tasted better than that evening in Huampami. Our meal was followed with a large bowl of sweet warm banana drink.

Darkness soon engulfed the rain forest in total blackness. Small wick lamps were lit giving off a smoky, yellowish-orange glow that cast eerie shadows around the hut. In the distance we heard the high-pitched sound of a large land snail shell being blown. Its sound broke the still quiet night, advising us that the church service would soon start. I grabbed my flashlight, Bible, and Aguaruna songbook and followed Alfredo and family down a dark damp trail. Looking down the path I could see many yellowish lights converging on a small building in the clearing.

Moving through the doorway, my eyes began accommodating to the dim light of several lamps placed high overhead at strategic points around the church. We had a wonderful service with many praying around the altar. As I knelt with that large crowd of people that night, isolated by time in a remote, almost forgotten part of the world, I realized once again that He was there in our midst and how blest I was to be His missionary.

The air was charged and filled with excitement as we were walking back to our huts under a beautiful sky filled with blinking stars. I climbed under my mosquito net, sunburned and tired, but happy to be in the center of God's will for my life. There was a light glow from the dying embers of the fireplace across the room. Outside I could hear the croaking of untold numbers of frogs and the rustling of trees from a small breeze that blew gently through the forest. A vampire bat or two flew overhead looking for a victim, but my mosquito net was firmly tucked under my bed and my tired body finally succumbed to a deep sleep.

At first I heard the low sound of talking and movement in the cookhouse, then the soft yellowish light from a wick lamp sketching shadowy figures on the bamboo wall. I was struggling with my subconscious state of sleep trying to awaken and focus my eyes in the semi darkness.

I knew that Indian men arise around four A.M. to rinse out their mouths and start a fire to begin a new day. 'Surely it is not time to awaken yet,' I thought. I grabbed my flashlight to see my watch. 'Why, it's only midnight, what in the world are they doing?' I heard someone outside chopping a small tree down with a machete.

Rolling onto my side, I could see Alfredo coming through the doorway with a long eight-foot pole about two inches in diameter. With his machete he began picking at the dirt floor making a hole not too far from the cooking fire. Several ladies were scurrying in and out of the hut talking softly. Alfredo put his machete aside and began driving the long pole into the hole at an angle of about 45 degrees. He would plunge the pole into the hole, pull it out and repeat the process over and over until he was satisfied that the pole was anchored solidly in the ground.

A water pot was placed on the cooking fire to boil. One lady left and soon returned with a freshly cut, large banana leaf and placed it on the ground in front of the pole. At this point I was fully awake, wondering what was going on. About that time Alfredo's wife was helped through the doorway by a lady friend and led over to where the pole was placed in the floor. Then it hit me, she was about to give birth in this cookhouse. I waited, thinking that they would be calling me at any moment to assist her in delivering this baby.

She knelt down on both knees, clutching the pole in both hands. One of the women stood behind her with her arms locked around the waist of the mother-to-be with her interlocked hands above the abdomen. When the contractions came the lady friend squeezed and pushed down hard on the abdomen as Alfredo's wife held the pole firmly and pushed against it until the contractions stopped. I watched this age-old custom that had brought countless babies into this world. I thought about all the fuss and sophistication of a modern hospital in the U.S.A. compared to the scene before me.

Another contraction came hard and fast, with low groans from the mother clinging to the pole and pushing with all her strength, while her helper applied downward force on her abdomen. Alfredo was rummaging through an old wooden box looking for a string he had saved for tying off the cord. I looked from Alfredo to his wife as another hard contraction came, accompanied by pushing and fast breathing.

Triumphantly he lifted his prize from the box and continued looking through it for something else. The next thing I heard was a gasp from the mother, and Alfredo came quickly to her side in time to receive the newborn into this world, laying it gently on the clean banana leaf. Evidently, Alfredo was not able to find the other object in the box that he was searching for, because he came to my bedside asking for my pocketknife.

'My pocketknife,' I thought, 'Oh, he wants to cut the cord with it.' The Indians usually use a sharp piece of bamboo or pottery shard, or if they have it on hand, a razor blade. Reaching into my pocket I extracted my Swiss army knife with one hand, while the other lifted the side of the mosquito net. I handed him my knife and instructed him to put it into the boiling water before cutting the cord. His wife was still clinging to the pole and a few minutes later she delivered the afterbirth.

The women made the new mother comfortable near the cooking fire where she soon was fast asleep with the newborn by her side. All was quiet again and I lay there for a long time thinking about how complicated life has become for us and how simple life is for them. Alfredo washed off my knife, came back to my bed and handed me one of my prized possessions. I held it for a moment remembering all the chores it had performed in its short lifetime, and then placed it once again into my pocket. I turned over and dozed off to sleep once more to the sounds of the rain forest just outside the comfort of my sleeping bag.

The Inevitable

Chasing those pesky baby chickens out the doorway of her one-room, bamboo, thatched-roof hut, she paused long enough to tell her four children that school would soon start. All four were squatting around a large banana leaf in the middle of the floor dipping pieces of boiled yuca in a mound of rock salt. Quickly they washed it down with bowls full of warm banana drink, and headed for the doorway. Goodbyes were exchanged as they scurried happily outside on their way to the little village school located down the winding trail that led them to the very heart of the village of Listra.

This picturesque village, situated in a peaceful valley two hours by trail from the Marañon River, takes one back to another world; one of intense beauty in this evergreen paradise. The serenity of this pristine valley was broken only by a noisy flock of parrots flying rapidly on their way to a new nesting ground, and the constant chatter of boys and girls on their way to the small bilingual school.

Soon her children rounded a bend in the trail and their voices trailed off in the distance. She looked for a long moment at the little two-foot long brush broom clutched in her hand. Bending over, she continued sweeping the dirt floor free of banana and yuca peelings. Standing in the doorway she noticed a beautiful cloudless sky and knew that this was a perfect day to harvest the first fruits of their new garden that had been planted about twelve months previously.

Ducking back into the hut, she retrieved a large open weave basket from the bamboo wall. A broad vine strap was attached to the stout rim of the basket that she placed across her forehead, allowing the basket to hang freely over her back. A rusty three-foot long machete knife was extracted from the wall and examined by her strong calloused hands. Her finger automatically ran along the thin cutting edge to determine if it needed sharpening or not. It did. Skillfully the machete was placed into the basket and a mental note was made to sharpen it when she reached the stream.

Her attention then focused on a small hammock tied between two slender poles stuck in the soft, damp dirt floor next to the split bamboo bed upon which she and her husband slept. Reaching into the hammock she tenderly lifted up the newest member of the family. Touching that soft cheek elicited a faint smile from the innocent face of this, her fifth child. Mutterings of adoration followed as she embraced this tiny bundle of joy next to her heart. Gently the child was placed inside the front of her dress, whereupon he began to nurse immediately, and would continue to do so as she walked a long trail to the garden.

Stepping outside the hut she felt the warm rays of a tropical sun on her bronzed, exposed shoulders and arms. Quickly she crossed the small clearing and carefully made her way down the steep embankment, using her toes as tiny claws, gripping the firmer soil that lay just beneath the light surface of mud that covered the ground. Once at the bottom of this ravine, she waded out into the cool, refreshing, ankle-deep, rock-strewn stream that flowed past their home and emptied into a larger river, disappearing into an eternal expanse of jungle. She stood there, allowing the cool water to caress her feet as small pebbles, carried by the slight current, danced across her toes.

She felt so happy and free this morning as she listened to the birds singing in the trees. Glancing up, she noticed thin shafts of light from a sun that was desperately trying to break through the thick heavy canopy of entangled vines and trees, but only smattering rays of sunlight penetrated the dense foliage and illuminated the damp soil around her.

To one side of the stream was a carved out recess where water pooled from a small spring that filtered through the porous soil. From this pool they obtained their water in large squash-like gourds for drinking and cooking. In the afternoons this water served as a bathing area for the entire family. Such pleasant memories flooded her mind as she mechanically drew the machete from its resting place and sharpened it on a nearby rock.

Mission accomplished, she began her ascent up the slippery mud bank on the far side of the stream and soon disappeared into the forest. Her feet nimbly carried her across the trail for some time until all of a sudden, emerging before her, was a large clearing composed of several small hillsides covered with cultivated yuca and banana plants. Stepping out into the clearing, she felt the intense heat of a blazing tropical sun on her back. She stood, as if frozen in time, admiring this new garden area that she and her husband had carved out.

Surveying the mature yuca plants, she spotted a large overhanging tree that provided a lot of shade just off to the edge of the garden. With machete in hand, she cut a path to the tree and cleared the area of weeds and overgrowth. Nearby were two small saplings growing about five feet apart which provided a perfect spot to tie the baby's hammock. This done, she took the baby, now full from nursing, and placed him into the hammock. Giving it a gentle nudge, he was soon fast asleep.

She gazed into that peaceful face for a long moment and then made preparations for the hard work ahead. Her eyes skirted this new garden and a faint smile parted her lips as she remembered the day they had cleared the ground. It had been a herculean task: the clearing of the underbrush, the felling of trees followed by a month of drying and then burning the cut vegetation. She remembered the intense fire as it consumed all the brush and limbs of fallen trees, leaving behind a smoldering, charred hillside ready for planting. Twelve months ago they had planted those small tender banana plants and the long cut twigs of yuca stems in the ground. Then came the long periods of rain, sun, and cultivation of those young shoots as they grew skyward.

She took one last look surveying this miracle of nature and hard work. Here and there were clusters of bananas with their long broad leaves, waving under a gentle breeze. Tall ten to twelve foot yuca plants, their small green leaves glistening under a tropical sun were waiting to be harvested.

She placed her basket on the ground close to several stems of yuca growing at slight angles to each other. The steel machete in her skilled hands dug into the soft, sandy, black, damp soil breaking the ground loose around those stems. Now in a squatting position, her hands clutched those stems just beneath the broken soil. She pulled with all her strength. Slowly, at first, the earth cracked and then gave way, as long dark tubers, attached to the stem at different angles, broke free from their underground prison. Each tuber or root was about one to one and a half feet in length and as big around as a man's arm. Each stem produced 3-5 tubers. She shook the dirt from the roots and then cut them loose at the stem and laid them neatly in her woven basket. This process was repeated until the basket was nearly filled.

Large beads of perspiration gathered on her brow and dropped onto the soft soil. She could feel the unrelenting heat of the sun on her back as she cut three pieces of the stems and jabbed them back into the cavities made by the extracted yuca roots. These pieces she leaned at a 45 degree angle and tamped the soft dirt around them for regrowth.

She now straightened up, and, wiping her forehead with a dirty hand, she squinted into the bright sunlight. Resting her back, she surveyed the garden and caught sight of a large sun-ripened stalk of bananas just waiting to be picked. With machete in tow, she cut a quick path to the banana plant and cut the soft stem halfway through about three feet from the ground. Gently pulling on one of the big broad leaves she drew the stalk of bananas to her side, allowing them to glide slowly to the ground. The stalk was cut into smaller sizes and placed in the basket.

Once more she looked around the perimeter of the garden and there, not more than one hundred feet away, she spied a large orange papaya. Approaching the papaya plant, she noticed that the birds hadn't gotten to it yet. Cutting a long two-inch-in-diameter pole from a slender tree she made her way to the spot. After blunting one end of the long pole, she stretched it overhead and nudged the ripened fruit and it fell into her waiting hands. Examining it closely she thought of how much her children would enjoy that sweet soft fruit when they returned from the village school. Into the basket it went, followed by a clean, fresh cut banana leaf to cover the papaya and keep the sun from spotting it.

Glancing at the sun she noticed that it was about 11:00 in the sky. Perfect timing, she thought, as she moved to retrieve her baby and head home to prepare lunch before the children returned from school. She was about to lift the sleeping child from his little swinging cocoon when out of the corner of her eyes she spotted the fresh tracks of some wild animal about fifteen feet from where she stood.

Garman Family - June 1974 (Chiclayo, Peru)
top row: Greg, Candy, Rusty
bottom row: Addie, Tim, Larry

July 1964 - Garmans left for
Mexico in Sept. '64

Family

Garman Family all grown up:
front row: Larry and Addie
back row: Tim, Greg, Candy, Rusty

The Garman's home on
New Horizons Mission Station

Kusu - Garman's home
the first 16 years

Home

Addie's Jungle Kitchen

Larry and friends with
9 foot bushmaster snake

Addie with
Smoky and Cheeta

Addie holding parrots

Larry holding
Boa and Anaconda snakes

Line at the clinic (1971)

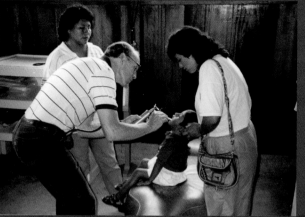

Larry working in clinic (1992)

Clinic

Larry and Addie in clinic

Larry napping in his boat- "This is the life."

Tim Garman watching Kusu lady spinning clay for pottery

Typical Amazon Hut

Life

Bible Institute Kusu

Kusu Mission Church

Church

Amazon Church altar call

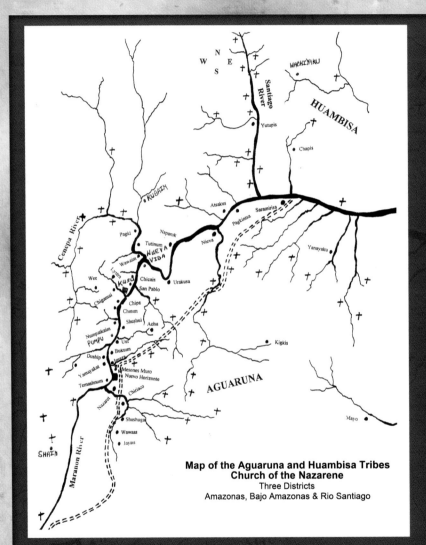

**Map of the Aguaruna and Huambisa Tribes
Church of the Nazarene**
Three Districts
Amazonas, Bajo Amazonas & Rio Santiago

**Villages Where the
Stories took Place**

Kusu
Chigamai
Chipe
Wee
San Pablo
Chinim
Lystra
Shushui
Kubaim
Nazaret
Tutino
Wachiaku
Shaim
Uut
Pumpu
Bellavista
Mesones Muro
New Horizons
Colalla
(mountain village not on map)

Crosses on map
represent Nazarene
Churches

Curiously she slipped away and moved toward the fresh-made tracks, wondering all the time as to what animal could have made them. Could they be those of a tapir *(largest animal of the rain forest)*, or deer, or perhaps those of a jaguar? That last thought sent cold chills through her trembling body. Her fears were relieved however when, kneeling down to examine the indented prints in the ground, she realized that they were the tracks of a large armadillo.

Immediately, thoughts of succulent white pieces of tender meat formed a mental image in her mind. She could see her children squatting around clean fresh banana leaves mounded up with boiled yuca, dipping armadillo meat into little coarse grains of salt and drinking broth from a clay bowl. Triumphantly she muttered almost out loud, 'That animal will be in my cooking pot today.'

Automatically she glanced at the tiny hammock still gently swinging beneath the shade of her garden tree. Grabbing the long pole she had used to knock down the papaya, she proceeded to make a stout point on one end with the machete. Jabbing the machete into the ground right next to the basket, she turned with pole in hand toward the tracks of the armadillo.

As she followed the tracks, a plan was formulated in her mind. She knew well the process of extracting an armadillo from its hiding place. She had accompanied her husband on many a hunting trip and knew exactly what to do. The tracks led to a steep hillside where they disappeared into a small hole at the base of that hill.

She knew that animal was holed-up in the recesses of the narrow tunnel deep in the earth. With the long pole poised over the entrance to the tunnel, she thought once more of her children and their need for meat. Ernesto, her husband, was a government-employed schoolteacher who received a small salary to teach in the village school of Listra. His goal in life was to have five wives and much money. He was well on his way, for she was one of two wives and each had five children. Meat was scarce. Anytime an animal was killed it was devoured immediately between thirteen people.

She plunged the pointed end of that stout pole into the soft ground over the opening of the hole, busting the dirt loose. Over and over she repeated the process, and then on all fours she retrieved the loose dirt with her hands, pulling it away from the hole, mounding it up behind her. Her arms ached from this laborious task. Perspiration-soaked clothing clung to her tired body. Stopping to rest a moment, she swiped a dirty forearm across her brow as drops of sweat stung her eyes.

Hesitating for a moment, she thought of trying to reach blindly into the dark recesses of the hole and grab that animal by the foot, drag it out, club it over the head, and take it home for the cooking pot. Quickly, however, she cast that thought aside, knowing the dangers of reaching blindly into an armadillo's hole. Many times the largest of all poisonous snakes of the Amazon will share the same hole and they never bother each other. They get along wonderfully well together. The adult bushmaster can measure up to twelve feet in length with very potent venom.

I will never forget the day I was treating patients in the clinic, when desperate cries for help outside reached my ears through the screened windows. Rushing outside, my eyes fastened upon an Indian lady holding a man in her arms. He was extremely pale and definitely in shock. Exhaustion showed on her face as she emotionally informed me of their plight.

"We were hunting deep in the forest when we came across the tracks of an armadillo. We followed the tracks to a large hole in the ground. My husband was digging out the hole with a large pointed pole, and then in his haste reached blindly into the dark tunnel and was bitten on the hand by a large bushmaster snake." Instinctively I looked at his swollen, inflamed hand as she continued, "I half carried and dragged him hours over the hunting trails back to the village and then here to the clinic." Bushmaster bites are very serious as they are capable of injecting large amounts of venom, up to 5 cm. at one strike. His blood pressure had bottomed out and his life was hanging by a thread, but that's another story.

Another day, desperate calls for help reached my ears again. Looking out the clinic window, I saw a man hurriedly tie up his long, sleek, black dugout canoe at the river's edge and make his way toward the clinic frantically calling my name. I went outside to meet this man who was desperately calling, "Docturo wamak tati," (Doctor come quickly). Excitedly he begged me to accompany him to the village of San Pablo where his aunt had been bitten by a bushmaster. He informed me that he had been on the river for hours fighting the heavy current paddling upstream to our mission station. He told me that his aunt went to the garden earlier that morning to dig up yuca for her family. She did not see the large coiled bushmaster resting in the shadows of a nearby plant. When she made that sudden move, pulling on the stem to break those tubers loose from the ground, the startled snake lunged, striking and biting her on the upper leg. The force of its blow knocked her down. While on the ground screaming and trying to escape the serpent, she was bitten a second time.

She plunged her pointed pole again and again into the ground making the hole wider and deeper, knowing that soon she would be able to safely reach in and extract the armadillo. Her muscles burned with each stroke of the pole. Her clothes and hair were matted with dirt and her parched dry lips begged for water. She felt the fury of a mid-day sun on her back, as exhaustion overcame her tired body. Dropping the pole, she sought the shade of a nearby tree to rest a moment before the final assault on the hole.

To relieve the monotony of the work at hand, she thought about the events that had shaped her life during the last year. Before moving to Listra, Ernesto, his two wives, and ten children lived in the village of Kucha, three long days away over a very difficult trail through dense jungle, where he taught in the bilingual school. Resting there under the shade tree her mind carried her back to that unforgettable night in the village of Kucha months before.

Word had spread like wildfire through the village and the name of Roberto Atamain Shunta was on the lips of everyone. He was the District Superintendent for the emerging Amazon District and that very afternoon he would be arriving in the village of Kucha, after three exhausting days crossing the mountains, to visit the pastor and church. Roberto was not an Aguaruna as were the people of Kucha. He was a Huambisa Indian and the two tribes had often fought among themselves in the past. For generations they had been archenemies and revenge-killing raids between the two tribes had been a way of life for many centuries. Peace, however, had come to the area as the Aguarunas had reached out to evangelize the Huambisas.

She desperately wanted to go to the church that night and hear this man speak, but her husband forbade his wives to attend. That night, however, Ernesto was with the other wife, so she slipped away and entered the door, sitting on the very last bench. The church was packed to overflowing. The people of Kucha listened intently to this humble man as he told of his miraculous conversion through the medium of the spirit world in the form of a vision. She remembered listening, spellbound to his account of how God changed him from drunkenness to Holiness. She found herself walking the dirt floor of this little church to the front, kneeling at a simple altar, and pouring her heart out to the Savior.

Returning home, excited to tell Ernesto of her newfound joy and peace, she was greeted with mocking and cynicism as he belittled the pastor and all things spiritual. He despised the church and all that it represented. His intense purpose to drive the church from Kucha had failed, and now, of all things, one of his wives had been converted to this faith.

A faint smile broke through the dry parched lips as she contemplated the days following her conversion. She remembered being so discouraged and down, but the Christians had prayed with and for her in the ensuing days and encouraged her to give testimony to her new-found faith. If my husband won't listen, she thought, then whom can I tell?

Shortly thereafter the other wife came to mind. They had not gotten along very well and a lot of jealousy had formed between the two families. Sometimes Ernesto would give meat to one family as opposed to the other, creating a lot of hard feelings. Ernesto had a drinking problem that involved both wives. Each one in her respective hut was required to provide him with masato. After prayer one day, she humbled herself and went to the other wife to share her testimony.

Her testimony fell upon eager ears and a hungry heart that soon accepted the gift of eternal life through Jesus Christ. Now both beer pots went dry, and Ernesto would never be the same. He was caught between a rock and a hard place with both wives praying for his salvation.

Standing to her feet, she clutched the pole one more time and plunged it into the ground. A few minutes later the hole was now ready to be entered. Her digging had provided a tunnel-like passage that she could crawl into and capture the armadillo. Dropping the pole, she inched her way forward into the dark damp tunnel. She could feel the coolness of the moist clay on her overheated body and it felt so refreshing as her eyes adjusted to the dimly lit area. There in the corner, cowering against the back wall, she could see the shadowy form of the object of her hard work. In one motion her arm stretched forward as the hand clutched the leg of the armadillo. As she was dragging the animal from its hiding place, the inevitable happened.

Late that afternoon Ernesto was returning from the fishing expedition and he was famished. Approaching his hut, expecting to find food, he entered the doorway, but to his surprise his wife was not there. He looked around the hut noting that the baby, basket, and machete were not in their familiar place. The cooking pot was empty and concern soon portrayed itself on his face. Calloused hands dipped a bowl into the large masato pot, but it too was empty. 'Where could she be?' he muttered half out loud. Turning to the doorway, he called to his children who were playing outside. "Where is your mother?" was his question.

In unison they replied, "We don't know. When we left for school this morning, she was sweeping the house, and when we came home she was not here."

His heart was racing now as he realized that something must have happened to her, as she should have been back hours ago. In desperation he quickly made his way to the only place that he could find what he was looking for, the church. Right inside the door, hanging on a cane pole, was a large land snail shell. The shell is fashioned into a horn used to communicate with the entire village. One long blast repeated at several second intervals is used by the pastor to call the flock together at church. Two long blasts means that there is a problem in the village and everyone must converge at a central meeting place. Trembling hands held the shell as he blew two long blasts. People came from nearby huts, converging on the scene. In chorus they asked, "What has happened?"

"My wife left for the gardens early this morning, but has not yet come back. She should have been here hours ago." The search party crossed the stream, climbed the steep muddy hill on the far side, and disappeared deep into the forest. They ran along the trail expecting the worst, when at last they emerged into the large clearing, eyes searching in every direction.

The sun was dropping behind the tallest trees, casting shadows across the garden area. The hammock was spotted and its small contents were handed to one of the women who soothed and loved the baby.

Almost simultaneously the basket of produce was found with the machete stuck in the ground next to it. Still there was no trace of the mother, until from the far edge of the clearing came a shout of triumph. Tracks of an armadillo were seen with barefoot prints following the tracks in a northeasterly direction. The men ran to the spot and hastened to follow the tracks that led them to a steep hillside and there they found her.

The women began to cry the death song as men frantically tore at the mound of dirt with their bare hands. The ground over the tunnel had broken through and she was buried under a tonnage of dirt. Eager hands agonizingly uncovered her lifeless body and carried their loved one back to the village. Ernesto was heart-broken and confused. He finally asked the pastor to perform the burial rites over his departed wife.

That night in a small semi-dark hut sat a lone man with his thoughts. His children were asleep on their split bamboo beds and only the night sounds of the rain forest interrupted the silence of his personal thoughts. His mind was in turmoil as pictures flashed through his mind.

One image that haunted him dealt with the time he had gone to her hut to eat and, upon entering the doorway, heard her praying with the children and for his salvation. Disgustedly he had turned and marched to his other wife's hut only to hear the same thing. He knew that night that his life would never be the same.

There was no denying the fact that both wives no longer fought among themselves and even the children were better behaved. His family was at peace and only he was at war with the Lord. Rising to his feet, he left the hut. The night was dark, but a gentle breeze was lightly blowing as he crossed the village, following a trail that led him to a small hut at the edge of a clearing.

Across the way he could see the three white crosses under a faint moonlight slightly illuminating the front of the church. He paused for a long moment realizing that in this little church his two wives had found so much happiness. Turning, he faced the hut where a yellowish-orange glow shone between the bamboo poles, casting broken shadows at his feet. Pausing, he called, "Yatsaju Pastoro pujamek?" (Friend pastor, are you there?)

"Ehe, yatsaju pujajai, yaitpau?" (Yes, friend, I am here, who is there?)

"Witjai, Ernestojai," (It's me Ernesto) replied the visitor. From the doorway Ernesto saw a shadowy presence emerge and a hand gesturing, inviting him to come and enter. Passing through the low doorway made of upright posts, he entered the dimly lit hut and was asked to sit down. There he sat, facing the man he had despised and rejected, but now he was looking to him for help. The pastor reached out to this confused and hurting man, patiently revealing to him God's grace, love, and plan of salvation through Jesus Christ.

That night, in the middle of the rain forest, a broken-hearted man came to the Savior and his life would never be the same. Months passed and Ernesto became an integral part of the church in Listra.

Then came that memorable Sunday night. Excitement filled the air as students from all over the upper Amazon gathered to begin a new semester of theological education in the large church on the campus of the Nazarene Bible Institute. The director presented the new first-year students as they lined up across the front of the church. It was exciting as the new students gave their names, a short testimony, and where they were from. The microphone was passed from student to student and finally it came to rest in the hands of an older man. "My name is Ernesto Chavez, and I am from the church in the village of Listra. I have resigned my state school teaching job, for God has called me to preach."

The Amazon Call

The Mysterious Vision

He stood alone that day in the front yard of our mission station located on the corner of the Kusu and Marañon rivers deep in the rain forest. He seemed a little uncertain of these new surroundings, as his keen eyes drank in the layout of our station. Approaching him, I immediately recognized the fact that he had traveled a great distance.

A broad friendly smile on a very pleasant face greeted me as I spoke to him that warm tropical afternoon. His feet were thick and calloused by endless trails, feet that had never seen a pair of shoes. His pants rode high above his ankles and the shirt was threadbare. Over his shoulder was a small bag tied to a pole, housing his meager belongings. The warmth of his strong but tired voice caught my attention while he told me that he had been on the river and trail for many days of endless travel.

"I have come," he said, "from the Wachiyaku village among the Huambisa Indians across the mountains between the Santiago and Morona Rivers." I couldn't believe my ears when he mentioned the words Huambisa and Morona Rivers, because that was another world from where we lived deep in the Aguaruna Territory.

He continued, "I have come to prepare for ministry and have been told that there is a Nazarene Bible Institute here on the banks of the Kusu River." His eyes moved from me to the Institute located on the high hill behind me that overlooked the beautiful valley below with the Marañon River meandering like a long serpent, snaking its way through the endless green jungle.

I responded affirmatively, extending my hand to this, our newest student. In our fondest dreams we never imagined the work reaching that remote and isolated corner of the jungle. We had made trips to evangelize on the lower Santiago River. They were exhausting trips in our long dugout canoe boat where we visited many villages on that large river. I had contemplated that mountain range which separates the Santiago and Morona river basin where he had come from, never thinking of reaching the Huambisa people. Our hands met and clasped for a long moment and he knew he was welcomed.

The sun was relentless on his near-naked body as he plunged into the turbulent muddy waters of the Santiago River to seek some relief from the unbearable heat of the tropical sun overhead. His balsa log raft drifted with the current following that serpentine twisting river ever downward toward the village where he hoped the answers to his many questions that plagued his mind would be answered. Crawling back onto the raft, he rested and his mind floated back to that night a few weeks before in the Wachiyaku village. He remembered very vividly that haunting vision which awakened him from a deep sleep.

Roberto Ataman Shunt, eighteen years old, asleep on a split cane pole bed, saw a man dressed in white standing before him that dark night. Visions were not new to Roberto. When he was five years old, his grandfather had instructed him in the ways of his people. Sitting near the small three-logged fire in the middle of the hut, the older man would tell him the history of his people. He was taught to fast sweets and observe other dietary habits according to age-old customs.

At seven years of age, he would have to sleep in the jungle with only one other companion, and at twelve spend seven days and nights alone in the forest. At night he would tie his hammock between two trees and drink Datem, tobacco tea, belladonna, and other drugs, hoping to receive his power from the spirit world in the form of the jaguar, boa, or eagle. He must sleep in a different place each night so that Iwanch (devil) and the demons might not snatch him away during the night, because they roamed in the dark. The greatest vision from the spirit world was to become a great warrior and participate in revenge killings and retaliation war raids. He memorized genealogies and the history of wars. The second best vision was that of becoming a great hunter to provide meat for his table. The third vision that every young man desires is that of becoming an authoritative powerful speaker.

Roaming the jungle during the seven-day period would prepare him to become a man. He was frightened to hear the owl hoot for that meant someone would soon die. When he looked at the stars he would shudder, because they represented those who had died. He talked to no woman, ate little, and fasted sweets, pineapple, crab, boiled eggs, peanuts, and soup with meat. He would learn the songs to drive away the demons and sing the war songs to be a warrior.

This night, however, the vision was unlike any he had ever experienced. The man dressed in white spoke to him about his drinking habits. Inside most huts would be a large clay pot about five to ten gallons in size sitting on a tripod affair with a clean green banana leaf covering the opening held in place with a vine. The jug usually is full of a local beer called masato. The women make the beer by chewing and masticating the boiled yuca root. It is chewed and mixed thoroughly with the salvia until it has the consistency of watered down mashed potatoes. The chewed mash is then spit into the pot and more yuca is chewed until the pot is about three-fourths full.

It takes several hours to make a large amount of masato. Maybe two or more women will help in the chewing process especially if there will be a three day and night beer-drink. Finally the mouth of the pot is then covered with the clean banana leaf. The enzymes in the saliva cause the fermentation process of changing the liquefied predigested yuca into a strong alcoholic beverage called masato. This process takes about three days.

After having completed their work and bathing in the river, the men are ready for a drinking spree. If the man of the house has invited his friends to help him clear a new garden plot, make a new hut, or drag a new canoe from the high country to the river's edge, he must provide the brew for all of them. His wife removes the banana leaf, dips a round gourd with small holes in it into the large pot, straining it into another bowl. She passes the bowl to her husband who turns his back on his guests and drinks it down. It is not polite to drink facing people.

The bowl is then refilled and each guest in turn participates, and then the process is repeated throughout the night. The men adorn their finery in the form of a crown of feathers, beetle winged earrings, and seedpod bracelets tied around their ankles and then paint their faces, arms, shoulders and chest with the bright red paste of crushed achiote seeds. To the beating of the drums, men dance with men carrying in one hand a spear or shotgun. The women don their waist bands made of large triangle pieces of land snail shells. Smaller bands of the same are placed on the upper arms and women dance together holding hands and jumping up and down in one place.

The man in white then held up a book and, pointing to it, said, "One day your name could be written here." The man disappeared and the vision was gone. Roberto awoke in a cold sweat, wondering what this vision could mean, for every vision has meaning and must have interpretation. He had never seen a man dressed in white, and the book involving his name, what could be its meaning?

His father had died many years before and Roberto had become the man of the house, caring for his mother, brothers, and sisters. He provided wild game for the family's table and gave direction to their physical needs. His mind searched for an interpretation to this vision, but none was forthcoming. He lay awake wondering what the spirit world was saying to him.

He looked around the familiar surroundings of his hut. He saw the large beer pot, the drum, feathered adornments, spear, and baskets of all sizes and descriptions as well as his long ten-foot blowgun standing near the doorway of his home. As his eyes focused on the dim light that emanated from the dying embers of the three-logged fire in the center of the hut, he saw his hunting dog curled up in a ball near the cooking logs drawing some warmth from their radiated heat. Immediately his eyes moved from the dog to those white, bleached out skulls of the many animals that he had killed, lining the wall of the hut.

Sleep would not come and soon the sun of a new day arose in the eastern sky, with the incessant chattering of untold numbers of birds in the canopy of the forest, awakening the entire household.

Roberto sought council with the elder men of the village regarding this mysterious vision, but none could give him meaning as the interpretation was hidden from them. He constantly thought of this vision and every waking moment his mind was in turmoil. 'What could it mean?' he thought to himself throughout the day. At night sleep would elude him as he would close his eyes and see the man dressed in white standing before him holding the book.

Two long weeks drifted slowly by and the torment was relentless. Then one day a great commotion was heard throughout the Wachiyaku village. The word passed like wildfire that in their midst a stranger had come from the distant Santiago river basin over the mountains bringing news of that far away place. Men, women, and older children gathered in the center of the village to hear this man, a distant cousin, tell them the news of their people living along the banks of the mighty Santiago River.

Whenever a man was preparing to visit distant relatives in a far away corner of the jungle, he would arise every morning before departing on his long journey and rehearse in a powerful sing-song way all the news items that he would share with them. They prided themselves on their ability to communicate orally with their peers. After all, this was one of the gifts from the spirit world after taking powerful hallucinating drugs.

On the fringe of the large group of people gathered that day to hear the stranger, stood Roberto with the other young men of the village. The man held them spell bound as he shared the events of the last few months on the Santiago in that sing-song forceful way of waving his arms and stepping forward then backward and occasionally spitting on the ground as if to punctuate his remarks.

Near the end of his speech which had left the people excited and animated, he paused and said; "I have been asked to deliver this message to the young men of the Morona, that there is going to be a Bible course on the Santiago River," naming the village and date and thus finishing his talk.

Roberto was fascinated by the last remarks of the stranger, so he approached him with the question, "What's a Bible course?"

Roberto had no knowledge of Jesus, the Bible, or the church, as his village was so isolated and remotely removed from the larger society. The man replied that they have a book about Apajui (God-creator), the Creator of our people and they teach about Him. Immediately Roberto's mind was drawn back to that night and the vision, and the man dressed in white holding a book and telling him that one day his name could be written there. Could this be the answer to that haunting vision? His mind was in a whirl, as his heart quickened and his feet carried him quickly to his hut. He told his mother of his plan to go and that he would return within a month.

He took his traveling basket from the wall and neatly placed the only shirt and pair of pants that he owned inside it. The basket was made of a double weave with a dry banana leaf between the two layers that sheds water on a rainy trip through the forest. The basket also has a top of double weave that slides down over the basket thus making it waterproof. A long, stout, broad vine is attached to the basket for carrying purposes. His mother handed him a large green banana leaf, folded and tied in place like a Christmas present, full of baked yuca, banana, and fish for the long journey. This bundle was placed inside the basket that was then covered with the top, swung onto his back, and carried over his shoulders by the long vine.

Taking the three-foot machete from the wall, he turned toward the doorway of his hut, paused, and told his mother, brothers and sisters goodbye. His mother watched as her son disappeared around the bend in the trail and was soon out of sight. She wondered what the outcome would be as she turned her attention to the duties at hand.

He quickly made his way up the steep thin-cut trail that led across several small streams, and hours later crested on top of the range of low mountains separating the Santiago and Morona Rivers. He only wore short hunting trunks accompanied by an old long sleeve shirt. His thick toughened feet nimbly glided along the rough terrain, avoiding the sharp palm thorns, bamboo shoots, and any other objects that might cut or penetrate the skin and thus impede his progress.

His one singular thought was to find an answer to the nagging questions regarding that mysterious vision. Occasionally he would have to cut heavy vines and clear the brush that encroached on the trail. Pausing at the top, resting his tired legs, his thoughts continually took him back to that night. The downward trail was easier going, and now at full trot, it took him closer and closer to his destination.

In the rain forest the ground floor never completely dries because the canopy overhead is so thick and entangled that sunlight barely filters through. The floor is in a constant state of decay, as leaves lie rotting along with fallen trees. One has to be careful on the downhill side of a mountain because the underlying dirt is damp and slippery.

Finally Roberto reached the Santiago where he spent the night, devouring the food items his mother had sent along with him. Cutting down some palm branches, he made a small shelter to ward off the possibility of a sudden rainstorm from threatening dark clouds that rolled overhead. Placing dry leaves on the ground floor his tired body succumbed to a deep sleep.

Early the next morning he began the laborious task of cutting down several large balsa trees, stripping them of their bark, and cutting them into ten-foot logs. Pulling the logs into the shallow water along the river's edge, he lashed them together with the long stout strands of bark. Skilled hands then fashioned out a paddle with the machete knife. A four-foot high tripod of pointed wild cane poles were jabbed into the soft balsa logs and tied together with thin vines. Roberto tied his waterproof basket on the tripod to keep it dry, and shoved his raft out into the main current of the Santiago River.

The hot sun quickly dried his body while he squatted on the front of the raft, steering it by dipping the paddle into the water and pulling deep broad strokes in the direction he wanted his craft to go, always trying to keep it in the heaviest part of the current and away from the many shallow sand bars that silently waited in hiding to beach his raft.

Slowly the afternoon hours waned on, as he was getting closer to his destination. At last he came around a large sweeping bend in the river that brought into sight the village mentioned by the stranger. He took his position on the front of the raft and fought the heavy current with the long balsa wood paddle. His muscles ached and burned with every stroke, but finally he broke the current, struck the backwater, and his raft skimmed the river's edge before coming to rest at the mud bank where several dugout canoes were tied. He jumped onto the shore, pulled the long twisted vine that was tied to the raft, and anchored it to a nearby tree.

Retrieving his basket, he climbed the steep hill and followed the trail that soon led him to the village. He asked about the Bible course and soon was led down another trail that dead-ended at a long thatched roof building with wild cane pole walls. He was introduced to the occupants, who welcomed him with open arms. After a meal of boiled yuca, bananas, and fish he fell asleep, exhausted from his long journey. The roosters crowed and Roberto was awakened to the bright sunlight that penetrated the long house where he slept. Opening his eyes, and examining his surroundings, he realized that the men who shared his hut last night were gone.

Then he heard men in a nearby hut talking and their conversation was rather strange. Upon investigating, he found them kneeling by benches with their eyes closed and talking out loud. After a breakfast of boiled yuca, egg, and warm banana drink, Roberto was introduced to the Bible course, and it wasn't long until he knelt and prayed to Apajui, the Creator of the Aguaruna and Huambisa people. His long journey to find answers had come to an end. Fear was replaced by faith and his name was written down in the Lamb's Book of Life. Roberto would never be the same. His life was radically changed as God called him to prepare for ministry.

Three months later on our front lawn when our hands clasped, Roberto began a new chapter in his Christian journey.

Upon finishing the three years of pastoral preparation, Roberto married a beautiful young lady from the village of Chipe which was located about thirty minutes from the Bible Institute. Her father was a Huambisa, but had come years ago to live in Aguaruna territory. He later married an Aguaruna girl from Chipe and the third daughter born into this family was Angelina, Roberto's new wife.

Together they felt called to plant the church in the Santiago River basin and reach out to the isolated Huambisa tribe. It was a difficult task to plant the church in this remote area of the jungle that was ruled by fear and superstition. Their struggles were many as Roberto encountered opposition from the spirit world of intense darkness that challenged them at every turn. He knew that God had chosen him "to open their eyes and turn them from darkness to light, and from the power of Satan to God" (Acts 16:15). He also knew that God had said, "I will live with them and walk among them, and I will be their God, and they will be my people" (II Co. 6:16).

The Santiago River area was malaria country and the hordes of mosquitoes and blood sucking gnats extracted a toll on their health. Many days and nights Roberto and Angelina comforted each other as their fevers, chills, tremors, and splitting headaches tested their faith in God as they lay prostrate on the bamboo beds for long periods of time.

They were faithful to that heavenly calling and successfully established a small mission on the edge of the Huambisa territory. Years later that church was the mother church and many churches were established among the Huambisa Indians. Angelina became so physically exhausted that they returned to Chipe to regain their health.

While in Chipe, Roberto became very active in this large church and then began to coordinate the many churches in this area. He was recognized and sought after as an outstanding leader and teacher. It wasn't long until he was appointed District Superintendent of the now emerging Amazon district. Under his twelve years of leadership, the Amazon district grew and was divided into three districts. The two newly formed districts included the Huambisa churches from the Santiago River and the other district incorporated those of the Morona River.

Roberto Atamain (in white shirt)

Along with their five children, they later moved to a very distant area of the high jungle to work with a part of the Aguaruna tribe that has been separated geographically from the main tribe. He now pastors a very successful church in Soritor, and is planting a new church in a neighboring village. All of their children are active in the church and three of them are studying in the famous University of San Marcos in the capitol city of Lima, Perú.

Yes, the questions were finally answered. Not only Roberto Atamain Shunta's name is written in the Book of Life, but hundreds of others whose lives he has touched as well.

Washout

From a distance we could see the many huts lining the bank on the opposite side of the river as our car pulled to a stop with dust swirling all around us. A beautiful scene unfolded before us in the valley below.

After hours of bouncing along on a rough dirt road, our destination was finally in sight. Looking out across the Marañon River, we saw the village of Tutumberros tucked away and nearly swallowed up in the thick, vast, green rain forest. Before stepping down from the car, we saw several Aguaruna men walk out of the brush, smiling, and making their way toward us. Immediately I recognized them as our Bible Institute students that had come from two villages to greet us and take us across the river to begin our long awaited trip to the far away village of Shaim.

Greetings over, we unloaded the Suburban Carryall of sleeping bags and equipment for the exciting journey ahead of us. We followed the students down a steep trail that led from the road where we had parked the car to the river below.

Bobbing up and down in the backwater was a long, sleek, black dugout canoe tied to a stout bamboo pole driven into the small sandy beach at the river's edge. The young men quickly cut two-inch round poles three-feet long with their machetes. These poles were placed on the bottom of the canoe, wedged in on both sides. Carefully they placed our equipment on the poles to keep everything up off the floor of the canoe, thus avoiding contact with water that would splash in along the sides.

Addie was led to the center of the canoe where she sat on a small hand-carved balsa stool. With the swaying and rocking of the canoe she clung to the sides, dreading the crossing of rough water that awaited us in the middle of this fast rolling treacherous river. I sat closer to the front of the canoe near one of the men who held a large wide-bladed paddle in his hands. Behind Addie were two men, one of which sat on a carved seat in the back of the canoe holding a large paddle to steer this frail craft across the river. We breathed a silent prayer as the trailing vine that was attached to the bamboo pole was untied and tossed onto the floor of the canoe.

Addie Garman preparing to travel on a balsa raft.

One of the men shoved the canoe away from the bank, jumped back into the craft, grabbed his paddle in one quick motion, and began paddling out into the main current. The canoe rocked heavily from side to side as we hit the strong crosscurrents. Our knowledgeable oarsman in the back steadied the unwieldy craft with his broad paddle and kept it in a steady path while the canoe cut across wave after wave at right angles. We were inching our way to the distant shore. Occasionally cold water splashed over the sides, striking our bare arms and faces, causing us to automatically cling to the sides of the canoe, hardly daring to breathe, as our little craft rode crest after crest of the turbulent Marañon River.

Once again, skilled navigators of the Aguaruna tribe had brought their cargo safely across to the other side. This was done without fanfare and almost as a matter of fact, since these people of the waterways had been doing this for countless generations.

Stepping from the canoe, we congratulated and thanked them for a job well done. Eager arms embraced us from the waiting crowd that lined the bank to receive us. Greetings were exchanged and we were ushered to the hut where we would spend the night. Along the way we were informed that the trail to the village of Shaim had been washed away in many places due to the recent heavy rains. However, they quickly added, they were making a large raft to float us downriver to a point below the great pongo of Yamakai where the trail would take us to the village of Shaim.

Addie, very concerned, excitedly asked, "Do you mean that we have to go through that famous pongo?" A pongo is a stretch of river filled with rapids, dangerous cross currents, and large whirlpools. The pongo Yamakai is notorious for its extremely dangerous water. In fact no boat, canoe or motorized craft of any kind can navigate its treacherous waters.

The Indians, when traveling through this great area, use large rafts made of huge multiple logs lashed together with thick stout vines. Just before navigating the pongo they will steer the raft out into the middle of the river, then proceed to tie themselves onto the raft with strong pliable vines.

When the raft enters the upper part of the pongo, it begins to spin from the swift cross currents and will be submerged into the swirling, silt-filled turbulent waters, finally emerging and surfacing downriver. They then stand to their feet untying the vines and continue their journey. They are spared the ravages of the river because they were tied securely on board.

Addie knew that I had heard of Yamakai for years and had always wanted to make a trip through it with the students on their way to the Bible Institute, and now was the time. She objected with fear betraying her voice to a ride through this great pongo. "Señora," responded one of her students, "don't worry because we are going to let you off at a point above the pongo. There is a trail leading around the pongo that joins the main trail to the village of Shaim."

The men had made a huge raft of fifteen buoyant balsa logs nearly twenty feet long. They were lashed together with thick vines and the bark from the same logs. In the middle of the raft they built a platform about three feet high to place all of our equipment on to keep everything dry. A log bench next to the platform was secured with stout poles for Addie and me to sit on for the ride of our lives.

Finally the raft was loaded, a prayer said, and goodbyes exchanged with the many people lining the bank. The sky was blue, the sun was hot, and all anticipated the ride downriver as our raft was untied and shoved out into the main current. Now we were on our way.

The raft was so large that it took four men with paddles sitting on the front end with their legs wrapped around a couple of logs apiece, knowing that they would be immersed in the cold waters of Yamakai. They used the paddles to steer the unwieldy craft away from the boulders, sand bars, and partially submerged logs and to keep it in the middle of the river where the current is strongest and the water is deepest. The raft picked up speed, being carried along by the strong currents flowing through the canyon that we were fast approaching.

The valley was green all around us until we entered the narrow canyon with its steep walls of layered rock lined with smaller shrubs and plants growing from the many crevices. Shadows fell across the water as the angle of the sun was diminished from the depths of the canyon walls. The four men on the front of the raft dipped their paddles in unison, steering our craft away from the many obstacles that lined the river.

We could see the beautiful parasitic plants lodged in cracks in the rocks and in the tops of small trees. Some of these had long thin vines that trailed down to the river and dangled right in front of us as our raft glided by. The ride was breathtaking and exhilarating as our raft bobbed up and down in the huge water troughs caused from cross currents formed by outcroppings of rocks that kept us from taking a straight course downstream. Recognizing how skilled our oarsmen were caused us to relax and the journey downriver became very enjoyable.

Sometime later, I remarked to Addie about the four men down on the front of the raft talking with each other and then turning to back look at us. I said to Addie, "I think they are going to go for it."

She replied, "No, I am on board and they would not risk it." Then she remembered that these were some of her students and they would like nothing better than to see her reaction.

The next thing we knew, one of them hollered back across the noise of the river saying, "We are going to go for it, and we think we can make it through the pongo!"

Addie responded with the words, "You think we can make it? I don't want to hear the word 'think.' I want to know for sure."

Up ahead we could hear the roar of the river at the entrance to Yamakai. Looking at the land, we could tell that the river was dropping quickly and picking up speed as we neared the rapids. One of the men down front yelled to the man sitting to one side of the raft to grab the Señora's shoulders and hold her down. I don't know if they thought she was going to jump overboard or what, but he clamped onto Addie's shoulders to steady her.

Quickly they brought a thick stout vine from the front of the raft to the back and said, "Hold on tight." They did not have to repeat that twice because we were already holding on for dear life. An older gentleman was accompanying us on the trip and he immediately began to pray out loud in an excitable voice. We could see the foaming fierce whitecaps in the river up ahead. There was no turning back now, and our four oarsmen were feverishly struggling to keep the front of the raft pointing downriver and not allow it to go sideways. All eyes were fastened upon this inferno that we were about to enter, and indeed our craft seemed so frail in the clutches of this tremendous force of nature.

As our craft entered one of the formidable canyons of the Marañon River, the cross currents rocked our craft and we were ushered into the very center of the river as large waves washed over our raft while swirling muddy waters trapped us in their death-like grip sending us into the heart of Yamakai's menacing whirlpool. Rocking, twisting, and rolling, our small floating island of security seemed doomed in this unforgiving force bent on our destruction. The raft was pitched and tossed in every direction while its precious cargo of human life hung on for what seemed like an eternity. Water poured in from every direction drenching us, our cargo, and everything on board.

The Amazon Call

The four men down on the front were partially submerged before the powerful tentacles of this pongo finally relinquished its death grip on our raft allowing us to strike the backwater and finally the safety of shore. The four men jumped ashore, securing the thick vine to a nearby tree as we all breathed a long sigh of relief. Looking back at the granddaddy of all pongos in this stretch of river, we wondered how we had been spared from a watery grave. On the lips of all was a grateful thanks to God for His protection and safety.

Safely anchored, our friends stated that we could step ashore and take the trail that would lead us to the village of Shaim. Addie, with shaky legs, stepped from the raft to solid ground, just grateful to be alive. The trail to Shaim was long and steep, but after several hours we finally entered the beautiful confines of this isolated, remote, and hidden village located deep in the rain forest. We spent two wonderful days with these gracious and hospitable people.

The time finally came for our departure and the long hike back to the river. After saying goodbye, we set out on the trail. A few men accompanied us back to the main trail, and the journey from Shaim to the river was uneventful and mostly downhill. Pausing to rest, Addie asked, "How are we going to get back upriver to where the car is? We can't take a raft upriver."

I responded that we would have to go by trail. "But the trail is destroyed," she countered.

"We will just have to make a new trail," I replied.

Rounding a bend in the trail, we could hear the rushing of water nearby. It was a stream that flowed by the village of Shaim in the high country. While staying in the village, we had bathed in its cold take-your-breath-away waters. Now from the heavy rains of the night before it had become a raging torrent, swirling along between large boulders lining its twisting crooked course. Fifty yards below us it emptied its angry contents into the Marañon River close to the pongo of Yamakai.

"How will we ever cross this raging stream?" we asked each other. To wade across was impossible as the current was traveling about fifteen miles an hour. It nearly made us dizzy to look on this swollen river that frantically carried its foaming waters to the main river just below us. Fortunately the men that had accompanied us from the villages had their machetes with them.

They began to cut down small three-inch diameter trees that they cut into ten-foot long poles. They each had a pole, and gave one to us to use as a walking stick to brace us against the onslaught of water.

Little by little the men inched their way out into the stream, planting their poles against the base of huge boulders at a forty-five degree angle back toward themselves (much like a pole-vaulter would do). Holding onto the poles, they slowly and methodically began crossing the stream with us right behind them. The heavy crush and pressure of tons of water pushing on our legs threatened to sweep us away in its rampant dash to the Marañon. The men, observing our unsteadiness and inexperience in this hostile element, came to our rescue.

They planted their poles securely in the streambed and took us by the hand, leading us across this life threatening force of nature. Our feet slipped on slippery rocks and we nearly fell sideways into the relentless force of water. Strong hands righted us and kept us upright. We were holding onto our poles for dear life. Finally we struggled onto the other shore on wobbly tired legs. The men grinned and said that they would be returning to the village now that we were safely across the stream and on the trail home. At this point, only three of us remained. Lucho Asangkay, a wonderful layman, was both guide and leader of our small group. Addie was in the middle following Lucho, and I brought up the rear.

The trail led us along the river for a great distance, and then began its ascent to cross the small mountains that lay between us and the end of the trail. At first the going was not too bad, but the further we went there were little washouts where the trail was obliterated and new footholds had to be found. Lucho would carefully plant one foot after another so that Addie would be able to place her feet in the impressions left by Lucho. At times she would have to hold onto vines and roots on the mountainside of the trail to keep from falling. Addie is very fearful of heights. She can look out at the horizon, but not straight down for fear of tumbling over the edge.

The going was painstakingly slow because we were now about two hundred feet above the river, and the trail was right on the edge. If you fell from that height into the boulder-strewn river below, it would be certain death. Addie was silently praying, 'Lord, please don't let me cry, please don't let me cry.' Looking only to where Lucho placed his feet, she did the same, step by step. I was cautiously following along encouraging her, knowing how dangerous our journey was becoming.

Suddenly Addie stopped in her tracks, because Lucho was not directly in front of her. Instead she froze, realizing that the trail had been washed out, and it was a straight drop to the river below. When she looked up, Lucho was leaning way out from the other side, hand extended and telling her to grab his hand and jump. She turned, looking at me, and said, "No way, I can't do it."

"Addie, you have to take his hand and jump," I said.

"No!" She replied, "I will go back down the trail and find another way across the river."

"There is no other way across," I told her. "Now grab Lucho's hand and jump."

"I can't," she responded, and began crying.

"Look," I told her, "Lucho will have your hand over there and I will have your hand on this side."

"Oh sure!" she said, "You are just going to dangle me out there. No way!" she cried.

She is well and alive today, but she has jokingly accused me of pushing her that day long ago on a dangerous trail. We don't remember exactly how she got across that chasm, but we do know that God definitely answers prayer.

Hole In One

Our large dugout cargo boat plowed through the water making its way downriver to the village of Uut where the Work and Witness team was headed to construct a church. We had loaded all of the necessary supplies at the port of our mission station. The team members had climbed down the steep slippery hill, some spending a few moments on one part of their anatomy that we won't talk about. Everyone donned a life jacket and we were on our way.

The boat swung out into the current and glided past the sheer rock cliff that stood like a lone sentinel in this treacherous part of the river. Navigating our way through the shallows and rounding the bend, our course was set on the middle of the river where the channel was deepest. Ten minutes later we passed the Peruvian army camp on the right. On the left was the Aguaruna village of Yama Yakat with its many thatched-roof bamboo-walled huts dotting the low hillsides.

Our motorist maneuvered the lumbering, unwieldy craft past the village of Duship. Rounding the next two bends in the river, we could see the choppy water ahead that was the opening to the pongo called Sasa. A pongo is a swift moving area of the river that takes us through a small canyon with many huge boulders, rapids, and finally a large menacing whirlpool that waits with devastation for any novice motorist. The boat picked up speed as we entered the gateway to this pongo. The water was boiling, muddy, and very treacherous, with repressive waves greeting our boat with great force, lifting the bow out of the water, then shaking the wooden craft as we all held onto the sides. Finally, the thirty-foot boat plunged into the swirling crosscurrents that led us to the edge of that powerful whirlpool. Our motorist skimmed the edge of the whirlpool by accelerating the motor and forcing our way past its greedy waters, waiting to gobble up any intruder. The boat was quickly righted and we emerged from the canyon on our way to Uut.

Around the next bend in the river, we could see the village of Uut in the distance. Pulling into the mud bank at the port of the village, we were greeted by a large crowd, welcoming us with open arms. After shaking hands, they carried our bags and led us up a steep hill to a hut that they had prepared for us.

Walking into our sleeping quarters, we found a long row of split bamboo beds down the long wall of the hut. Immediately we began hanging our mosquito nets to ward off the vampire bats that fly at night looking for a free meal. While tying the nets, the pastor of the Work and Witness group asked me where the latrine was located, as he needed to visit it. I pointed to the lower level where we had left the boat, asking him if he could see the two small lean-to buildings in the distance. He responded affirmatively and left in a hurry, leaving us to the work at hand.

Sometime later he returned and seemed quite concerned, pulling me off to the side, relating the following: "Doc, I have a big problem now and you have to help me. I walked into that little latrine, dropped my trousers, and my billfold fell into that hole."

"Oh no," I replied, half laughing. I have been asked to do many things as a missionary, but there are limits.

"Please," he repeated, "help me, but do not let the team know what has happened, because they will never let me forget it."

We quietly slipped away leaving the team to finish tying the mosquito nets in place. Arriving at the lower level, he pointed to the latrine that now harbored his lost billfold. The two latrines were covered only on the side facing the village. The other three sides were open for good viewing. Latrines are made by digging a hole about five feet deep and four feet in diameter. The hole is then covered with large round logs with the two middle logs cut in a half moon fashion thus making a hole about six inches in diameter. The logs are then covered with dirt.

I knelt in the dirt, peering into this dark, forbidden hole with the pastor looking over my shoulder. There was his billfold, lying in a folded position. 'How,' I wondered, 'do we retrieve this object from its precarious predicament?' Taking a long seven-foot branch from a nearby tree, I tried to lift the billfold from its surroundings, but to no avail.

While we were intent on this project, the villagers were carrying our toolbox, portable generator, and building materials from the boat to the building site. There also was a long line of men, women and children carrying sheets of corrugated roofing on their heads and looking over their shoulders, wondering why the missionary would be kneeling, looking into a latrine hole. Curiosity getting the best of them, one by one they laid their cargo on the trail and migrated to where we were intent on our work at hand.

The inevitable question was asked, "What are you looking at?" I responded that the pastor had tragically and involuntarily dropped his billfold into the hole.

The next question was obvious, "Why would he want it back?" I tried to explain to them that it contained his driver license and credit cards, and that he desperately wanted it back. Try to explain to villagers in the middle of the rain forest about credit cards. To them nothing was of enough value to fish out of that hole. I finally convinced them that it was very important to the pastor and that he really did need to retrieve his billfold.

Village of Uut

One of the men immediately produced another long branch and took the one I was fishing with and attacked the folded object from two sides.

Up on the hill, one of the Work and Witness team members stepped outside to view the beautiful rain forest. While looking around, he spotted a large group of people congregated on the lower level, and wondered why so many people were gathered around the two tiny buildings. Had they killed some wild animal, seen a snake, or was someone hurt? Ducking back into the hut he informed the other men of his sightings. One by one they left their work of tying mosquito nets, walked outside and then down the hill to inspect this unusual phenomenon.

Now the picture looked like this. The Indian man was skillfully maneuvering the two branches, with the pastor and me looking intently over his shoulder, and the entire village was looking on. The Work and Witness team strolled up just in time to see the man successfully, gently, lift the mysterious object from the bowels of the earth and hand it to him in full view of all.

The moral of the story: please button the pocket where your billfold is housed when entering small buildings with holes in the ground.

The Amazon Call

Second Chance

In the distance, sharp high-pitched crying in a singsong fashion penetrated the dark, quiet, humid night. Our attention was immediately drawn to the screened window that overlooked the Marañon River. We listened intently as the crying came closer and much more animated. Peering out into the inky blackness we could see nothing, but yet we could hear the splash of paddles frantically propelling a dugout canoe toward the lights of our mission, and the desperate calls for help followed by the death cry. I grabbed a flashlight while making my way to the front door.

Once outside, I could hear the excited commotion of people talking loudly as the canoe glided into our port. We were located on the quiet waters of the Kusu River just before it emptied its contents into the larger turbulent Marañon River. Following the beam of my light I could make out a group of men scrambling up the steep muddy bank carrying someone on a small bamboo litter.

A group of women followed, crying that Susana was dying. I hurriedly opened the clinic door and ushered the group inside. Lying on the open litter was Susana, pale, lifeless, and drenching wet. She was in a coma and her vital signs were failing rapidly. I reached out my hand automatically, taking her pulse that was fast but extremely weak. It was obvious that she was dying.

I asked what had happened, and was told that Susana had taken a very toxic alkaloid poison called Barbasco to commit suicide. Barbasco is a root plant that the Indians use to poison the streams to stun the fish. When women are distraught and life has no more meaning, they will chew a large piece of the raw root and within two hours their life will be taken from them. Her breathing was shallow and the vital signs were ominous as death was a very real presence.

In the village she had been carried to a nearby stream and great amounts of water had been poured over her shivering body that nearly turned blue as she sat shaking and chilled to the bone while she sat upon a large boulder. They forced copious amounts of water down her throat and then made her throw it up. The men formed a circle around a large gourd bowl into which they all spit masticated sugar cane juice. She was then forced to drink the bowl full of sugar cane juice followed by forced regurgitation.

Since there was no improvement, they had come by night to the clinic as a last resort. Her life hung by a thread as she slipped into a deep coma. I did all I could and told Addie who was standing by, nearly in shock, that Susana was in the Lord's hands now and only a miracle could save her. After learning the circumstances of her attempted suicide, Addie ran to the house, falling on her knees by the bed, pouring out her heart to God on behalf of Susana.

We had known Susana since her early childhood. She was a bright beautiful girl who accompanied her father to the clinic three days a week for many months. Her father, Oracio, had a dreaded parasitic disease called Leishmaniasis. It is caused by the bite of a nocturnal sand fly that bites on some exposed part of the skin while people are hunting or fishing near the sand beaches at night. It begins as a small pimple-like sore that soon erupts into a very large and deep crater-like sore that will weep and seep for many months. It will not scar over until months have passed. I knew of a man who took a hot rock from the coals of the fire and seared the flesh to make it scar.

Eventually it will heal, but the parasite remains in the blood stream where it has an affinity for the septum of the nose. It will begin eating away the septum and finally destroys the entire nose, upper lip, part of the cheek and even the eye socket, thus disfiguring the face.

When the people heard that the new missionary doctor had the medicine for Leishmaniasis, they came from everywhere. We were overwhelmed by the numbers of people that came to the clinic looking for treatment for this devastating disease. Some came from great distances, so we had to build a hut to house them since the treatment required as many as one hundred injections. Oracio was a kind, loving father and Susana enjoyed accompanying him to the clinic every Monday, Wednesday, and Friday for his treatment. She would sit in the back of the canoe with a huge paddle that would be used to steer the long sleek craft back to their village. Oracio plunged the long twelve-foot cane pole into the river bottom, pushed on the pole, and propelled the canoe upriver as Susana used the large paddle as a rudder.

Susana began attending Sunday school classes and it wasn't long until she gave her heart to the Lord, as did her father, mother, and the entire family. Oracio's life was prolonged for a short time, but the devastating ravages of this disease finally cut his life short. His wife continued coming to church and, as always, there was Susana with that contagious smile sitting with the children in Sunday School. Oracio's widow had a number of children and it became increasingly difficult to maintain and care for them all, so she gave Susana, now a young girl of perhaps thirteen years of age, in marriage to a young man from the village of Chipe by the name of Walter Katan. We were so disappointed to hear of her marriage to Walter because he was not a Christian. As time went by Susana had several children, but remained faithful to the Lord and the church, even though Walter cared nothing for spiritual things.

I looked upon the ashen white face of this mother of three wondering why, why had this happened? I asked those standing by what had taken place this day to cause Susana to take Barbasco poisoning. I was told that a few months earlier Walter brought home a new wife and announced to Susana that she would be living with him also. Now both wives lived in separate huts, but he began to cater to the new wife and neglected Susana and the children.

Walter stared into space that night, terrified with the scene unfolding before us. He knew that if Susana died he would be held accountable for his neglect of her and that her uncles would probably take his life in revenge. Early this morning Walter had gone hunting and had killed a rather large animal. Susana saw him coming with the large woven basket hanging from his back attached to his shoulders with a stout broad vine. Inside the basket she noticed the bulky package wrapped in banana leaves with blood dripping through the open weave of the basket. She was very excited as he approached the hut thinking that at long last there would be meat for her and the children. Without looking up, Walter passed by Susana and delivered the entire animal to his new wife. She was so disappointed and hurt that she reasoned to herself that if she were gone, maybe he would care more for his children. She decided to end her life.

She slipped away to the gardens some distance from the village and dug up the root plant Barbasco. Crushing pieces of the root and drinking it with water, the effect was rapid. They later found her that afternoon, alone, and near death's door.

I once again looked upon that pale, expressionless face and cold body, waiting for the end to come. The exhausted family hovered nearby with horror displayed in their tired, anxious eyes. Addie was fervently praying for God to intervene and give Susana a second chance. She knew the custom all to well of taking Barbasco when the women felt rejected and alone. Her tears stained the bedspread as she intervened for Susana. Soon Addie felt a peace come over her and arose knowing that God had heard her prayer. I, too, had prayed for Susana and for her people living under the bondage of customs that held them captive to the fears of the spirit world. How many times I had assisted those dying from Barbasco poisoning, and heard the death cry that always followed.

The silence was broken only by the night sounds directly outside the clinic in the forest that surrounded our little lighthouse in this isolated part of the jungle. Erie shadows were cast upon the walls of the clinic from the dim light coming from a small lantern. Women stood by with arms folded across their chests ready to give the death cry, since they knew that the end was so very near. I readied myself for what would follow during the ensuing moments.

At first there was a slight stir, a movement of the eyelids, and a few almost inaudible words coming from this ghost of a person lying on our examining table. As of one, we all drew near and focused our attention on this miracle that was taking place. She was coming back from the brink of death. A few moments passed, the clinic door opened and in walked Addie. Her first question was, "How is Susana?"

Excitedly I responded, "Addie, she is talking."

At that moment one of the ladies asked Susana, "Who just walked through the door?"

Susana, turning her head sideways, replied, "Why the Señora did." We all rejoiced and had a prayer of thanksgiving. Later that night, Susana, with the help of others, walked to the river with the small, happy, relieved group and returned to Chipe by canoe. Walter, so terrified from this experience, sent his second wife back to her family and never lived with her again.

We came to the United States for our year of furlough and solicited prayer for Walter that he might become a Christian. Upon returning to Perú, we moved the mission station further upriver and lost contact with Susana and Walter for a long period of time. Years passed and word filtered up to us that Walter had finally given his heart to the Lord and was serving on the church board in the local congregation. We rejoiced greatly over this answer to prayer. Several more years went by and our retirement loomed in the near future, however we had requested an extension to allow us to continue. The extension was granted and we returned to New Horizons to continue our work.

In September of 2001, the director of the Bible Institute asked me to substitute for one of the absent teachers that day. Upon entering the classroom, I noticed a large number of young men and women who were beginning their first semester of a three-year program in ministry. I was excited to know who they were and from what village they had come. One by one they stood to their feet giving me their names and the names of their villages. I was thrilled to know that they came from the Morona, Santiago, Cenepa, and Marañon Rivers and other areas of the upper Amazon. There were Huambisa and Aguaruna Indians sitting in the same classroom. Many years before they had been mortal enemies.

A slender, handsome young man stood to his feet and stated that his name was Demetrio, and that he was from the village of Chipe. "Chipe," I responded. We had lived our first sixteen years just downriver from Chipe and we had known everyone in that village. "Who are your parents?" I asked Demetrio.

"You know my parents," he replied, "Walter and Susana Katan."

My mind quickly traveled back across the years to that night in a small remote clinic isolated by time and distance in an almost unknown part of the world, when God had again manifested Himself to a group of people, proving that indeed He loves the whole world. Demetrio was born several years after that unforgettable night on the banks of the Kusu. He graduated from the Bible Institute and took his place among the ministers in the church of Jesus Christ.

The Amazon Call

Snake Bite

"Doctor, doctor," the call came from the small canoe as it glided into the soft mud bank of the Kusu River, about one hundred yards from our clinic. I ran to the screened-in window in time to see the man jab his long cane (bamboo) pole into the soft soil at the river's edge. After tying up the canoe, he reached into the dugout and lifted a small child into his arms and rapidly approached the clinic. I ushered him inside, placing the child on the examining table. Excitedly he informed me that his five-year-old son was playing barefooted and did not see the small coiled snake on the trail. He felt the sharp burning pain and began to cry. His father came running, saw the snake, and immediately killed it with a stout pole. He then produced the snake with a long thin vine tied around its neck.

Upon examining the snake, I recognized it as a Boash (pit viper). Its brownish black color blended in well with the ground covering. The triangular shaped head and round eyes with vertical shaped pupils, along with four small orifices, two at the nose and one between each eye and nose, making this a mortal enemy of man. The venom from the Boash is a hemotoxin that causes bleeding and in many cases hemorrhaging, which can lead to death.

The child's foot was swollen and extremely painful. I administered treatment and monitored his vital signs very carefully. For three days it was touch and go as serious signs of life-threatening symptoms developed. His life hung in the balance, and his father never left his side. We prayed and asked God to perform a miracle in this little boy's life. We were accustomed to praying with our patients every night and many times in between. There were many moments in our clinical experience when we felt overwhelmed and desperately relied upon God's intervention, and this was such a time.

The Amazon Call

On the third day there was marked improvement and we were cautiously elated, believing that God had once again demonstrated His healing power to a people who lived in great darkness. By nightfall it was evident that this brave little boy was out of danger and on the road to recovery. My heart went out to both father and son. They never complained and were very grateful for any little thing we did for them.

Later in the evening I made one last visit to the clinic before retiring for the night. Upon opening the door I saw the father shaking his son and gently slapping him on the face trying to keep the now-exhausted boy awake. The little boy desperately wanted to sleep, but his father continued shaking his shoulders and talking to him. In the world where superstition abounds, certain customs have to be followed. The father was a victim of his people's belief system.

Whenever a Boash snake bites a person, you never allow them to sleep, because in their dreams they will be bitten again and not awaken, thus the father continued shaking his son. There are many customs to be followed in the treatment of snakebite. This father could not eat certain foods like salt, sweet potato, etc. because if he did, his son's condition would worsen. He cannot leave his son's side for more than a few moments, or his symptoms will be aggravated. A pregnant woman is forbidden to look upon a snakebite victim, because that will cause the swelling to increase where the bite occurred and the flesh will become gangrenous and rot away.

Once again I checked the child's vital signs and told the father that he was fine and to let him sleep. The anxious, weary man locked onto my eyes with a sad look of fear and despair. Again the child closed his tired eyes as his body craved sleep. Again the father called his name and shook him until the exhausted son reluctantly opened his heavy eyelids and stirred lethargically on the bed.

Knowing the child's great need to sleep and also of the father's deep-seated fears, I quickly formulated a plan in my mind that might solve both situations. I removed the stethoscope from my neck and hung it from the shoulders of the startled father. I then plugged the earpieces into his ears while placing the round diaphragm over the boy's heart. His eyes lit up as he heard for the first time in his life the loud audible sounds of a beating heart. He listened intently to the lup-dup, lup-dup rhythmic tones of his son's heart with great interest and obvious excitement. After praying with them, I said to the father, "Allow your son to sleep and you can use my stethoscope to listen to his heart all night. As long as you hear the heartbeat loud and clear, let him sleep," I instructed. "If you hear no sounds, please come and call me."

Early the next morning as I entered the clinic, I noticed that all was quiet and peaceful. I quickly found out why as I observed that father and son were both sound asleep, with the stethoscope still dangling from dad's neck. The young boy soon returned home and later on became one of our son's closest friends. Aren't we glad that we support clinics and hospitals around the world?

The Amazon Call

The Death Cry

They stood motionless, staring at the ground as the sun rose from the eastern sky. Warm soft rays of sunlight broke through the heavy canopy of entangled vines caressing the ground in a beautiful patchwork fashion.

A faint breeze broke the monotony of the stifling humid heat that seemed to engulf the rain forest on that most wretched of all mornings.

She looked at those five fresh mounds of dirt with fixed agony in her dark sad eyes, partially hidden by multiple strands of uncombed hair. Her dirt-streaked face reflected a countenance of anguish, despair, and utter hopelessness as she contemplated the events of these last short weeks of mystery and death.

Her eyes were red and swollen. She felt exhausted from endless hours of crying. Her voice was hoarse from the spasmodic death cry, which emanated from a throat now too weak to even speak. A hand mechanically and spontaneously reached into that one-piece soiled dress knotted over her right shoulder and gathered about her waist by a thin belt-like vine, to caress the baby that was no longer there. She glanced once more at the last little mound of dirt and then turned to make her way across the trail as her shoulders heaved, and great sobs weakly pierced her dry parched lips.

He watched as she disappeared around a cloister of banana plants and returned his attention to the sad task at hand. He was as utterly tired from the sleepless nights of the past two weeks, his mind in constant turmoil as he pondered the recent events and subsequent deaths of their five children, deaths that were so mysterious and sudden. Bending low, he clutched a handful of dirt and gently sprinkled it on this last little and recently dug grave. His tears mingled with the soft mound of dirt as he slowly rose to his feet and turned to follow the footsteps of his wife that led down the path to their hut.

He paused outside the hut while his eyes searched the clearing and its immediate surroundings. The hut sat on a small flat knoll overlooking the little stream that traversed the village of Pumpu. A well-manicured path led to the stream where bathing was performed and water was drawn to supply the family's needs. On the sloping hillsides were mature plants of cassava root waiting for the harvesting with large orange-in-color papaya ripening under a tropical sky.

The sun was bathing the clearing in all of its early morning glory. He glanced at the hut that occupied the middle and prominent place on that peaceful knoll. His mind went back to a better day when he had cut those long poles for the framework of his house and the leaves were brought from the high country to weave onto the latticed rigging that formed the thatched roof. He remembered those little dark, naked bodies running around the clearing, laughing and playing while he worked. How could he forget the day his little daughter stuffed a stick doll in the front of her dress and followed her mother down the path, dragging a broken piece of machete with a small basket strapped to her back, imitating her mom on the way to the gardens? A faint smile creased his lips, and then dissipated rapidly.

He snapped back to reality and was met with deafening silence and the fact that little feet would no longer run along these paths. Slowly he turned and walked through the small doorway that led into the now quiet hut. Silence filled the air, broken only by the soft hoarse sobs of his wife who sat on one of the three logs that formed her cooking fire on the dirt floor in the middle of the hut.

Trembling hands clutched a feathered fan that she waved near the coals of a small fire. Flames and smoke arose, leaping around the small clay pot sitting on the spot where the three logs were butted together. Methodically she dropped an egg into the now-boiling water. Upon entering the hut, he sat on a split bamboo bed and was now deep in thought. He reached way back into his culture trying to find some answers as to why all five of their children had died in such a short space of time.

His thoughts went back across the years when, as a small boy, he sat at the feet of his grandfather listening to the myths, legends, genealogies, and war songs that were such a vital part of his training as a growing Indian boy. Grandfather had said that you do not die from natural causes, but because of witchcraft. He remembered hearing of how certain witchdoctors had been killed because of using witchcraft to cause someone's death. Could the local witchdoctor be responsible for the deaths of five innocent children? His mind raced and reasoning told him that it was so. Then he will pay, he thought to himself.

His eye caught the little hammock still tied between the two poles located at the foot of their bed. The hammock was flat and empty. His eyes moved rapidly to his wife sitting on the log, but her bosom carried no child. He stood to his feet, walked to the wall of his hut, and retrieved a large woven hunting bag. Searching the bag he found two shotgun shells wrapped in dry banana leaves to keep the humidity out. His fingers came across the good luck charms poised in one corner of the bag and he rubbed them together knowing that he would need power from the spirit world to complete his mission. Throwing the bag over his shoulder, he glanced once more at his wife who sat motionless and stared into space. He removed the old rusty shotgun from the wall and walked out into the stillness of a new day, determined to avenge the deaths of their five children.

The trail led up and over a steep hill then twisted and turned, gently sloping downward across the stream and disappeared into the jungle. His mind and legs raced along that crooked, uneven path filled with obstacles of decaying trees and roots that jutted from the ground as if they were waiting to trip the unsuspecting and inexperienced. The trail led down into the forest and its final destination, the Shimutas River. Long before it reached the banks of the Shimutas, the path emerged at the foot of a hill where a smaller trail forked off to the right, winding its way to the hut of the witchdoctor. It was now late afternoon and the shadows of early evening began to engulf the rain forest as the sun dipped in the western sky.

There was nothing now to do but wait. Near where the trail forked was a large mahogany tree that afforded protection from both trails and yet allowed great visibility in either direction. Behind that tree his long vigil began. Patiently he waited as darkness completely swallowed up the last faint rays of day, turning the rain forest into an eerie presence.

Slowly he followed the path leading to the home of the witchdoctor. Carefully he threaded his way along, knowing that any noise might betray his presence to the occupants of the hut. His bare feet gracefully glided along the rough trail, avoiding any dry twigs that might snap under his weight and awaken the fierce hunting dog that he knew would be asleep next to the dying embers of the three logged cooking fire. He did not want to face the wrath of that animal in the darkness or run the risk of its owner leaping from his bed with his shotgun in hand.

Rounding the last bend in the trail, he could see a very faint, pale, shadowy moon that was desperately trying to peek its way through heavy clouds that swirled overhead. The outline of the hut could be seen in the clearing, not more than a stone's throw away.

Cautiously he moved with painstaking slowness, approaching the backside of the hut. He knew exactly where the witchdoctor's bed was located next to the wall opposite the doorway. The darkness sent a shiver along his spine as he focused his attention on the bamboo wall that was lashed together with thin vines. He surveyed the wall until he found what he was looking for. It was a place where the vines had been frayed and two bamboo poles were slightly separated leaving a small opening about the right size to squeeze the barrel of his gun through.

Quietly he pushed the barrel into the small opening and was ready to pull the trigger when the moon broke through the clouds and shone upon the wall of the hut. His heart nearly stopped beating as he noticed that the bed was empty and the witchdoctor was not at home.

Quickly he retracted the gun and retraced his steps back to the main trail again, standing in the shadows of the huge mahogany tree. 'The witchdoctor must be gone, but will have to return to his home sooner or later,' he contemplated. 'I will wait for his return no matter how long it takes,' he reasoned to himself.

It seemed as though an eternity passed as he stood motionless, waiting for some indication of the witchdoctor's return. The ants crawled on his bare feet and mosquitoes nibbled at his skin as he stood frozen in time. The night air was cool, damp, and chilled his near-naked body. Patiently he waited into the long hours of night. He knew what it was to wait. He had spent many lonely nights while hunting, hidden and waiting for the forest animals to come and feast on the fruits and nuts that dropped to the jungle floor from overhanging trees.

His mind raced back in time, when as a twelve-year-old boy he took the most powerful of hallucinating drugs made from a vine extract that produced his visions from the spirit world to become a great warrior and hunter. He remembered roaming the forest for seven days and nights searching for his spirit power that came on the wings of the eagle or in the form of a boa.

His thoughts were interrupted by a noise coming from far up the trail. Every muscle tensed and the adrenalin flowed as his hand touched the cool muzzle of the gun. With his heart racing, he peered cautiously from behind his vantage point in time to see a shadowy figure emerge over a distant rise on the trail. His eyes strained in the darkness for a better view. Could it be the returning witchdoctor or someone hunting at this hour? For a fleeting moment, his mind wandered back to those five little mounds of dirt and his wife's crying night after night. Quickly he snapped back to attention when he heard the nearing footsteps of this shadowy figure.

The faint light of a pale moon broke through the heavy clouds and illuminated the face of… yes…it was the witchdoctor! Carefully and slowly the man picked his way down the trail knowing the dangers of animal life that might lurk in the darkness ready to strike an unsuspecting victim. In an instant the man sprang from his hiding place and pointed the gun into the horrified eyes of the helpless witchdoctor.

Surprise and stealth have always been the hallmark of revenge killings raids. An eye for an eye and a tooth for a tooth was ingrained into him since early childhood. To avenge the death of a loved one, at least one member of the offending party's household must be killed. It can be a brother, uncle, nephew or even a cousin will do, but at least one male must be sacrificed. These revenge attacks usually occur in the dead of night when one least expects an attack.

The witchdoctor froze in his tracks, knowing that his life would soon be over as he looked down the barrel of the gun. Quickly the trigger was pulled and there was the echoing sound of metal on metal but no explosion. The gun had misfired. The witchdoctor, realizing what had happened, turned and fled across the darkened trail leaving the man with shaky hands fumbling into his hunting bag for another shell to place into the chamber of his gun. By the time he placed the shell into the gun, the witchdoctor had disappeared and would not soon return.

He stood in disbelief for this gun had never failed him before. His hut was lined with white bleached-out skulls of animals proving his skill as a hunter. Slowly he turned and stumbled down the trail as exhaustion plagued his every move. The sun was rising on yet another day in the rain forest when he finally arrived home. Upon entering the hut, his eyes adjusted to the semi-darkness that betrayed the shadowy presence of his wife still sitting on one of the logs of her cooking fire. The silence was broken only by her soft sobs.

He said nothing as he approached the bamboo wall where a hunting bag hung by its long shoulder strap. Removing the bag from its resting place, his mind went back to happier days in that little home. He remembered rising early around three a.m. and rinsing his mouth with water to cleanse it of saliva which is a nasty body waste. He then would shove the three logs together and fan their almost dying coals back to life. That small cook fire provided enough light for him to make a new hunting bag with the thread he himself had obtained from the thin fibers taken from the mid-rib of a long broad leaf. Those fibers were hung over the support beam of the hut where they were dried and then twisted into a stout thick thread. The thread was placed through the eye of a long curved needle made from the bone shaft of an animal.

In those early morning hours he would look at the newborn baby lying in its tiny hammock tied between the two poles right next to their bamboo bed. He could still see the older children asleep on their beds, as his wife would soon arise to begin cooking yuca and bananas for breakfast. Oh, how he longed for those days again. The events of the past weeks seemed like a nightmare that would not end.

He reached into the bag and removed two more shotgun shells wrapped in dry banana leaves with a thin vine tied around them. Placing those shells into his shoulder bag, he glanced one last time at the small empty hammock and the bed where his children had once slept. He saw only the small blanket of rags sewn together and the empty flat hammock. Immediately his gaze turned to his wife sitting disconsolately and softly crying, as she had done for endless nights.

He was so tired and confused. For days now he had followed her nearly every time she left the hut. He knew that she would try to take her life by digging up the poison root, Barbasco, and chewing that alkaloid substance to commit suicide. Her grief was so heavy and life had nothing more to offer. When she went to the nearby stream to wash, he followed her, knowing that she was capable of wrapping a stout vine around her neck and leaping from a rock to hang herself. Her desperation was so complete that he feared for her life.

He left the hut that morning with only one recourse left. Hope was gone and despair had taken its place. He did not take the trail to the Shimutas River, but the one that led up into the high country. The trail was long and he finally emerged into a small clearing where the hunting trails crossed deep in the jungle. He stood for a long moment, contemplating the hopelessness of his situation, and then pointed the gun into his midsection, closed his eyes, and squeezed the trigger.

Silence filled the air, broken only by the sounds of the forest. There was no explosion as again he heard only the sound of metal on metal. The gun had misfired again. 'This is impossible,' he thought, taking yet another shell from his bag and plunging it into the chamber of that old shotgun. His hands trembled as sheer exhaustion and mental anguish clouded his mind. He felt an emptiness engulf his very soul. The gun was once more turned toward his tired body. His eyes were closed and his finger automatically moved towards the ancient trigger of that weapon, when he heard a noise above him where the hunting trails crossed. His mind reacted quickly and his hunting instincts came alive as he glanced up as if to see some large animal emerge in the clearing. Could it be a tapir, the largest of all Amazonian land animals or perhaps a wild boar breaking through the brush?

Every muscle tensed as he surveyed the trail to identify this intruder into his silent world of affliction. Bewilderment reflected itself on his countenance. It was not an animal emerging onto the trail before him, but a tall Indian man. He carried a large hunting bag across his shoulder, wore hunting shorts, was barefoot, but carried no gun.

Questions tumbled from his already overloaded mind. What would this man be doing here deep in the forest without a weapon? Who was he and where did he come from?

The stranger stopped about twenty yards away and spoke. "Yatsaju Pujamek? *(Friend, are you there?)* he asked.

"Ehe, Yatsaju, Pujajai," *(Yes, friend, I am here,)* he replied.

The next question was his to ask. "Yatsaju, Yamai minamek?" *(Friend have you just come?)*

The stranger answered, "Ehe yatsaju yamai minajai." *(Yes, I have just come.)*

The man with the gun spit on the ground and said, "Chii dekas?" *(Really?)* Both men in authoritative animated voices exchanged pleasantries.

The stranger spoke and stated that he was from the village of Numpatkaim which was across the mountain range. He pointed in that direction. "I am on my way to the village of Pumpu, but I do not know which trail to take. Could you point me in the right direction?"

The man with the gun quickly contemplated the situation and said, "I am from Pumpu. I will take you to my village." In silence they walked under the heavy canopy of the rain forest. The air was very humid and stifling as the sun's rays barely filtered through the entanglement of vines, limbs, and leaves. The floor of the jungle was damp and cool as their bare feet nimbly dodged roots, rocks, and other obstacles along the trail.

They crossed the Pumpu River and entered the garden areas dotted with patches of yuca and bananas ripening under a tropical sky. Around the next bend in the ever-winding serpentine path they saw the first of many huts basking in the heat of a new day. Little naked, bronzed-skinned boys were playing soccer with a small round gourd. Little girls were following closely behind their mothers, making their way to the gardens that lined the perimeter of the Pumpu village. The women were carrying their babies in the front part of their one-piece dresses. There were large woven baskets strapped to their backs with a broad vine placed across their foreheads holding the baskets in place. Each lady had a long, three-foot machete for cultivating her garden plots.

Men were leaving the village with blowguns and quivers full of poisonous darts hanging from a shoulder strap. Skinny mongrel dogs ran in front of the men, skirting here and there, anxious for the hunt.

Finally their path led to a thatched-roof bamboo-walled hut in a well-manicured clearing. The stranger waited as his companion removed about five or six upright poles held together between a two-poled wedge strapped on top of the doorway. The stranger was invited inside and instructed to sit down on a long, slatted, split bamboo bed.

He placed his gun across a low-slung hand carved stool and immediately walked to the middle of the hut where his wife sat on one of the small fire logs. Her quick glance passed from her husband to the stranger, and then the blank stare focused again on the damp dirt floor. Her husband spoke in soft tones that seemed to fall on deaf ears. "Please prepare something for the stranger to eat," he requested, as his eyes surveyed this once happy mother. Her appearance portrayed the days and nights of prolonged anguish. Mechanically she acknowledged his request by picking up the large feathered fan and moving it vigorously back and forth until the tiny flame leaped around the blackened clay pot sitting atop the three logged fire. Methodically she dropped an egg and two green bananas into the boiling water.

The stranger waited patiently, knowing that he must eat the food that was so graciously being prepared before they could initiate conversation. His keen eyes unobtrusively drank in the all-familiar scenes displayed in this hut. It reminded him of his own home. He saw the small hammock tied between the two poles near the bed where this couple slept, but the hammock was empty. Immediately his gaze moved to the lady sitting on the log, shielding her eyes from the thick smoke that arose from her cooking fire. He looked into that sad face and then realized that she was not carrying a baby.

His instincts warned him that something serious had taken place in this family. On the back wall was attached another split bamboo bed with a blanket of rags sewn together that obviously covered their small children at night. Near the bed was a stout vine tied between two poles that sagged with the weight of a few children's clothes. The clothes were thread bare and stained from much use. 'That's it,' he pondered. The absence of children nearly screamed at him. 'What has happened to the children of the family?' he puzzled. Glancing around the hut he saw the five-gallon beer pot sitting on a tripod near the cooking fire. A green banana leaf was tied across the opening of that vessel which housed the masticated and now fermented brew. The drum clung to the wall waiting as it were to call the men for a three-day and night beer drink.

Instinctively she arose slowly and tipped the clay cooking pot, allowing the water to run onto the dirt floor, and then retrieved the boiled egg with the two cooked plantains. These she deposited on a clean fresh cut banana leaf and placed it on the floor in front of the stranger. From a black, soot-covered woven basket hanging from a pole directly over the cooking fire, she unfolded a dry banana leaf and pinched a jagged piece of brown brackish rock crystal salt that she placed on the clean banana leaf and then motioned for the stranger to eat. He ate alone and in silence. When he finished, she brought him a gourd bowl filled with water that he poured onto his hands, washing them, and then drying them on his hair. It was now time to talk.

The stranger was asked why he had come to the village of Pumpu. Before answering, he, in turn, asked the man a question. "I see that your wife has been crying for many days and there are no children running about in your home, please tell me what has happened." The tired man looked warily at his wife and as if to purge his mind of the last few weeks, blurted out his story. He told of how all five of their children had mysteriously fallen ill and died within a two week period and that only yesterday they had buried the baby, the last child.

The stranger looked into those tired eyes and felt a deep sense of compassion for this man and his wife. He knew the agony and hopelessness of his people, for he, too, at one time had lived in that vacuum of despair. He also knew that the only hope his people had clung to for centuries was that a loved one might be reincarnated in the form of an animal someday and that wasn't much to look forward to. For that reason he had come to Pumpu.

He took a well-worn New Testament in their dialect from his hunting bag. Quietly he read those beautiful reasons for living and the hope of eternity with Christ. "Let the little children come unto me," "Let not your hearts be troubled, you believe in God, believe also in me." Perhaps it was these or verses like them that caught her attention. She arose from the log and moved over to sit with her husband. She had never heard words like these before and a spark of light shone from her eyes as she drank up every word of hope that this stranger spoke.

Gently he led them to the knowledge of the wonderful Savior who came to bring hope to broken hearts. That day, deep in the rain forest, two lives shattered by death were mended and changed forever. This couple would never be the same again.

The stranger instructed them in the ways of the Lord and promised to send believers from his church in Numpatkaim to help them from time to time. He encouraged the man to go to the mission and purchase a New Testament in his dialect. He challenged him to build a small hut and invite his friends to come and listen to their testimony of God's love.

He bought the New Testament, built the hut, and began conducting services in the village of Pumpu. It wasn't long before the masato beer pots went dry and the drums stopped beating. The village was slowly changing from darkness to light and from the power of the devil to God.

Some months later, with a growing congregation, he felt the need to prepare in the Bible Institute for ministry. God had called and he obeyed. Finishing his studies, he pastored the church in Pumpu for many years until God called him home.

Who was that stranger? Canicio Tsakim Kugkumas was pastor of the Numpatkaim church when God placed on his heart the urgency to cross the mountains that day where the hunting trails cross and thus meet a man in his hour of desperate need. Canicio later became the District Superintendent of the large Amazon District. He shepherds over one hundred pastors and their flocks in those very remote and isolated regions of the rain forest.

Was it a coincidence that Canicio crossed the mountains to visit Pumpu that day? No, God had a plan. He always has a plan to save the world.

NOTE: A Work and Witness team from Kentucky built a beautiful new church in the village of Pumpu. To God is the glory.

The Amazon Call

From the Mafia to the Pulpit

He could see the military checkpoint up ahead and the armed soldiers standing nearby as he approached the lowered bar blocking the road. 'This will just be a routine check of my personal identification papers,' he thought. 'I will be on my way to Pucallpa in no time.' He could hear the crunch of gravel with each step he took along this lonely stretch of road.

His backpack contained a fairly large amount of folded bills tucked away under a sewn flap of material hidden from the naked eye. The air was stifling hot, laden with humidity that he could almost reach out and touch. Glancing here and there, Felipe's senses came alive. There was the usual stray dog wandering around looking for tidbits of food. One could almost count the ribs on these mangy, emaciated creatures. On either side of the road, small temporary makeshift houses haphazardly placed on tiny clearings filled the empty spaces between the army camp and military headquarters. Chickens were wandering along the road, pecking and searching for insects of every description and size to devour. His muscles tensed as he approached the lowered bar blocking his progress.

"Halt," came the retort of a soldier clutching his automatic with two hands. "Report to the control desk and show your identification papers." The soldier motioned with his weapon the direction to the table. He approached the table, noticing that this day a sergeant was sitting there rather than the usual corporal. A gruff voice demanded to see his personal ID. Felipe was careful not to place his backpack on the table, but on the ground by his feet, shielding the backpack from suspicious eyes with his body. He unzipped a small pouch removing his ID papers. He nervously wiped dry his sweaty palms before handing the paper to the sergeant. His heart was beating faster and he hoped that the officer didn't notice the slight tremor in both his hands and voice.

"Felipe Montoya," the sergeant said, in a tone that aroused suspicion. Felipe shifted from one foot to the other nervously. Silence filled the air for what seemed an eternity. He observed the sergeant writing something on a piece of paper and handing it to a nearby soldier who immediately disappeared. "Wait here," exhorted the officer in no uncertain terms. The words rang in Felipe's ears and beads of perspiration gathered quickly on his forehead.

Felipe was born the oldest of seven children. He was raised close to the village of Bellavista in a beautiful fertile valley watered by the great Huallaga River in the state of San Martin. His parents were farmers with an expanding family, struggling to make ends meet. His was a pleasant childhood, working in the rice fields long and often exhausting hours. When the harvest was over Felipe and his friends would ride inner tubes down the fast moving streams under a blazing hot tropical sun. These little frail crafts would sweep around the many sharp bends in the river, bouncing occasionally off the surface rocks, causing the tubes to tip over, and throwing their laughing occupants into the cool refreshing water. Splashing wildly, they would climb back into those round objects and repeat the process over and over again along several miles of waterways before finally making the long trek back upstream to their homes. What freedom he experienced during those carefree long afternoons! Attendance in church with his parents was more out of respect and obligation rather than a personal desire of his own.

A new year brought many changes to the now twenty-one-year-old Felipe. He began experimenting with another lifestyle that was to alter his future forever. His parents heard about land grants in the growing city of Pucallpa, far away on the Ucayali River. They decided to move and buy land in this new and exciting area of the jungle that held great promise for homesteaders.

Felipe decided to stay in San Martin and continue to work his father's farm. At last, alone and free of his parents' influence, he soon tired of just making enough money to live on and determined that he would enjoy the finer things of life. In February, he planted his first seeds of coca in a hidden valley near the Huallaga River. Harvest time brought an abundant crop of coca that he sold for a very good profit, and life was looking up. It wasn't long until he realized that more money could be had, not only growing and harvesting coca, but also much better returns could be his by making the paste and joining the drug trafficking mafia. Three and one half years passed and Felipe had sold and dealt in cocaine for a very good profit.

The sun was unbearably hot and Felipe felt sick to his stomach when he saw the soldier returning with an army officer by his side. He knew something was wrong when he noticed the officer had three bars on his shoulder, a Captain in the Peruvian Army. Approaching the desk, the Captain spoke to the Sergeant and carefully examined Felipe's ID papers and many questions followed. Finally the Captain stated that there was a warrant out for his arrest for drug trafficking and being a member of the Peruvian Mafia.

Felipe felt the blood flush his face and his heart was racing rapidly as those words sank into his mind that day. He struggled for words, but none came forth, as his world came crumbling in around him. His mind was swirling and searching for something to say, but to no avail. "Place your backpack on the table." He stood motionless, frozen with fear and unable to respond for a long moment. "Put your backpack on the table," came the impatient command of the Captain. Slowly his fog-shrouded mind responded almost mechanically to the command. The Captain unzipped the large compartment and his experienced hands began rummaging through the contents of this well-worn canvas bag, spotted with streaks of recent perspiration. Felipe stood helpless on legs that threatened to cave in as the officer continued his methodical search of the suspicious backpack.

His mind conjured up images of a similar day when he was arrested and placed in jail for two days for possession of cocaine. While in jail, alone and afraid, he thought about his father and mother in Pucallpa. They were wonderful Christians and he knew that they prayed for their wayward son. Felipe remembered praying to God while in jail, but only out of desperate fear of the long prison term that surely awaited him. He asked God to help him gain his freedom, with the vacant promise to serve Him, if he could only be free. But trusting in his own power, he bribed the police and was soon on his way.

"What is this?" he heard a voice say. Quickly his wandering mind was snapped back to the present situation, as he saw the Captain removing something from deep within the backpack. His heart was racing wildly, thinking that the drug money had been discovered in the secret compartment. The color drained from his face and he felt faint as the Captain's hand slowly withdrew from the bag, clutching something in its grip. Felipe's life had been filled with surprises of late, causing him to reflect on the events of the past months.

Since joining the drug mafia, he had been assaulted on four different occasions and once they had threatened to take his life. On one of those occasions they had stolen his motorcycle, leaving him stranded and without transportation. Twice he had been arrested by the police for drug possession and twice he had bribed his way to freedom.

"Is this yours?" he heard the Captain ask. The officer held in his outstretched hand a worn black Bible.

"Yes, that is mine," Felipe responded dumbfounded. His parents had given him the Bible years ago and he carried it with him on long trips. He never read its contents, but had carried it as if it were a good luck charm.

"Are you a Christian?" the Captain asked.

"Yes," Felipe, quickly but falsely, responded. The Captain then extracted a used airplane ticket stub from the backpack. It was for a flight from Pucallpa to Tarapoto.

He asked, "Are you from Pucallpa?"

Conditioned to lying, Felipe falsely stated, "Yes."

"Then you are not from Tarapoto?"

"No," he replied, hoping that his voice would not betray him. The Captain believed his story that he was on his way home to Pucallpa after visiting family in Tarapoto.

"There is a warrant out for your arrest, so you will have to spend tonight in our military jail. Tomorrow your accuser will be here to identify you as a member of the drug mafia."

That dark night, hungry, lonely, and sitting in a dingy cell, Felipe felt a wave of depression desperately sweep over him. Images of his life flooded a tormented mind. He saw his parents, family, church, mafia, drugs, police, and the Captain, and soon guilt overwhelmed him that night.

'Who could be the informant who has accused me before the authorities?' he wondered. The night passed so slowly and Felipe's tormented mind, along with the fear of the unknown future, caused him to spend a restless night. Roosters crowed and another day dawned in the Amazon. Tired and anxious, Felipe waited, welcoming the light of day. He paced nervously back and forth, wondering who could have informed on him. He knew that the mafia was a cutthroat group that would stop at nothing to bring down one of their own and thus take over their portion of the lucrative drug trade.

He heard the soldiers approaching his cell and now the moment of reckoning had come. They led him down the narrow hallway to a small room where he would soon be interrogated. Many and varied thoughts ran rampantly through his tired confused mind while looking out the only window in this drab and dreary room. Suddenly a face appeared out of nowhere peering in at him. Their eyes met for a fleeting moment and recognition was immediate. The face disappeared quickly and Felipe knew why. This man was also a member of the elusive mafia with whom he had previous unpleasant encounters. 'So he is the informant,' Felipe said almost out loud. 'Two can play this game and we will both go down together if he identifies me to the Captain.' Long moments passed before the Captain entered the room. Felipe felt the tension rise in every muscle of his body, waiting for the man to speak.

"You are free to go," the officer said. The words echoed in Felipe's ears 'free to go?' He sat stunned for a long moment, unable to speak. The Captain spoke again. "Mistaken identity," he said. "Your accuser has returned to his home." Felipe strapped on his backpack, shook the Captain's hand and walked out into the freedom of a new day. Soon he was on his way to Pucallpa and his family.

It wasn't long, though, until he was again living in drunkenness, forgetting all the promises he had made to the Lord. The next four years brought only misery and problems. During this time he had a daughter by a woman that he was living with. Then he had a dream. In this dream he heard the words, "Repent or death is coming." The dream was so real that it left him terrified. He desperately wanted to go to the church where his family attended, but he was ashamed to go because of his drunkenness and live-in wife.

At that time, Felipe was working on the highway. A speeding fuel truck passed by, spinning a rock from its wheel. The rock struck him on the head right behind the ear. The force of the blow knocked him out. When he came to, he realized just how fragile life is. On Thursday of that week, he told a friend about the dream he had. The friend was not a Christian, but he sensed the desperate spiritual need Felipe had. "Let's go to the church tonight and I will accompany you," he said. Felipe reluctantly agreed.

"I will meet you tonight at eight p.m. in front of the church." As the day wore on, Felipe had second thoughts about just showing up at the Thursday night prayer meeting, so he went and sat in the park nearby. His friend arrived at the church at the appointed time, but no Felipe. He immediately went looking for him, and soon found him sitting dejectedly alone on the park bench. He insisted that they attend the service, which they did.

The singing was beautiful and spontaneous and Felipe soon found himself kneeling, weeping and asking God to forgive him of a long sordid past. He arose from the altar that night, a changed man. His family and church friends hugged him warmly that incredible night. One of the outstanding laymen embraced Felipe and, looking into his eyes said, "Welcome home, we have been praying for you for eight long years."

Felipe's common law wife who was not a believer left and took her daughter with her. Felipe was trying to put his complicated life back together again under the Lord's leadership and made a trip to the far away jungle city of Iquitos on the Amazon River, about five hundred miles down stream from Pucallpa. He went to this port city looking for work and a fresh start in life. While in Iquitos, he met a wonderful young lady who was attending church with her father, but she had not yet accepted the Lord. She had been deceived by a young man while studying in high school and was now raising her little boy by herself.

It wasn't long until they fell in love and each accepted the other with all of their flaws. After they were married, she gave her heart to the Lord and they formed a wonderful Christian home. Work was scarce in Iquitos and they decided to move back to Pucallpa. Felipe bought some land in a small community a long way from Pucallpa in Pampa Verde. They both attended a small church and were growing in the things of the Lord. His testimony was vibrant and contagious. Together they farmed and supported the little church.

Later, the pastor moved to another city and the leaders asked Felipe to become the pastor. He accepted the assignment and God has blest them beyond imagination. A Work and Witness team built a lovely church in the village of Pampa Verde under the leadership of Felipe Montoya. Everyone fell in love with pastor Felipe and his beautiful Christian wife. Yes, miracles continue to happen in the jungle of Perú.

The Amazon Call

Baptized

The crunch of gravel under his feet broke the silence of a tropical night as he made his way home with only the pale dim light of a moon desperately trying in vain to break through the heavy layer of clouds. Damp moist air clung to his skin as he laboriously staggered up yet another hill on his way home from the little sleepy village of Mesones. His eyes were glazed and his step was unsteady as he struggled to maintain his balance on this rugged dirt road bordering the thick jungle on either side. His mind was clouded and oblivious to the sounds and dangers of the rain forest on this dark night. There was a hint of rain in the air as black clouds swirled overhead and a warm wind blew gently through the trees announcing the imminent arrival of a rainstorm.

On and on he walked in a daze caused from the deep stupor of the intoxicating liquor he had consumed just hours before. His gait soon became unsteady and those wobbly legs withdrew their support. José fell into the weed-infested ditch alongside the road. The crumpled body lay motionless through the long wet night as mosquitoes freely nibbled on his skin while ants paraded up and down on their unconscious sleeping victim.

The dawn of a new day swept over the Amazon with soft rays of light penetrating through the entangled forest overhead, dancing lazily on the damp jungle floor. Birds were singing from the branches of a thousand trees and insects scattered, escaping the sudden movement of hands desperately scratching untold numbers of raised welts on the irritated skin of their once hapless victim.

With mud-covered hands, José managed to roll himself over, looking into a bright sun that automatically caused him to cover those red swollen eyes with those same hands, all in one excruciating motion. The splitting headache seemed to find its way into every joint of his tired body as he struggled to his feet. Immediately he sought the shade of a small tree to escape the inferno that raged within his body. Once again, José began the long walk home.

Small groups of children on their way to the village school giggled and pointed to the disheveled man approaching them on the opposite side of the road. "It's José, the town drunk," they whispered to one another. They kept a safe distance between themselves and this sad looking man with dirty clothes and uncombed hair.

José finally made it to the little room he called home on the edge of the rice fields. He picked up a small mirror that was lying on a tiny crude table and looked into its shiny reflection. What he saw shocked him to the depths of his soul. He determined that he would free himself of this devil of drunkenness that had so long held him in bondage. He muttered to himself that he would not taste another drop of liquor, while preparing a cup of strong black coffee to shake this splitting headache that caused him to feel sick to his stomach. He looked around his room of meager belongings, wondering what life was all about. His was a life of vicious cycles. Work in the rice fields provided him with the bare necessities, which most of the time was wasted on liquor and gambling.

Working in the swampy fields planting rice was backbreaking and monotonous under a fierce, unrelenting, tropical sun. Harvest time was not better, since he had to stand long hours chasing the hordes of birds away from the ripe grains of rice waving in the breeze. Cutting, separating, and drying the grains took great patience and was very time consuming. Finally, bagging the grain in huge one hundred pound sacks and carrying them to the truck was almost unbearable. How many times José wanted to quit the fields and make a living some other way were too numerous to count, but there was no other work to be had.

That evening, after laboring in the fields, José bathed in the nearby stream, ate supper, and found himself walking that lone road back to the village of Mesones to gamble and drink the boredom away. He was all of twenty-three years old and on the path of destruction. It wasn't long until José began dabbling in drugs and witchcraft. He was searching for meaning to life in all the wrong places. He sought out a prominent witchdoctor to become a student of witchcraft. He was immersed into the world of the spirits, trying to find something that would satisfy the empty void in his life.

One night, while walking to Mesones, José heard some strange singing coming from a small building on top of a hill near the edge of the village. He paused for a long moment, wondering what this singing was all about. He had participated in drinking and dancing before, but this had a different ring to it. Since it was dark, he continued his journey to the gambling table to drink the night away with his friends.

A few nights later, he heard singing from the top of the same hill. Curiosity aroused, he climbed some steps that had been dug out in the side of the hill. Reaching the top, he approached a small bamboo building with a corrugated metal roof. Peering inside, he noticed a group of people intent on singing music about, of all things, God. They seemed happy enough, but the room was rather dark, as the only light came from some little wick lamps placed strategically around the walls on tiny boards nailed to the posts that held up the roof. He listened for a moment then turned and left, making his way into town to follow his nightly routine.

This night José had come to town riding his fourteen-year-old brother's bike. His brother had asked José to buy him a can of evaporated milk for his breakfast the next morning. José had been pretty much on his own, because his mother suffered from tuberculosis and was not able to provide and care for her children. His fourteen-year-old brother, Manuel, lived with an older sister and her family that farmed the rice fields near the Marañon River. There was an older married brother, Felix, who lived just a short distance from José, however his marriage was on the rocks and they were about to separate and go their own ways. Manuel waited into the long hours of the night for José to return, but to no avail. He, too, worked in the rice fields in the afternoons and on Saturdays. Every day Manuel rode his bike four miles on that same dirt rock-lined road to attend high school in the little port town of Imaza.

He was so thin from exhausting days at school and the hard work in the fields that he finally succumbed to sleep. Upon awakening early the next morning Manuel dressed and had his usual breakfast of coffee and bread before departing on his journey to school. Stepping out into the small clearing, he felt the warmth of a bright sun that was breaking loose from the entangled forest around him. Rounding the corner of the small home he shared with his sister, brother-in-law, and their children, he could not find his bicycle that was always parked in the same spot each night. Immediately he remembered loaning the bike to José and the money he had given him to buy the can of evaporated milk.

He hurriedly made his way to José's hut to pick up his bike and begin his long journey to Imasa and the school. Approaching the hut, he saw no sign of his bicycle and the house was unusually quiet this time of morning. He called to José, but there was no reply. 'Where could he be?' Manuel thought as he continued calling. He was perturbed that José had not delivered the promised can of milk. He had had to drink his coffee black this morning. The bike was nowhere in sight and time was slipping away rapidly, so Manuel began the long walk down the dirt road, knowing that he would be very late to school. His mind flashed back to the many nights that José had come home late and drunk. Climbing one steep hill after another, he wondered if José had fallen off of the bike in a drunken stupor, and if so, where could he be?

Rounding a sharp bend in the road, something shiny caught his attention about ten yards from the road down a steep incline in the entanglement of bushes. Upon inspecting the area, he found that it indeed was his bike lying there, half buried in the undergrowth, but there was no sign of José. Moving branches and pulling thick weeds aside, he found a bruised, sleeping brother lying in a heap, oblivious to the lush plant and insect world that had been his bed for the night. Manuel looked sadly upon his brother and felt deep pity for this man, lost and broken by the ravages of liquor. He awakened those blood-shot eyes by gently shaking José by the shoulders, calling his name.

Staggering to his feet, his hands automatically rubbed welts raised by hungry mosquitoes during the warm tropical night. Sheepishly José handed Manuel the slightly dented can of evaporated milk as if to say, 'See, I am not a total waste.'

Manuel straightened out the front wheel of his bicycle, stored the can of milk in his well-worn backpack, and headed off to school, leaving José with his sad, lonely thoughts of failure. That day José decided that he must change and be a good example for his younger brother.

That afternoon as the two brothers worked side by side in the fields, very few words were exchanged as disappointment showed on both men's faces. Manuel was disappointed in his older brother and José in himself. After bathing and eating, José felt that deep mysterious tugging of his addicted body to repeat his age-old custom of drowning his troubles in the familiar brown bottle that had so enslaved him. He struggled with his inner self, but to no avail, and soon, under a beautiful starry night, his feet once again were crunching small pebbles on their way to Mesones.

Approaching the village, José again heard the melody of music coming from that now-familiar bamboo building on the hill. Reluctantly his tired troubled mind urged his legs up the well-worn steps leading to the door of this place where peace and happiness seemed to abound. He looked longingly upon the faces of these seemingly happy people who sang as if it came from their hearts. Slipping quietly into the little church, José sat on a backless bench near the door, listening to the testimonies of people he had known for years.

The message was age-old and uncomplicated coming from the lips of Rev. Abiatar Roncal, pastor of this new fledging congregation. He had met Pastor Roncal on occasion, but had tried to avoid him as much as possible. His younger brother attended services on the New Horizon mission station where Rev. Roncal was the director of the Bible Institute. A deep hungering for the peace and joy demonstrated by these humble people drove José to the altar and his knees, where he poured out his heart to God for a measure of what they had. A sense of God's presence flooded José's heart and soul that night in the village of Mesones.

He began the long walk home that night under the influence of God's forgiveness. He felt so unworthy, but the joy that filled his life made the long walk pass quickly. The next few weeks brought great changes in José's life. He attended all the services and showed wonderful promise in his new life, but it wasn't long until the claims of his former lifestyle surfaced and the deep struggle with alcohol robbed him of his joy.

Late one night, José was staggering down the dirt road wondering what had happened to him. He had struggled for many months, making frequent trip to the altar, only to be followed by bouts of drinking with his old friends.

Christmas was approaching and Addie prepared a drama for the young people in the Mesones church. José had one of the main parts. Practices went well and José was holding steady and everyone was excited about the very first Christmas drama to be presented in the Mesones church.

Two weeks before the presentation, we had to leave for the coast and would not be returning until after Christmas. However, Addie had left the direction of the drama in very capable hands. Upon our return to the jungle, we anxiously asked how the drama went. To our dismay, we were told that they had to call it off at the last moment because José had gotten drunk the night before. Such was the life of José, the town drunk. We all despaired and gave up hope of him ever being delivered of the demons of alcohol, drugs, and witchcraft. José sensed that people had given up on him and again resumed his old habitual way of life.

One warm humid night José was drinking with his buddies in a small one-room restaurant where the owner offered roasted chicken as the only item on the menu. While downing a glass of beer, José looked up and saw Pastor Roncal approaching the doorway. He immediately crouched down behind the rough wooden table, hiding so that the pastor could not see him. He did not want the pastor to see him drinking and drunk.

Pastor Roncal ordered a plate of chicken and fries and proceeded to enjoy his meal. José shifted from one cramped leg to the other as his muscles screamed for relief. It seemed like an eternity passed before Pastor Roncal finished, paid his bill, and left the restaurant. José stood, rubbed his sore legs to restore circulation, and quietly left for home, embarrassed about his hopeless and helpless lifestyle.

Sunday morning found José in church once more. The pastor announced that next Sunday morning the first baptismal service for the new converts in the Mesones church would take place. The baptism would take place in the Kusu Chico River about a one-hour walk from the village. Excitement filled the air that morning as everyone was anticipating a great service on the banks of the Kusu Chico River next Sunday. José left the church that day forming a plan in his mind. He knew that if he could be baptized, everything would change and he would be accepted as one of them.

ONE WEEK LATER

Birds were singing and the sun rose from the eastern sky, bathing the jungle in its warm glow. Through the bamboo walls, soft rays of sunlight danced up and down across the bed where José lay in a heap, snoring loudly. His room suddenly was bathed in sunlight, and two hands covered those red swollen eyes protecting them from this unwelcome intrusion. His head was pounding and the slightest noise produced an unbearable headache. He slowly swung his legs to the floor and sat up all in one motion, cupping his head between his hands for support.

Slowly and painfully his mind floated back to the night before, not able to count the number of drinks he had imbibed. He thought about the last visit to the witchdoctor, his teacher in witchcraft. Upon arriving for his lesson, he remembered the witchdoctor asking him why he was there. The man said, "You have been going to that Evangelical Church. There is something different about you. Therefore, I cannot teach you the art of witchcraft. Go home," he said, "and don't come back." His head throbbed and despondency filled his heart.

Rejected by the local witchdoctor and embarrassed by his failure to change his life, tears flooded those blood-shot eyes in the loneliness of that moment. Scenes of the past flooded his tormented mind: the many times he had knelt at the altar, the bicycle incident, failure with the Christmas drama, kneeling in the chicken restaurant, and the announced baptism. The baptism, "Oh no!" he said, jumping to his feet, standing for a long moment waiting for his head to stop spinning. "This is the Sunday for the baptism," he muttered out loud. Quickly he put water on to boil, for he desperately needed a cup of black coffee. While the water was heating, he grabbed a bar of soap and headed for the nearby stream to bathe. The water felt so cool and refreshing on his tired body.

Gulping down two cups of black coffee, combing his hair, and changing clothes, José was soon on his way to Mesones. 'I wonder if everyone has left the church yet on their way to the baptismal,' José thought, as he hurried along the familiar road to the village. He hardly noticed the few people walking with machetes on their way to various gardens scattered along the little valleys lining the river. He longed for the few shaded areas in certain spots along the road to escape the intense heat of a sun bearing down from a cloudless sky. Perspiration saturated his clothing, but a light breeze produced a rapid evaporation that cooled his overheated body. Soon the outskirts of Mesones were in full sight as he hastened his step.

Coming upon the steps that led up the little hill to the church, José finally stopped, panting, out of breath, and stood before the closed doors of the church. Quickly he turned, bounded down the steps and headed for the river one hour away. Passing a small store, he stopped, entered, and purchased a box of chewing gum that he emptied into his mouth. When the gum was thoroughly masticated, he spit into his hands and rubbed the sweet smelling residue on his face and hands to stifle any lingering smell of alcohol on his person. The long hour to the river passed slowly and with every turn in the road, José's heart leaped within him as he anticipated being baptized. He prayed that he wouldn't arrive too late.

Jose (in white shirt)

Up ahead he heard singing coming from the direction of the river. His steps hastened, and there below him at the edge of the river was Pastor Roncal, baptizing the last of the candidates on his list. José arrived just in time to hear the pastor ask if he had baptized everyone on his list. Edging his way through the crowd, José approached the pastor, turning his head slightly so that the pastor would not detect the slight smell of alcohol on his breath. "Pastor, I want to be baptized," he said, shielding his mouth with his hands.

Pastor Roncal, taking a long look at José, asked, "Are you sure you want to be baptized?"

"Yes, please," José responded.

Reluctantly the pastor placed his hands on José that Sunday morning in the waters of the Kusu Chico. In the name of the Father, the Son and the Holy Spirit, José was baptized as the whole crowd stood by with bated breath. When José came up out of the water, it was evident that he would never be the same. José later testified that when he came up out of the water, it was not that he didn't want the pastor to see him drunk, but that he never wanted God to see him drunk again. A miracle took place that moment long ago, because José never touched another drop of liquor again.

He enrolled in our Bible extension course and prepared for ministry. Sometime later Pastor Roncal resigned the pastorate of the church in Mesones and José Lopez was unanimously installed as the new pastor. His ministry reached into the heart of untold numbers and the church grew and started new satellite churches in the area. José pastored the church for nine years before becoming an itinerant evangelist and working full time in our Nazarene Clinic where he finished his degree in nursing.

Today José administers the clinic, does traveling clinics and encourages many churches by visiting, preaching, and treating the sick. He later married a beautiful Christian girl named Maria. Their first son was born in December and they named him Jesús.

The Amazon Call

Smoky the Bandit

We were on an evangelistic trip trying to plant churches on the Santiago River. We were days from our home upstream. One morning our son Greg came to me holding in his hand a little baby orphaned animal. The Indians had shot and eaten her mother. "Dad, please, can we buy her? I have always wanted one of these, please."

I looked at this small, cuddly, orphaned, future tree swinger and said, "You can have her, but you will have to take good care of her." He paused thoughtfully for a long moment and then gave her to his sister. She fed the little fuzz ball with a teaspoon of sugared water, milk and egg white. It rode on her shoulder, slept in her bed and thought she was a person. Unfortunately, the little animal lived in our home and destroyed our house.

We named her Smoky since she was coal black. She later became Smoky the Bandit, because she would steal anything her greedy little paws could get hold of. Smoky was a wooly monkey. The woolies are well formed and extremely intelligent. We have a variety of monkeys in the rain forest. There are the spider monkeys with long gangly arms and legs, known as the trapeze artists of the Amazon. The howler monkeys are well named, because you can hear them calling from a great distance, and for that reason they usually end up in the cooking pot.

When Smoky grew to about two feet tall we no longer allowed her to stay in the house. "Smoky, outside with you, and don't come into this house again," we told her. She lived under the roof eaves, eating bugs, spiders, grasshoppers and anything that moved.

Her favorite food was a hot homemade roll cooling on the kitchen table with butter dripping down the sides. Where we lived there were no bakeries, so every Saturday morning Addie made

Smoky and Addie

these beautiful hot bread rolls. Smoky could smell the bread a quarter of a mile away. You could see her swinging from tree to tree, finally walking hand over hand the length of the clotheslines and thus landing on the front porch, staring at the bread cooling on the table. She wanted that bread in the worst way, but knew that she was not allowed in the house. Pressing her nose against the screen door, she would determine the distance between the door, the bread, and us.

Making sure that no one was watching, she would open the door with one of her hands and stick her head in between the open door and door jam. Smoky quickly surveyed the situation, observed that no one was watching, and made her move. She slid across the floor on her belly, closing the door quietly with her long tail. She would lie there until everyone was distracted and then bolt for the table, retrieving one hot roll and retreating to the door with me in hot pursuit. "Smoky, put that bread back you silly monkey."

Out the door she bolted, running down the short sidewalk as fast as her legs would carry her. The sidewalk ended at the base of a steep hill beyond our home. Holding the bread high above her head, she would run up the hill where I could not get to her. Turning around, she would sit on her haunches, munching the bread, looking at me as if to say, 'What are you going to do about it?'

The next Saturday I was prepared for this bread-stealing fuzz ball. I took off my belt and hung it over a small wooden bar on the screen door, ready to teach her an unforgettable lesson. Beautiful brown rolls were cooling on the kitchen table. I looked up and there she came swinging from tree to tree, heading for the front porch. I turned my head away from the door, but watched her from the corner of my eye. Smoky, thinking I was distracted, opened the door, stuck her head in and then slid across the floor on her belly, closing the door silently with her long tail. I thought to myself, 'Smoky, if you steal that bread, you are going to receive a swat with my belt.'

Cautiously, she jumped to her feet and quick as a flash headed for the table. She grabbed the bread and in one motion turned for the door. I leaped from my chair and ran to the door. We arrived at the door at the same time. As Smoky was leaving the door, I reached for the belt and swatted her on the rump. She froze in midair, screeching and rubbing her bottom all at the same time. She fussed and scolded me, crying all the way down the sidewalk. I watched her disappear into the jungle madder than a wet hornet. I congratulated myself and thought that this will teach her not to steal bread again.

The following Saturday, the pleasant aroma of fresh baked bread floated out through the screened windows of our little house in the jungle. Guess who I saw swinging hand over hand on the clothesline? The temptation was too great as Smoky made her way towards the front porch. The belt was still hanging there just in case she came back. I turned my head away from the door, but again watched her from the corner of my eye. Cautiously Smoky approached the door, looking longingly through the screen at the bread on the kitchen table. 'Monkey,' I thought, 'if you steal another bread today, I will give you a spanking that you will not forget for a long time.' The door opened and a round head poked inside, followed by a belly slide across the floor and the door being closed silently by a skilled long tail. I waited patiently, and then breaking all speed records Smoky ran, grabbed a roll, and turned to flee the scene of the crime. We both got to the door at the same time. I reached for the belt just as her tail flashed past my outstretched hand and pulled the belt from my reaching grasp. She sprinted down the sidewalk, pulling my belt behind her. I chased her to the end of the sidewalk where she promptly dropped the belt and scurried up the steep hillside where I could not reach her. She sat on her haunches, munching her bread and looking at me with those cold black eyes as if to say, 'Now, what?'

Please pray for us, because "It's a jungle out there."

Smoky Rides Again

It was a typical day with numerous patients lined up at our clinic, waiting their turns to be treated. Opening the door to admit a new patient, I observed a familiar scene. The Indians were sitting on the low stone retaining wall between the hill and the clinic on the shady side of the building. Mothers were carrying nursing babies in the front of their one-piece dresses. The dress was a large rectangular piece of cloth wrapped around the body, tied over the right shoulder and cinched around the waist with a stout vine. Little dark eyes betraying fear peered at me over the top of the dress. There were a few small naked boys clinging to their Mom's legs in abject fear of the white-skinned doctor. Their abdomens were distended, hair tinged red, skin pale, and very listless. It was obvious that they suffered from malnutrition.

I noticed an elderly woman standing near the door. She was perhaps sixty years of age and maybe four feet six inches tall. Her leathery-wrinkled thin face exhibited round nickel-sized blue tattoo marks on her prominent high cheekbones. Long stringy hair hung loosely down over her stooped shoulders. Dark kind grandmotherly eyes met mine for a fleeting second. I greeted her in the dialect and she politely responded by raising her two thin bony arms and pointing in my direction. Immediately I noticed the swollen joints of her small hands and knew that she suffered with arthritis.

Next to the hillside lay a young man on a bamboo mat. His eyes were listless and sunken deep into a pale, nearly ashen white face. He appeared so frail and lifeless. Slight contractions pulled the muscles of his extremities in a tremor-like fashion. With great effort, he managed to roll onto his side just as a violent shaking of his body took over. He gagged, vomited and gasped for breath as his mother responded immediately to his desperate situation. With the help of a couple of men, we admitted him and began hydrating him with intravenous measures. I felt so overwhelmed that day by the constant stream of needs passing through our clinic.

A few minutes later, I heard people laughing outside and making loud comments. Wondering what was so funny, I looked through the screen window. Smoky, our pet wooly monkey, had jumped on the back of a large dog and was pulling his tail. The dog was jumping in circles trying to buck off an unwanted rider that kept pulling his tail every few seconds. When the frustrated dog became furious and determined to rid himself of this intruder, Smoky would jump, climb up a pole, and sit on the roof, waiting for the dog to be distracted. A few minutes later when the dog was not watching, Smoky would jump on his back, pull his tail and start the fun all over again. The people were laughing and gesturing wildly at the antics of Smoky. I smiled and felt the tensions of another challenging day dissipate. Thanks, Smoky, for bringing a little joy to our lives.

Many forgot just how sick they really were as Smoky entertained them for nearly twenty minutes. We soon learned that she was good medicine for most of our patients, that is until a patient would exit the clinic, heading for the village carrying their pills in a small clear plastic sack. Smoky would run up behind the unsuspecting person, grab the sack, and sprint for the front porch. She would climb up on the roof, open the sack, and watch the pills roll down the roof and fall onto the ground. Helplessly, I would watch her disappear into the jungle as the patient returned to the clinic pointing to the empty plastic sack. I had to replace the medicine on more then one occasion. Thanks a lot, Smoky (the Bandit).

The Tormentor

Our communication with the outside world was by Ham radio. Behind our house stood a tall tower anchored down with strong guy wires, holding it securely in place on the steep hillside about fifty yards away. On top of the tower was a large multiband antenna. Connected to the side of the tower was a small strand of wire attached to another tiny antenna for local contacts. This small strand of wire hung loosely under the roof and ran through the wall to our radio.

Addie was sick and lying in bed one day when she heard a noise outside near the roof. Ricky, our parrot, was perched on the small strand of wire enjoying life. We had clipped his wings so that he couldn't fly away. His tiny feet were tightly gripped to the wire that gently swayed in a light breeze. To Addie's amazement she saw the wire lose its swing-like arch and begin to rise higher and higher.

From the corner of her eye she saw Smoky sitting on the roof, reeling in the wire like he was pulling in a fish. When the wire was taut, she let go of it and watched with glee as the wire dropped with a thud, vibrating and shaking uncontrollably, while the poor little parrot fluttered his stubby wings desperately trying to hang on. The terrified little bird clung to the wire as Smoky reeled him in once more. Again, Smoky let the wire drop and the parrot struggled to stay on the wire and not fall to the ground. Smoky repeated this game until she was bored and soon swung away into the trees and disappeared. Visibly shaken, the parrot quickly exited from the vibrating nightmare, never again to perform on the high wire.

Smoky soon appeared again, just outside the clinic door. Patients were milling about, waiting their turn to be treated when a big red rooster walked by. Big Red was scratching the ground looking for insects and any tidbits of food to devour, unaware of Smoky's presence. Smoky ran up behind the rooster and tried to pull his tail feathers. Monkeys cannot grasp objects the way humans do, because their thumb cannot close on the index finger. She followed the rooster trying to pull the feathers, but they would slip right through her hand. Smoky tried over and over to grab a handful of feathers, desperately wanting to torment the animal, but without any success. The people were laughing and gesturing wildly at the unsuccessful antics of this foolish monkey.

Nothing New Under the Sun

(Hair Tinting, Tattoos, and Body Piercings)

Among the Indians of the Amazon, hair tinting is even done by men. Tinting is done by women and little girls to keep their hair black with a slight sheen to it. There is a lot of malnutrition among the Indian populace, causing the hair to have a reddish tinge to it. The hair also loses its shine and becomes dry and dull in appearance.

A liquid dye is made from the extract of a plant called Suwa in the Aguaruna dialect and Huito in Spanish. It comes from the genus Genipa of the Rubiaceae family. This liquid is clear and transparent until it comes into contact with the hair and skin. It is applied to the hair with the fingers and everything that it touches immediately turns black. Naturally, when it is applied to the hair it runs down the face, neck, and upper arms, turning them black, also, along with the fingers, hand and forearm. The dye is not washable and has to wear off with time. We see many people with this new shiny hair, but their skin is stained as black as coal. Finally after a week or two, the dye, little by little, fades away. The dye is used not only to tint the hair, but also to paint the body black for revenge war raids, and for insect repellent.

Tattoos are symbols of beauty for both men and women. They are usually etched on their high prominent cheekbones leaving a permanent mark. The tattoos are round and about one inch in diameter made from a plant extract. They are blue in color and consist of small dots. Painting the face with a paste made from the crushed bright red Achiote seeds highlights these beauty marks. These seeds are from the Annotto tree. They are greasy and red in color. They grow in a small pod and, when mature, the seeds are extracted, crushed, and made into a paste that is painted on the face, chest, and upper arms with a finger. The Indians paint themselves for social occasions, war raids, and dancing.

Body piercing takes place even in the jungle. Young Aguaruna girls traditionally would puncture a small hole on the lower lip halfway between the mouth and chin. This hole would be expanded to accommodate a round two or three inch length of bone or palm wood. This adornment is used for social occasions such as dancing or special communal activities. When they talk the bone moves up and down drawing one's attention from the eyes to the bone or palm wood.

The Aguarunas pride themselves on their appearance. The hair is usually well combed and cared for. Traditionally the men have had long hair flowing down over the shoulders, cut in bangs across the forehead and at right angles over the ears, exposing interesting objects attached to their earlobes. These adornments consisted of beautiful beetle wings or feathered earrings. The bright, shiny and green iridescent wings of the beetle strung together on homemade thread provide the most desirable earring worn by the men. They are about six inches long and tipped with red and yellow parrot feathers. The Huambisa men place three-inch shafts of bamboo about the size in diameter of a pencil in the large holes that penetrate the earlobes.

The most intriguing of all earrings are large rusty safety pins. Chimpa, the aged witchdoctor, wore a safety pin in just one ear. On one occasion I was visiting with a man in a local village who sported a large rusty safety pin in one ear, while the other was empty except for the large slit in the lower lobe. Visiting us at the time was a young lady from the United States who wore two lovely golden antique earrings. The scene was a lesson in cross-cultural settings. The Aguaruna man wore the typical (itipuk) homespun skirt cinched at the waist by a thin vine. His hair was long, hanging loosely over broad shoulders and cut in bangs across the forehead. Our lady friend wore pants and her hair was gathered in a ponytail. Desiring to have some fun, I asked him if he would like to trade his safety pin for those two lovely golden antique earrings. He looked at me with stoic, penetratingly kind eyes and empathically said, "No."

Again I asked him, adding that he would only be giving up the old rusty safety pin in exchange for the beautiful golden earrings. Looking me in the eye, he said, "Nakitajai" (that's enough, I won't do it). Pointing to his thick calloused feet that had never felt a pair of shoes and never would, and whose toenails were split from endless trails, he told me the following: "Many times I spend days and nights in the jungle hunting for wild game to provide food for our table. The trails are filled with many dangers and I have to be very careful especially at night when walking on the dark damp floor of the jungle. Occasionally I step on a long sharp black palm thorn that penetrates deep into my foot causing excruciating pain. I have to limp over to an old tree stump, sit down, take out my earring and open the skin to pick out that palm thorn." He pointed to the golden earrings and stated emphatically that they wouldn't do him a bit of good.

How you define life depends upon your cultural point of view.

The Amazon Call

The Gates Are Opened
Paulina

He came running up to our house calling my name, "Doctor!" I looked up from my desk and through the screened-in window I saw Antonio from the village of Nazaret. He was out of breath, perspiring profusely, and obviously very tired. Excitedly he told me that one of my favorite people had just passed away. "Paulina has died."

The words weighed heavily on my mind and I responded, "When is the funeral?"

"Tomorrow," he replied, "and we want you to help bury her."

"I will be there in the morning," I assured him. Antonio turned to hurry back to the village to make preparations for a proper burial.

A few yards down the trail he stopped and called me once again. "Doctor, could you please make a small casket in your wood shop and bring it with you tomorrow? You know that she isn't very big and it won't take much lumber. We don't have anything in the village with which to make a casket."

"No problem," I replied, "we will bring it tomorrow." Antonio took a few short steps and then yelled again in my direction, "Could you bring the message tomorrow?"

"Yes," I said and then I saw him rapidly disappear around a bend in the gravel road leading away from our house.

I stood for a long moment as images of this precious little lady named Paulina flooded my mind. She was probably all of four feet eight inches tall, thin as a rail, wearing the typical one-piece dress knotted over the right shoulder and cinched at the waist with a small thin vine. Dripping wet she might have weighed eighty pounds. At night when she slept on her split bamboo bed (no mattress), she would untie her dress and use it as a blanket. On cool damp tropical nights she would have a little fire going on the dirt floor right at the foot of her bed to keep her arthritic feet warm.

She lived in a one room, thatched roof, bamboo walled hut with her son, daughter-in-law and two grandchildren. She tended a tiny garden that produced yuca, bananas, and papaya. She also cared for a few chickens. All of her earthly possessions could have been placed in two large baskets with enough room for her well-worn machete. She had been a widow for many years and a dear friend of mine for about six.

She had long hair that hung way down over her thin bent shoulders. You could see the blue round dotted tattoo marks on her prominent high cheekbones. The hole in her lower lip had once sported a two inch long piece of palm wood or a thin animal bone for dress up occasions. Her eyes were dark, but kind and grandmotherly. When she looked at you, it was obvious that she had a deep inner strength.

Returning to the house, I thought to myself that the church in Nazaret would never be the same, because we had just lost a saint.

Early the next morning we loaded the little casket with the white cross into the back of our Suburban Carryall for the short trip over the rough bumpy dirt road to the village of Nazaret. Several of the third year students from the Bible Institute accompanied me, since we had been teaching them how to conduct a funeral.

Our trip took us along the Marañon River and afforded a breathtaking view of the upper lush green valleys that folded into the rising mountains in the background. The rich vegetation stretched as far as eye could see and disappeared into the fog-shrouded hills in the distance. The road turned rather sharply around another bend and we could see the mouth of the Chiriaco River where its clear waters were rapidly gobbled up by the larger swift muddy Marañon. The road led us around innumerable curves before we arrived at the village of Nazaret. Rounding the last bend in the road, we saw the little church with its three white crosses hanging there in plain view for all passersby to see.

I was amazed by the size of the crowd that had gathered to pay their last respects to this dear lady that had departed from us. The church was overflowing and people were standing outside. I knew that Paulina was deeply loved, but I was not prepared for the large number of people that had come from nearby villages. Stepping from the car, I was immediately ushered inside the church. It was packed and every backless bench was fully occupied.

Soon a space was made for me on the front bench where I quickly settled in after greeting many familiar faces on my way. Observing my surroundings, I noticed the large group of little widowed ladies occupying the first couple of rows.

Off to my right I caught a glimpse of Paulina wrapped in the white sheet that Addie had sent with Antonio the day before. She was lying on a split bamboo woven mat placed across two benches with her open New Testament lying next to her head. There was a deep sense of peace and reverence in that setting that immediately commanded my attention. There was not the feeling of borderline hysteria that accompanied so many burial scenes in the tribe.

The singing began and the whole church was filled with hope, joy, and a sereneness that I had not anticipated. Something was unusual here in the Aguaruna church of Nazaret. After prayer and introductions, I was invited to speak to the people. Standing there in the wonderful presence of Jesus, I was overwhelmed by what He had done in the lives of these precious people and especially in the life of Paulina. My message was simple and consisted in retelling her story.

Behind me, attached to the bamboo wall of the church, was a small blackboard similar to the ones in most of our village churches. I had preached on many occasions in this church and this blackboard had served me well. Since our people were just learning to read and write, I would write the text on the chalkboard and many times use stick drawings to illustrate my message. It was my custom that after writing the text for all to see, those of us who could read would fan out across the congregation to help the people find the text in their Aguaruna New Testaments.

The Amazon Call

I remembered with great fondness those services when, like a magnet, I was always drawn to help Paulina find the indicated verse. Every Sunday she occupied the middle space on the first bench surrounded by a host of widowed women like herself. She brought her New Testament to every service the church had to offer. She could not read a word, but thought that to be a Christian you had to take God's Word into His house. Every one of those widowed ladies did the same. After helping her find the verse, she would place a little bony finger on the page, squint her dark eyes like she was reading every word, and couldn't read a lick. All the other ladies did the same thing and none of them could read.

I then mentioned her giving and how she supported the pastor and the church. Every Sunday when the offering gourd bowl was being passed, Paulina would stand, reach under her bench and pull out a large woven basket of produce. It would probably weigh more then she did. The basket might be full of yuca, bananas, papaya, pineapple or raw sugar cane cut into one-foot long lengths and tied with a stout vine. Her offering on occasion was a skinny chicken tied by the feet, deposited at the altar where it would scratch and peck during the rest of the service. Paulina would then dump out the contents of her basket in front of the altar, with a long line of ladies following her example and doing the same. The pastor would take this produce home to feed his family for the week. Paulina never had money, but she never came to a church service without an offering. She had taught all of the other ladies by her quiet example, as she was one of the first converts in the Nazaret church.

One Sunday, after the service, they gave me the offering. It was a large, still-warm banana leaf, folded and tied with a piece of vine. It had been cooked in the coals of a fire early in the morning. Taking the package in my hands, I observed a large group of widowed ladies surrounding me with their bony arms folded across their chest, anxiously waiting to see if the missionary liked the delicacy that he held in his hands. They wanted me to sample their offering that morning. I proceeded to untie the vine, unfold the banana leaf, and expose to all the contents inside. It contained one of my favorite foods, baked palm heart. Between pieces of succulent white pieces of palm heart were what had been big fat juicy grub worms. They now were shriveled and yellowish-white in appearance. Every eye fastened on my hand as I took out a grub and began munching it before them.

I evidently made quite an impression as they all broke out in big grins, raising their hands in excitement as if to say, 'See, he likes them just like we do.' Swallowing the warm grub I thought to myself, 'Lord, why did they have to tithe today, anyway?'

I learned a great deal about giving from Paulina and the widow gang from Nazaret. She probably never had the equivalent of ten dollars in her life, but she never came to church without an offering. She thought that to be a Christian, one had to give the best to the Lord.

I looked over at her open Bible. There was a large white card lying on top at a slightly turned angle. Knowing what it was, I picked up the card, holding it up for all to see. It was well worn and soiled around the edges. I proceeded to read the card out loud for all to hear. It was Paulina's baptismal certificate. She carried it in her Bible, no doubt thinking it was her passport to Heaven. In the Indian culture it is tradition to bury a loved one with their most beloved possession; it might be a new blanket, a machete, or some other item that they highly treasured. In Paulina's case, they would bury her with her Bible and Baptismal Certificate over her heart, as she would have wanted to meet her Lord with His Word close by.

The certificate had her name written at the top, and the date of some six years previous to her death. No one had any idea as to when she was born, since birth certificates were unknown to her generation. We judged her to be about sixty-six years old at death. She had no doubt heard the name of Jesus for the first time at about age sixty when she gave her heart to Him. She was one of the first converts in the village. To plant the church in Nazaret was a great challenge, because drunkenness reigned and the drums beat long into the nights. Witchcraft was prevalent and revenge killings were not uncommon in their long history.

I related to the people that day my memories of the very first baptismal service in the village of Nazaret. After the Sunday morning service six years ago, fifteen new converts lined the bank of the Chiriaco River, receiving my instructions for that memorable occasion. A large crowd gathered to observe this moment in history. Men and women stood together in small clusters, with little girls standing very close to their mothers. Naked boys sat in long dugout canoes tied to the bank. The boys were diving and swimming in the backwater. The day was beautiful and the waters of the Chiriaco were cold as I stepped carefully into her dark depths. Positioning myself sideways against the swift current, I called the first name on the list. Digging my toes into the slightly sloping drop off, I braced myself, waiting for the first one to be led to where I was precariously standing. Occasionally I had to use my hands to push against the current to balance myself. One by one we baptized the group that day after they each gave a personal testimony of their faith in Christ, while those standing along the bank sang in their own language.

Finally it was Paulina's turn to be baptized. A young man helped her out to where I was waiting. I took a few steps closer to shore so that the water would not be over her head. Looking down into those dark eyes I said, "Dukuwachi (little grandmother), please give us your testimony."

She said, "I love the Lord with all my heart, and aim to serve Him until I die." She never spoke publicly, or taught a Sunday school class, but everybody learned from her example, especially the widows that filled the front benches every service. She faithfully served the Lord in those short six years as few people do.

We buried Paulina that unforgettable day in the village of Nazaret. Before returning home, I asked Antonio a question that weighed heavily on my mind. I wanted to know how she died. Does this Gospel we preach really change the lives of people that had for generations been enslaved to witchcraft, bound by superstitions, and shackled by the fears of the spirit world? I knew the answer, but I wanted to hear it from one of them.

"Doctor," Antonio began, "two nights ago Paulina took deathly ill, and we desperately wanted to take her to your clinic, but we had no mode of transportation. Darkness was settling in, so a great group of us went to her hut and asked if there was anything we could do for her."

She responded, "Please take me to the church."

Antonio continued, "We carried her on a split cane pole litter with a long procession of people following. Once inside the church, Pastor Alias Danducho asked Paulina what they could do for her now.

Alias was a wonderful pastor and loved his people very much. He was a miracle of God's grace, since before his conversion he had killed five people over the years. His was a life of revenge killing, and being greatly in tune with the spirit world.

She asked that they sing to her in the Aguaruna dialect the beautiful melodies that she had learned in the church. Singing filled the night as voices proclaimed the wonderful grace of Jesus. "Dukuwachi, can we do anything else for you?"

"Oh," she said, "please read God's Word and then pray for me." Our people usually pray out loud in unison, and that special night they prayed with great fervor and supplication on behalf of this dear lady. Shadowy figures were etched on the bamboo walls of the church that night under the faint yellowish, smoky light emanating from small wick lamps placed around the congregation. Silence filled the air as the service concluded. The men started to pick up her mat to carry her back to her home, when she stopped them with an upraised hand. "Don't take me home. Please leave me here in the church." She raised a little bony finger, pointed up to the sky, and in one breath said, "The gates are not open yet."

They went to their homes to eat and left her with her family. Later that night, a great crowd came back to the church to see how Paulina was doing. It was obvious to them that she was much weaker and that the end was very near. Pastor Alias asked her if there was anything that they could do for her. Paulina's skin was pale, her breathing labored, but a light penetrated through those dark, deeply sunken eyes as she responded, "Yes, oh yes, please sing to me." Again that great crowd joined in singing the glorious hymns of the Aguaruna church. The Bible was read and prayer offered up for this saintly woman of Nazaret.

Sensing that the end was near, the women folded their arms across their chests and their crying would soon begin. Paulina, with a weak soft voice, asked all of the women to gather around her bed. She then did the most unusual thing that we had ever witnessed among these people of the rain forest. Crowding in around her with anxious and surprised looks of anticipation, silence filled the room.

Every eye fastened on the frail little lady lying before them, wondering why she had called them together. Paulina spoke slowly, but with passion as she instructed these ladies in the ways of the Lord. "I am going to a better place," she told them, "and I want no crying, for I am going to be with Jesus." She then lifted her hand skyward, pointing with that bony finger toward the heavens, and said, "The gates are open." Closing her eyes, she traded that dirt floor, thatched-roof, bamboo-walled hut for a mansion in the sky.

I returned home rejoicing in the privilege of being a missionary in the northern Amazon of Perú.

Some weeks later I was back visiting in the Nazaret church on a Sunday morning. While speaking, I noticed the absence of Paulina. However, her place on the front bench had been filled by another little widowed lady. The offering was taken and all the ladies brought their baskets of first fruits to the altar of the church as per the example of Paulina. After the service, one of these dear ladies handed me part of the offering. It was a beautiful ripe fruit of which I am very fond. I said, "Thank you, lady friend."

She replied, "On my way to church this morning, I passed through the old garden of Paulina, and found this lovely fruit on one of her plants. Had she been here, she would have brought it herself."

'Yes,' I thought to myself, 'the spirit of giving lives on.'

Believe It or Not

Nurse Vicki's voice was full of emotion and bewilderment when she entered our house. "I was leaving the clinic," she said, "when I saw a casket sitting out front on the grass. Approaching the casket, I was startled when a pale-as-death man sat straight up, looked at me, and then lay back down."

"Vicki," I replied, "you have been in the jungle too long and you are beginning to imagine things." I had left the clinic earlier, leaving Vicki to attend to a few of the patients who were recovering from surgery. The rest of the medical team had followed me to the house leaving Vicki alone in the clinic.

Her story sounded bizarre, so I went to check it out. The clinic was a good quarter of a mile from our home and was located close to the dirt road that passed our mission station. Approaching the clinic, I noticed that there was a strange looking box-like object lying on the ground. Without warning, a thin emaciated looking form arose from the casket, sitting straight up looking at me. I looked into the ashen white face of a man with expressionless eyes that fixed their stare on me and then lay back down peacefully.

Immediately I recognized him as a patient who had come to our clinic several days earlier. His family had brought him from the distant Cenepa River, miles downstream, for me to examine. I remembered telling the family of my suspicion of abdominal cancer and that the prognosis was very grim. They were extremely frightened by this and wanted to know if there was anything that could be done. Desiring to give them every option, I said that they could take him to the regional hospital in Bagua many hours away over a very rough road for exploratory surgery. They left that day in the back of a fully loaded pickup truck for the distant city.

Exploratory surgery was performed, my diagnosis was confirmed, and the surgeon told the family that their loved one would probably not make it through the night. With heavy hearts, they bought an inexpensive casket to transport him back to the village. The next day, to their surprise, he was still alive. Their limited funds were running out so they paid passage on a pickup truck back to the jungle and their long trip home. The most comfortable place for their patient was in the casket. The truck was loaded with people, animals and the casket. Now they had to make the bumpy ride to the river where they would continue their journey by boat.

Hours later, the tired party arrived at our clinic and the man was still alive, lying in his casket. They knew that he was weak and dehydrated and desperately wanted to help him. They unloaded the casket, placing it on the grassy area in front of the clinic and set off looking for me. That is when Vicki came out of the clinic and saw the casket.

I was now kneeling down on the grass, taking his blood pressure and checking his vital signs as he lay in the casket. We decided to remove him from this

Vikki Briggs, Plymouth, Michigan

restricted space, place him in our recovery room, and begin intravenous feeding. In the recovery room, another man was connected to a catheter. To protect the casket from rain etc. we stood it up on end, leaning it against the wall between the two men. I don't know what was running through the minds of both men, but they probably thought that the one who goes first gets the box.

Two days later the man was still alive and they decided to take him home by boat. He was loaded into the casket, and we watched as if pallbearers were carrying a deceased loved one to be buried. The boat was loaded and downriver they disappeared. Several days later word reached us that he had indeed passed away. He was a wonderful Christian and had given a glowing testimony to his faith in the Lord. However, the experience lives on in the memory of two North Americans.

The Amazon Call

Persecution

"Doctor, Doctor," came the call that unforgettable night in the sleepy little mountain village of Colalla, Perú. The call had a certain ring of urgency to it and my tired body struggled to respond. "Doctor, we have to leave immediately and escape the area." My mind was trying to grasp the seriousness of the situation while fumbling around in the dark feeling for my flashlight.

Elvin, awakened from a deep sleep, slowly pulled back the heavy blankets, automatically scratching the raised welts from untold bites. "What is going on?" he asked. I quickly looked at my watch. It was two o'clock in the morning. The air was cold and clammy and we were engulfed in blackness. "Hurry," I said, "and get your things ready because we have to leave immediately and get down off of this mountain."

Pastor Rubio of the large Central Church in Chiclayo, Perú, had asked me if I would accompany Brother Tirado, a lay pastor, and Elvin, Pastor Rubio's sixteen-year-old son, to visit a new work in a very isolated part of the mountains. He asked if I could take my dental supplies and a small battery operated projector to encourage the new group of believers. Brother Tirado was a very patient older man who had planted several congregations in this distant area. He was tenacious and persistent and deeply loved these forgotten people of the highlands.

The Central Church would take offerings to help with his travel and he would go for a couple of weeks at a time. There were no evangelical churches in the area, but a deep hunger prevailed in the hearts of many for God's Word. He had a string of preaching points and many converts in Colalla, Santa Lucia, Guayllabama, Naranjo, Chiami and Wanama.

The people were fanatically attached to traditions and superstitions and had a great fear of the spirit world. It wasn't long until persecution of these new converts began to surface. At first it was just verbal threats, but it soon turned into physical violence. Word had filtered back to the Central Church of the suffering our people were going through. Their meeting place and several of the believers' homes were stoned in the dead of night, with the Christians huddling together in desperate prayer.

Pastor Mario with bandaged head

One dark night the home of Mario (the lay pastor) was attacked. They tied his arms and legs and carried him to the hacienda where they tried to force Yonqui (a very strong fermented beer made from sugar cane juice) down his throat. He struggled and resisted until his strength gave way. At that moment his wife burst upon the scene covering his mouth with her hand. The men finally in exasperation lifted him up in the air and let him fall to the ground with a thud. They left the scene and the members of the church helped him back to his home. Undaunted, Mario continued to preach.

On another occasion they threatened to burn Brother Tirado, but he escaped to Santa Lucia and continued preaching to his flocks high up in the mountains. Three of our young men were attacked and beaten one night. These new Christians needed encouragement.

The church in Chiclayo fasted and prayed for these valiant and determined Christians who counted their suffering but a small price to pay for their Lord and Savior.

Finally the day arrived. Supplies were purchased and my medical equipment was packed and readied for the journey to the little town of Colalla. I told my wife goodbye and not to worry, that everything would be fine. My mind was processing all the events of the last few months and the suffering of God's people. We drove the mission car along the northern desert area and turned east onto a dirt road that led us out across the flatlands and then ascended into the desolate hill country. The road became extremely rough with sharp narrow curves.

On the way to Colalla

The Amazon Call

At long last we came to a small open clearing at the end of the road where Mario was waiting. I looked all around and saw nothing but rocks, sand, and mountains that arose in the distance. It was so quiet and peaceful that one could hardly believe that persecution awaited us in these valleys and on the mountaintops.

The sun was overhead when we began our trek up the mountain. Elvin and I followed Brother Tirado and Mario single file around the innumerable curves on that hot dusty trail that led us deeper into the heart of the low mountains. At long last we came across a few scattered huts made of adobe clay. Some of the roofs were made of a thick straw-like material and others sported galvanized sheets of metal roofing. Along the way greetings were exchanged between the weary travelers and the local inhabitants.

Finally our small procession stopped at a beautiful adobe house situated on a hill under a cloudless blue sky. Suddenly a large crowd of people who shook our hands, exchanged hugs, and greeted us as if we were special dignitaries surrounded us. The sincerity and warmth of these wonderful people was overwhelming. All tiredness evaporated from my body and I felt invigorated and ready to work.

Soon our equipment was up and running. My dental chair that afternoon was a backless crude bench placed under the shadow of the roof. Who knows how many teeth were extracted from waiting and willing jaws. Most of these precious people had perhaps never seen a doctor before. The sun began dipping in the western sky announcing the soon arrival of a dark night. Supper was served, consisting of a huge plate of boiled potatoes, rice, and guinea pig.

We hung a sheet outside on one wall of the house and a great crowd gathered to view the life of Christ. The service went on into the night and was terminated at eleven o'clock. What a wonderful and blest evening it had been. I watched as people faded into the darkness, returning to their homes some distance away. I was standing alongside Brother Tirado and Pastor Mario when a voice called out in the darkness for Brother Tirado. Pastor Mario stepped forward telling us to wait while he went to see who would be calling for Brother Tirado at this hour.

Mario walked toward the voice that was calling for Brother Tirado, when all of a sudden the silence of night was broken by a piercing cry followed by the sound of feet running in the distance.

We stood frozen in time wondering what had taken place. Out of the darkness came Mario with blood coursing down his face from a huge gash on his forehead. His white shirt was covered in blood and he was holding his head. Immediately I retrieved my medical bag.

"What happened?" I asked while working feverishly to clean up the wound and bandage his head. He named the individual who was calling for Brother Tirado.

"When I approached him," he said, "I recognized the man as one of the strong opponents to the Gospel. I tried to reason with him, but he swung his saddlebag toward my head without warning. Inside the bag was broken glass that caused this terrible wound." The man turned and ran away into the night.

"Hurry, Doctor. You, Brother Tirado, and Elvin have to leave immediately, because he might come back with his friends who are capable of inflicting bodily harm," Mario insisted.

I turned on my flashlight and slowly climbed out of the flea-infested bed where I had spent a very restless night. Elvin and I had slept in the room that housed the saddles, blankets and gear for the pack animals. The fleas jumped from saddle blankets onto me and over to Elvin. It was a regular flea market with me being their chief source of food that short night.

"Mario," I said, " you come with us to the coast so that Pastor Rubio can see first hand what these people are capable of doing."

Some men of the church guided us down the mountain that dark cold night in complete silence in case they were lying in wait for us on the trail. Hurriedly we walked as the hours passed by. It was just about daylight when we reached the car. We arrived in Chiclayo at about nine o'clock Sunday morning.

We went directly to Pastor Rubio's home to inform him of the events of last night. When he saw Mario with his head bandage and shirt covered in blood, he said, "Don't clean him up yet," and he proceeded to call the missionary, Clyde Golliher, who came right over and took several photos of Mario.

Pastor Rubio took Mario under his care and I went home and prepared to attend the service that was to begin shortly. Addie and I were sitting in church surrounded by hundreds of people. Pastor Rubio was a very unique man, filled with the Spirit and extremely dynamic. His church had planted numerous new churches in the area. Chiclayo Central was truly a missionary church.

Soon the service began. Pastor Rubio went to the pulpit and began speaking about the new churches up in the mountains and the persecution that they had been facing. He continued in that vibrant way of his, reminding the congregation of our very recent trip to Colalla. "You know how some of our people there have been beaten, threatened, and their homes even stoned," he stated.

At that moment, he walked over to the edge of the large platform where a door led to one of the rooms that were used for dramas, etc. The door gave entrance to the platform. He paused, and then opened the door. Every eye focused on that door wondering what the pastor was doing. Pastor Rubio extended his hand and out walked Pastor Mario, head bandaged and shirt covered with blood.

Silence filled the air and instantly the entire church went to its knees crying and praying. The service was electrifying and the church was determined more than ever to support and nurture these valiant, courageous Christians of the mountains.

Monday morning Pastor Rubio went to a lawyer, presented the photos, and papers were immediately drawn up and presented to the Judge. Orders were sent to the police station to capture the perpetrator of this violence. He was brought before the Judge and in no uncertain terms denounced and sent back to Colalla to inform the people that any further disturbances would result in severe punishment.

That ended the persecution of our people and the churches were liberated from further hostility. Brother Tirado, Mario, and so many like them became instant heroes of mine. It has been my privilege to be associated with so many dedicated Peruvian Christians who have built the kingdom of God in their country.

The Amazon Call

Antivenom and Answered Prayer

The director of the Laboratory of Venomous Animals in the capital city of Lima visited our home on the Kusu River and asked me to collaborate with them in sending poisonous snakes to their facility in Lima so that they could extract the venom and prepare antivenom for use in the treatment of snakebite. Since I was treating the local population for snakebites, I agreed to do so.

The plan was for the Indians to bring me poisonous snakes that I would have to place in wooden boxes. He taught me how to identify the various species and label the boxes with names, dates etc. The key component to this enterprise was financial assistance for the people, since they would receive money for each snake according to its size and class. This was an excellent opportunity for our people to make some cash and also for us to receive antivenom.

Addie was very reluctant, because it was dangerous work and we would have to take the many boxes loaded with poisonous snakes in our carryall vehicle out to the coast to send them on to Lima. Sometimes we took the boxes all the way to Lima ourselves.

On one such trip we had several boxes loaded with over fifteen deadly snakes in the back of our vehicle. The road was rocky, rough, and full of huge potholes. Occasionally we would hit a big pothole and the boxes would fly into the air and then crash to the floor of the car with a thud. "Check the boxes, check the boxes!" Addie would scream to one of our children to make sure they were still intact.

That day we hit a huge pothole and every box flew into the air and crashed back to the floor of the car. "Check the boxes!" Addie screamed. At that moment she felt something wrap around her ankles and she shattered both of my eardrums with her desperate cry for help. She immediately looked down and saw that it was her sweater.

It wasn't long until our clinic became the main center for the treatment of snakebites in the entire upper Amazon. We instructed the people to bring the head of the guilty snake, so that it could be identified and thus administer the proper antivenom. There are three distinct families of poisonous snakes in the upper Amazon and thus three classes of antivenom to combat their poison.

Of the three families, two are of the pit viper variety with distinguishing features. They all have the common triangular head, vertical slits in the pupil (much like those of a cat), two nasal pits, and two sensory pits, one on each side between the eyes and nose (four pits altogether).

These pit vipers make up the largest classification of poisonous snakes in the Amazon. Of the two families the largest is the Bothrops with a large variety of snakes. The Bothrops are the most numerous of all pit vipers. Eight out of every ten snakebites in the Amazon are from this family. The venom is hemolytic, causing severe hemorrhaging. It breaks down the coagulating factor in the blood and thus the victim is bleeding intestinally and through the gums, eyes, ears, nose, and pores of the skin. If untreated, it can cause circulatory collapse and death. These snakes range in size, color, scale markings and habitats, but the symptoms are similar and the antivenom is inclusive.

"Teodoro was bitten by a snake!" came the call at the window of our home that Saturday morning.

"What kind of snake was it?" I asked. "He was bitten by a Boash," came the reply. Of all the pit vipers, the Boash is greatly feared. It is a small snake about one foot long that camouflages well with the ground covering. It's very difficult to see and I call it a heel biter. Immediately I retrieved a vial of antivenom anti-botropico from the refrigerator and headed for the clinic.

Teodoro was experiencing a burning pain in his foot. The fang marks were plain to see and the antivenom was administered. There is always a risk with the antivenom in that it is prepared from horse serum. The snakes we sent to the laboratory in Lima were milked and the liquid venom placed in a centrifuge, spun out and formed into crystals that were then processed and inoculated into horses that developed antibodies against the venom. The serum is extracted from the horses and thus the antivenom is prepared. The risk is an allergic reaction that can lead to anaphylactic shock and death. Teodoro was treated with antihistamine to ward off any allergic reaction. Adrenalin was always on hand in case the patient developed a severe reaction.

His vital signs were monitored all morning to determine how much venom he received from the bite. A large percentage of bites are not fatal as there are various factors to consider. If the snake has recently eaten, then his venom supply is limited. Once a snake is milked, it takes about fifteen days to restore its venom supply to full capacity. If an individual has been bitten after the snake has recently expended venom in killing its prey, then chances of survival are greatly increased.

If the patient has been bitten on the hand or face the consequences can be serious because of the abundant venous blood supply in these areas, thus the venom can reach the circulatory system faster and symptoms present rapidly. I believe that the amount of venom injected can depend on whether the snake is biting from an aggressive, defensive, or startled position, thus determining the amount of venom injected.

Two hours later, Teodoro began spitting up blood from bleeding gums. Each hour that passed the bleeding increased. Two days earlier we had extracted a molar tooth and now the hemorrhage migrated to this weakened spot in the tissue, and the bleeding from this socket increased. We knew that we were now in for a formidable battle. With the blood loss, his vital signs were weakening and his condition became very serious. We worked feverishly and prayed that God would touch this young man who was preparing for ministry to reach his people on the distant Santiago River.

The second class of pit vipers is the family Lachesis muta "shuchupe" or more famously known as the "Bushmaster." This adult snake can measure up to twelve feet in length with the capabilities of injecting as much as five cm. of very potent venom. The Bushmaster is extremely strong and nocturnal. Fortunately it accounts for a low percentage of bites, since it hunts at night and rests during the daylight hours.

I remember one instance when the helpers brought a nine-foot-long Bushmaster in a basket. Addie saw that snake and became very nervous, because she knew how dangerous they could be. The large box was prepared as well as my lasso and forked pole. I cut the vine that held the basket closed and let the unhappy penned-up snake crawl slowly out of the basket. Once out on the ground I quickly placed the fork end over the stout neck of this now mad snake. His coloring was beautiful with thick scales placed one over the other covering most of his body.

My helper prepared the lasso to place around the large triangular head at the neck level. In the blink of an eye that snake lifted my pole and freed his head and instantly coiled into a striking position. In that moment my helper turned and fled the scene leaving me frozen with fear only two feet from this awesome creature of the rain forest.

The afternoon hours waned on with no improvement in Teodoro's condition. Blood was seeping from the vacant tooth socket. In desperation we packed and sutured the gum together. It was tedious and time consuming but helped to stem the tide while God did the rest. The bleeding subsided and his vital signs improved. It was a close call, but God miraculously spared his life.

Bushmaster bites are notorious for their effect on the human body. The venom is a neurotoxin that can shut down the nervous system with dire consequences. The symptoms are severe pain, extreme swelling of the affected part, followed by collapse.

I stared into the large eyes with the vertical slits of this coiled serpent wondering when it was going to strike. They can strike about one third of their body length, and I knew that I was in that range. It seemed like the whole world came to a standstill. My helper was about thirty feet away, stunned into silence. Addie was standing on the small front porch of our home in stark fear.

His head was raised about ten inches higher than that strong, coiled body. At any moment I expected that quicker-than-a-flash movement when his head would thrust forward and sink two large hypodermics like fangs into my flesh. In that moment of indecision on the snake's part, I quickly jumped back out of striking range. He moved slightly, daring me to come closer. I managed once again to pin the head to the ground. My helper, with renewed courage, placed the hoop over the snake's head and we guided that incredible serpent into the box. I wasn't sure after that if I wanted to continue sending snakes to the laboratory, but as time wore on, and with more experience, I felt more comfortable dealing with these unusual creatures of nature.

The third class of poisonous snakes belongs to the Elapid family. They are rear fanged and must cling to their victim for a short moment while the venom runs down a grove along the fangs into the flesh of its prey. In the Amazon the most notable is the beautiful black, yellow, and red banded coral snake. The coral is very shy and usually found under rocks or debris of some kind, thus very few bites are reported.

It was the night before Thanksgiving and Addie had just turned off the Ham radio for her contact with our missionaries on the coast. The contact was set for 6:00 that evening, but there was no response to her call. Leaving the radio she stepped into the living room and glanced back over her shoulder to see the clock on the wall. It was 6:20 and at that moment she stepped on something rubbery. Addie was barefoot and knew instantly what it was. She felt the sharp burning pain in her toe and saw the snake slither away. Her screams awakened the dead and brought our son, Tim, and me running to the house. "What happened?" I asked.

Addie was crying uncontrollably and said, "I was just bitten by a cobra." She knew that we don't have cobras in the Amazon and hurriedly changed it to a coral snake. I asked her where it bit her. "On my toe!" she said.

Upon examination I could see the two fang marks. "Where did it go?" I asked.

She said, "Under there," pointing to our china cabinet. I flushed out the snake, pinned it down, and extracted the yellow, greenish venom from its fangs. It was a true coral snake, which has to be distinguished from the false coral that is not poisonous.

"Tim, get the ice. Addie, don't worry, you are going to be okay" I said, but I knew in my heart that this was serious. Coral venom is a neurotoxin, that if left untreated leads to a progressive deterioration of the nervous system and finally death. I usually maintained a good supply of antivenom on hand for the three classes of poisonous snakes.

Addie said, "If I'm going to be okay, why is Tim getting the ice? You don't have the antivenom for the coral snake do you?" she asked. She knew what was in the refrigerator, because when a snakebite case came to the clinic I would send a runner to the house, asking Addie to send me the appropriate antivenom.

"You are going to be fine," I said, trying to reassure her.

"You don't have the antivenom, do you?" she asked again.

"No, I don't," I stated with a voice that portrayed fear. "You are going to be okay and we are going to pray." All three of us prayed desperately that God would intervene and perform a miracle.

Word of Addie's condition spread like wildfire and students from the Bible Institute came to the house to pray for Dukuwa (Mother). They affectionately called her mother, because she was always doing special things for them and they loved her dearly. They returned to the library and had another season of prayer. I encouraged her to sleep while I monitored her vital signs all night long.

She awakened the next morning on Thanksgiving Day and we had a lot to be thankful for. Her foot was slightly swollen and it felt like a thorn was stuck in her toe. Addie complained of a film over her eyes. I told her that it was the end of the school year and she was grading a lot of papers. She said, "Yes, that is probably the reason." I didn't tell her until about two weeks later that the eye problem was one of the symptoms of coral venom.

We furloughed sometime later and happened to have services in Virginia. A wonderful layman who had been with us on several Work and Witness trips to Perú asked Addie if she had a problem at Thanksgiving time. "You haven't heard?" she asked. She then proceeded to tell him of the coral snake bite story.

He was absolutely amazed and related to her the following: The day before Thanksgiving he and his family went to visit his folks. In the afternoon he felt bothered and went to pray. He said Perú was brought to his mind and then Addie. He told the family to go ahead and eat while he continued to pray. He later told Addie that he finally felt relieved of the burden he carried for her and peace came over him. He looked at his watch and it was 6:20 P.M.

GOD STILL ANSWERS INTECESSORY PRAYER.

The Amazon Call

Monkey Mischief

Our washhouse was a tiny screened-in building between the house and clinic. It housed the old Maytag wringer washing machine and also doubled as the place where we hung huge stalks of bananas to ripen.

Every Saturday we cranked up the old diesel motor for Addie to do the weekly wash. Entering the washhouse, Addie said, "Hi Smoky." Our beautiful spoiled wooly monkey was sitting on the low roof, devouring a grasshopper. Addie never knew what she would find in the washhouse. There were at times large tarantulas, the occasional scorpion, and even a rare snake.

We also kept a large box of onions in the washhouse because our kitchen was so very small, leaving us no place to store them. While Addie did the wash, Smoky would inevitably eat a piece out of several onions then climb up on her shoulder and blow onion breath in her face.

One day she was pulling an article of clothing out of the water to run through the wringer, when she screamed loud enough to awaken the dead. Her hand shot up out of the water, shaking her finger violently and running into the house yelling that something bit or stung her.

Esteban, a young Indian boy who lived with us, ran to the washhouse and rapidly poked his hand into the water searching for the mysterious animal lurking in the soapy water. "Yeow," he yelled flinging his hand out of the water throwing the offensive object to the floor. Tim, our four-year-old son, came running into the washhouse and spotted the little four-inch-long fish lying on the floor and gleefully announced that it was "in my pocket." Tim was forever keeping souvenirs in his pockets.

The clothes were soon hung out on the line with clothespins holding them beautifully in place. The tubs were drained of water and Addie walked back to the house past the lovely clean wash drying under a bright tropical sky. A short time later she looked through the screen window just in time to see Smoky pinching the last few clothespins with her mouth and watching the last items of clothes bite the dust. She screamed at Smoky who looked at her with those innocent coal black eyes as if to say, "What fun!" Back outside, Addie went to hang up all of the clothes again.

Monkey Tales

"Doctor, would you like to buy this monkey?" I turned and looked into the eyes of a scared, shy, wooly monkey. She was definitely afraid of people. Her fur had a tinge of red indicating that she was malnourished. The stout vine around her neck had rubbed the skin raw and a light pale scar had formed. When I approached her with outstretched hand she pulled back, turning her head and shoulder as if to protect her body. It was obvious that she had been severely mistreated.

Addie couldn't stand the thought of this little terrified fuzz ball ending up in someone's soup, so she talked me into another act of insanity. With one hand I paid the man and reluctantly took the vine in the other. Immediately Addie, knowing that the way to win any heart is through the stomach, went straight to the house and brought out some food. This new addition to our family hesitated for a long moment, but hunger won the battle. She ate with great gusto but kept a wary eye on our every movement.

"What shall we name her?" Addie asked. I thought for a long moment, remembering that when we obtained our other wooly monkey, we wanted to name her Cheeta from the many Tarzan films that we had seen.

However, the children had said "No, let's name her Smoky because of her beautiful black coat of fur."

"Let's call this one Cheeta," I replied.

It wasn't long until she was swinging through the trees with Smoky the bandit, the monkey we had raised as a little orphaned baby. Smoky felt it her duty and obligation to teach Cheeta all the tricks of the trade. She taught her how to beg, cry, and steal. One day Addie made a delicious apple pie for the family. This was a real treat because apples were very difficult to find. "Please cut me a piece and put it on the table," I asked, "and I will eat it when I come back from the clinic."

Upon arriving back at the house, mouth watering for a piece of fresh apple pie, I was greeted with an empty plate. "Addie, I thought you were going to cut me a piece of pie."

"I did," she replied, "it's on the kitchen table." I looked out on the front porch and there was Smoky with that innocent look on her face.

Addie would take a bowl filled with red jell-o outside and then call the two tree swingers. Eyeing the bowl, they came swinging across the clothesline, plopping down on the front porch, desperate to see the contents of the bowl. Immediately Smoky climbed up one side of Addie's dress and Cheeta the other until they were on her shoulders, pulling her outstretched arms toward them to see what treat it held. Excitedly they plunged their faces into the cool squirmy Jell-O and slurped for all they were worth. They didn't stop until every last bite of this delicious sweet treat was gone. Looking at Addie with red plastered all over their faces, those mischievous eyes seemed to say, "Is that all?" From her shoulder they would jump onto the front porch railing and climb up under the overhanging roof to see what bugs and insects they could find to finish off their meal.

Natural Instincts

Every morning at 6:00 a.m., I would climb the 325 steps cut into the high hill that overlooked the Marañon River Valley below to attend the early prayer meeting with the students of the Bible Institute. We would meet in our little church to sing, pray, and begin yet another day of studies. After the service I said goodbye to the men and started back down the hill to have breakfast and participate in the activities of a new day. One fourth of the way down the steps I noticed something lying across the pathway perhaps ten feet below me. I stopped and saw a huge Jergon snake (pit viper) nearly five feet long stretched out and bathing in the early morning sunlight.

I called for the students to help dispose of this very poisonous serpent. I had treated many patients with antivenom for snakebite and thus wanted to remove this danger from our walkway. The students quickly terminated the life of this venomous animal with a powerful blow to the back of its head with a large stout pole. They were going to toss the dead snake over the hill, but I stopped them, because I wanted Addie to see it to remind her to always be careful when climbing the steps to the Bible Institute.

I carried the snake on a pole back down the hill to our house and stretched it out on the sidewalk right next to the front porch. The head was large and triangular in shape. There were two round pits on either side of the nose and two more between the eyes and nose. All pit vipers in the Amazon have the distinguished triangular head with the four pronounced round pits. Another prominent feature is the vertical slit in the pupil of each eye. All pit vipers have these vertical slits while most non-poisonous snakes have rounded pupils and only two nasal pits on a more rounded head.

Addie had prepared homemade donuts for breakfast that morning. Smoky and Cheeta were playing over by the clinic and had not seen me bring the snake home. Addie came outside to see the snake and carried a fresh sweet donut in each hand. She held the donuts in outstretched hands and called to the monkeys. They both loved sweets, especially homemade donuts. Smoky led the way with Cheeta bringing up the rear. Onto the clothesline they came, chattering and swinging hand over hand, rapidly approaching the porch. One last swing and they would be on the railing to grab their prize and head off into the jungle.

Just before jumping onto the porch, they spotted the snake lying on the sidewalk between them and the donuts. Both monkeys froze in midair, holding tightly onto the clothesline for dear life. They stared at the snake and didn't move a muscle. I picked up a stick and touched the head of the dead Jergon. The head jerked sideways with mouth open. Many times after killing a snake there can be a delayed nerve muscle reaction to a physical stimulus, thus causing the head to react. Smoky and Cheeta reacted automatically to that head jerking and were gone quicker than a flash. About twenty yards away they stopped, holding onto the clothesline in mortal fear, keeping a watchful eye on the snake.

Addie called for them to come and get the donuts, but to no avail. Both monkeys started crying, holding out their hands, begging Addie to come to them. They cried and came closer, but upon seeing the snake, retreated to safety. They desperately wanted the donuts but their natural instincts told them that this was a mortal enemy. It is interesting to note that although Smoky was orphaned when just a baby, and had been raised by humans, she still had that built-in fear of snakes. We watched with great anticipation as to what the monkeys would do.

Cautiously Smoky slowly walked the clothesline, keeping an eye on the snake. When she came to the end of the line, she jumped up onto the roof and then slid down to the railing, never setting foot on the ground. She leaped from the railing to Addie's shoulder, grabbed the donut, and exited the same way. Cheeta, the follower, did likewise and both tree swingers escaped into the jungle to enjoy their hard-earned treat.

Betrayed

Classes were over for the day and the students were heading down the trail to play soccer. Cheeta was high up in a tree that hung right over the trail leading to the soccer field. There was a large nest of wasps on a lower limb just above the trail where the students would pass by. She waited until they were right under that hidden nest of large black wasps, and then violently shook the limb. Angry wasps swarmed over the panic stricken students who were now running for their lives to escape their painful stings.

Cheeta watched with great amusement the yelling and flight of the students whose arms were flailing in every direction to ward off this angry mob. A few minutes later Cheeta saw another student approach the tree and she was ready to shake the limb and terrify the unsuspecting victim.

The students, now standing on the soccer field, saw what Cheeta was about to do, so in unison yelled to their friend, "Run, Cheeta is in the tree and she is going to shake the limb housing a wasp nest." The student ran as fast as he could before she had time to shake the limb. When she saw that her prey had escaped she was irate and screeched, fussed, and scolded the students for spoiling her fun.

Later that afternoon when the students returned from the soccer game they noticed that Cheeta was under the same tree, distracted, and looking for insects. One of the students quietly climbed the tree and was poised to shake the limb housing the wasp nest when Cheeta looked up and saw him there. She knew what he was going to do and started to cry. Frozen with fear Cheeta stood there shaking and unable to move. Needless to say, she never got that close to a wasp nest again.

No Name

"Yatsaju pujumatai, wainyami, Apajui yaimpakti." Goodbyes were being exchanged in the Aguaruna language as I turned toward the trail that led to the Kusu River where my boat was tied to a long cane pole jabbed into the soft mud at the port.

We had just concluded an afternoon service in the village of Chigkamai with the hope of planting a new church in this remote area. The sun was setting in the western sky as shadows engulfed the clearing, and still the formal goodbyes had to be said.

I faced each individual adult one at a time repeating the phrase, "Pujumatai." *(Goodbye, I am going, you stay).* And "Wainyami," *(I will see you later),* with "Apajui yaimpakti" *(God bless you)* being attached to it.

I waited patiently as each one repeated, "Ayu yatsaju, pumumatjai." *(Okay, I stay and you go).* And "Wainyami."*(I will see you).*

The last goodbye was uttered when the headman of the village called to me, asking if I could see a very sick girl in a nearby hut. Looking at my watch and checking the last rays of light I asked, "Where is she?" He pointed to a thatched roof hut on a hill not too far away.

Together we crossed the garden area, passing by the beautiful banana plants with their green-gold fruit ripening under a tropical sky. Finally we approached the hut and greetings were exchanged between the headman and the inhabitants inside as he told them that the doctor had come and was going to examine the sick girl.

Several lightweight upright posts were removed from their frame and a wedge opening was obtained, allowing us passage into the dimly lighted hut. My eyes soon accommodated to the semi-darkness as I observed my surroundings. It was a typical hut tucked away on the edge of their garden plot. The roof was made of thatched leaves tied onto the roof stringers with thin-stripped vines. The roof was designed to shed upwards of one hundred and fifty to two hundred inches of rain annually, withstand high winds, and provide coolness under a hot tropical sun. The walls of this one large room were made of bamboo (wild cane) poles lashed together with a stout vine. These poles were cut and trimmed from the low beaches and islands on the Marañon River. They had been tied into bundles and carried by dugout canoe to the village where the people shouldered them to the construction site. The straightest poles were selected and cut to make the split bamboo beds. The beds were located along the walls of this rounded hut.

Lying on the dirt floor not too far from the three logged cooking fire was the sick girl. Her dark sunken lifeless eyes fastened onto me as if to say, 'Can somebody please help me?' I returned her gaze and felt a sudden rush of sympathy for this emaciated child wrapped in dirty rags resting on a split bamboo mat. Her long black hair engulfed a frail thin face that portrayed long hours of suffering, giving her the appearance of an old woman in a child's body. Time was forgotten and not important as I contemplated one of the many reasons why I had come to the Amazon.

During the ensuing moments, the hut became a beehive of activity. Most of the men were ushered from the home, as it is not polite for a man to be present when a girl or woman is to be examined. Soon the last man disappeared through the opening left by the removed posts and I continued waiting, while sitting on a small hand carved stool. The women constructed a curtain of rags draped over a thick vine tied to two posts, thus shielding the sick child from the eyes of the world. With this done, I entered the parted curtain on the invitation of one of the ladies.

Kneeling down on both knees, I asked where she hurt. Under the scrutiny of many eyes, I examined the upper thigh area of the affected leg to find a swollen, hot, inflamed and seeping sore. The range of motion was limited, the infection rampant, and the diagnosis of osteomyelitis was made. 'This child needs immediate attention,' I softly whispered to myself.

Upon arising and looking at my watch, I turned to the headman and told him that she must be brought to the clinic tomorrow to begin antibiotic therapy. Again, goodbyes were exchanged and

I turned toward the trail that led to the river and home. Returning to the mission station just before darkness settled in over the rain forest, I wondered if they would bring her in the morning.

Days swiftly passed and with the heavy responsibilities of clinic and church work the young girl's face was crowded from my mind. Her family failed to grasp the importance and criticalness of her condition, so she was not brought to the clinic. Two weeks later we made another trip to the village to encourage the growing group of believers. After a wonderful service, goodbyes were exchanged and again I was heading for the trail that led to the river and home when the headman stopped me in my tracks.

"Doctor," he asked, "do you remember the young sick girl you examined sometime back?" as he pointed to the hut on the hill. Looking in that direction past the gardens to the bamboo hut located in the clearing, I replied affirmatively. My mind quickly retreated back two weeks as images of those haunting eyes were called to memory.

"How is she, and why didn't the family bring her to the clinic?" I asked. He lowered his gaze, visibly embarrassed, and replied that the local witchdoctor had been treating her as the family believed her to be bewitched. The now-familiar story of yet another critical case being treated by the witchdoctor caused me to ponder the deep spiritual darkness that our people were enslaved to. They lived under the bondage of the unknown and intense fear of the spirit world. The family had given him animals and gifts and now had nothing left to give.

He continued, "The nights are long in our village as her desperate agonizing cries awaken the entire populace. Her screams cause the dogs to bark and the children cry out in fear. Everyone is unnerved by sleepless nights. Would you please examine her again, since it is evident that the witchdoctor is not having success?"

We climbed the hill overlooking the village and once again entered the same hut we had visited two weeks earlier. Immediately my attention was drawn to the emaciated, dehydrated child lying on the same mat among the filthy rags. Her sunken dark eyes pleaded for help. Her plight was one of the most pitiful that I had witnessed in the tribe. Her skin was as pale as death and her bones protruded from her fever-racked body. Rapidly the women prepared her for examination.

The Amazon Call

My previous diagnosis was intact and she was in agonizing distress from this acute inflamed osteomyelitis. The slightest touch produced unbearable pain, causing her to scream out for relief. I turned to the family and reminded them of my diagnosis of two weeks earlier. I had warned them that if they didn't bring her to the clinic that she would end up a crippled little girl.

Now I told them that she will be a cripple and if they don't bring her soon, she will lose her life. "She must be brought to the clinic no later than tomorrow," I stated and prepared to leave them pondering the consequences. The family considered my words with great concern as I bid them goodbye.

The next day I was busy in the clinic when a great commotion was heard from the direction of the river. Looking out of the screened window, I saw a large dugout canoe loaded with excited people pulling into our port. There were men in the front of the canoe and then a large space in the middle with another group of men sitting in the back of the craft. The space in the middle was covered with a small canopy of leaves and I knew that the little girl was lying on a bamboo mat in the middle of the canoe, protected from the hot sun by the shaded canopy.

Another canoe pulled alongside and it was filled with women, crying that the little girl was going to die. I watched as the men lifted the mat from the bottom of the dugout and made their way up the two hills toward the clinic. I hurriedly prepared the examining table to receive her, hoping that we could spare her life.

Every jolting step they took extracted screams of agony from her pain-racked body. The clinic door was thrust open and the patient was ushered in. Immediately I prepared an injection to relieve her suffering as she had been in pain far too long. Her body had wasted away until there was very little muscle tissue left to receive the injection. We tried to gently roll her over to give the intramuscular shot in her hip, but the movement brought forth immediate screams from her dry parched lips.

Several people helped suspend her body from the table, and the injection was finally given in that suspended position. Soon her frail body relaxed for the first time in perhaps months from the severe pain that had held her captive.

The family members left for the village, leaving her in our hands and the care of her ancient grandmother. We soon learned that she was an orphan girl being raised by this elderly lady. This precious little woman stood about four-feet six-inches tall, maybe weighing ninety pounds. She wore the typical one-piece dress made of a large rectangular cut of material that was drawn around her body and knotted over the right shoulder. It was gathered at the waist and held there by a stout strand of vine.

Since she was very poor, at night she would untie the knot and use the dress as a blanket to ward off the cool damp tropical air. She never spoke, but observed everything we did. She had never been inside a clinic in her entire life. The absence of teeth made her thin lips pucker inward. She would stand nearby with bony arms folded across her chest watching every move I made with those small dark eyes. She lovingly cared for her granddaughter, tending her every need. The treatment was long and tedious, but the young patient's progress was good, and grandmother nodded her approval with each passing day.

Approaching the clinic one morning, I noticed a small group of people gesturing and laughing just outside the door. Grandmother was popping little round objects into her mouth, obviously enjoying a special treat that her family had brought from the village. I greeted them and then was invited to participate in the food fest as they gave me several of the round little objects. Hesitatingly I popped one into my mouth munching a crusty, crunchy, smoke flavored ball of unusual taste and smell. The taste was minimal except for the wood smoke they had been cooked on, and the consistency was like that of burnt pie dough. I politely turned down a second helping, leaving Grandma gumming the little tidbits with a satisfied grin. Grandma finally finished eating her delicacy and bid the visitors goodbye as they were ready to return to the village.

She followed the age-old custom of her people by grabbing each woman and child by the shoulders and blowing into their mouths. Evidently this was her way of giving her blessings to loved ones. She watched with loving affection as her family descended the hillside, entered their waiting canoes, and headed for home. I was so glad that I wasn't leaving that day.

We found out later that the little round objects were flying termites. During the month of April each year, a special termite leaves the large hole in the ground where they are housed to explore the world around them. The Indians have prerecorded this event and date in their minds. They are ready to harvest these large insects by reaching into the hole before they have a chance to fly away, and gather them in large quantities. They rip off the wings, legs, and antenna and toast the large round head and body of these flying insects over an open fire.

We realized very soon that our young patient did not have a name. It was custom to not name a baby girl until another child was born into the family, thus warding off the evil spirits. Our patient, now about twelve years old, was accustomed to being called 'she,' 'it,' 'her,' 'nawanta' *(daughter)*, and 'uchi' *(child)*. She responded to all of the above since she was an orphan and being raised by her little grandmother.

One day Addie decided that it was time to give our patient a name, as she was tired of referring to her as the little girl. She made up a long list of names and was ready to leave the house for the clinic when she thought of one last name that she jotted down before exiting the house.

Arriving at the clinic, Addie asked if she would like to have a name. She was so excited over the prospect of having a name that her dark eyes lit up with joy. As each name was read, Addie waited for the response. "Nakitajai" *(not that one)*, came the reply. The end of the long list was coming nearer and 'nakitajai' had been repeated so many times that Addie felt a little distressed. Finally the last name, Ester, was pronounced and a light flashed in the girl's countenance and her face lit up as she triumphantly said, "Wakeajai" *(I want that name)*.

From then on she became Ester *(Esther)* of the jungle. How fitting that she unknowingly would take the name of a great beloved, sacrificial missionary who gave her life for these people called Aguaruna many years ago. Esther Carson Winans began translating the Aguaruna language in the middle of the 1920's just before her life was shortened immediately after childbirth in 1928.

For a number of days now, Addie had been delivering food items cooked in her kitchen to help supplement the meager and starchy diet of our two precious ladies interned in the clinic. Protein in the form of meat had been almost non-existent and grandmother would receive the food offerings with eager hands, and then proceed to remove pieces of tomatoes, onions and anything else of a suspicious nature that she thought might cause harm to her already sick granddaughter. Custom dictated the abstinence of certain foods, both on the part of the patient and the family to ensure full recuperation. We had struggled with these concepts so many times in the past that it was rather amusing, but in many cases presented serious consequences. Sometimes the prohibited foods were exactly the ones we felt they needed for tissue repair.

Ester and the little grandmother had only one dress each, made of the one piece of local fabric that was well worn and stained with many years of constant use. One day Addie observed grandma washing Ester's dress in the river, and then spreading it out over the branches of a bush to dry. With that done, she went into deeper water and removed her dress, washing it, and then handing it to a lady friend to spread it over another bush to dry. Grandma remained in the cold water until her dress was dry. Then a friend handed it to her and she emerged from the river, draping the dress over her wet body little by little.

Later that day when I returned home, Addie was taking two dresses from her closet, announcing that she was going to the clinic to give each of them a dress. She said, "I am so much larger than they are, but at least they will have something else to wear." As she entered the door, Grandma automatically backed up to Ester's bed and watched as Addie approached. Their eyes and smiles told it all as they each clutched a dress, and eagerly drew it to them as if they had received a million dollars. This was the first present they had ever received. Now they each had a new dress and this was time for spontaneous chatter between them as Addie left the clinic for home.

Days lazily passed as time seemed to stop in this part of the world. With each passing day, Ester was healing. The pain had subsided, the fever was abated, and the lost smile returned to rosier cheeks. To the joy and answered prayers of many, another life had been positively touched through the compassionate ministry of the church. Grandma's smile reflected the trust that had replaced the fear of the unknown. Her life had been deeply touched by the prayers and concern shown by so many.

The infection was under control, Ester was sitting up and some resemblance of health was returning to that now-radiant face. Their departure date and return to the village was nearing. We and other Christians who lived on the mission station had prayed with them every night during the long road to recovery.

The Amazon Call

One dark, dark evening Addie announced that she was going to the clinic to share Jesus with Grandma and Ester. She took her Bible and a young girl to help translate and they disappeared into the night. I sat dumbfounded, for Addie never went out into the night unless I was with her. It had to be the Lord speaking to her as she went to harvest a well-cultivated crop. A loving compassionate ministry will always pave the way for positive results. Addie opened the clinic door and Grandma immediately migrated towards Ester with those two bony arms folded across her chest wondering what this late night visit meant. She had never received a visit from Addie in the dark of night before. Ester turned on her side, and then sat up, smiling, as Addie approached the two ladies. Greetings usually consisted of Addie speaking and both of them nodding their approval.

With formalities over, Addie preceded to share with them the wonders and faithfulness of Jesus Christ. Ester and Grandma listened intently that beautiful tropical night to the claims of Christ on their lives. These last two weeks had been a whirlwind of activity centering around a group of people intensely involving themselves in the life of a young orphaned girl. They had seen the church in action through its compassionate ministry and desire to share. The seed had been planted, watered, cultivated, and now was the time of harvest.

That night, in a little clinic in the middle of the jungle, two precious people came to know the Christ of Calvary, and their lives were changed forever. Addie was deeply moved by their positive and simplistic sincerity in accepting the Lord. She was leaving the clinic, excited to share the news with her family of the response of Ester and Grandma and their desire to follow Christ. As she turned the doorknob, ready to exit into the darkness of night, she was stopped by the first words Grandma had spoken in two weeks. "Nawanta" *(daughter)*! Addie recognized the endearing expression used affectionately only between two women and stopped. She turned to face Grandma and listened as the older woman began talking. "Thank you," she said, "for no one ever told me this before." Addie looked into that ancient face, smiled, and the bond was cemented cross-culturally between two of God's choicest creations. She gently closed the clinic door and floated home to share the good news with her family.

Ester was terribly crippled and would have to bend over, swing her leg way out, and plant it before taking another step. The day finally arrived and she was released to go back to her village.

I watched from the clinic as she proudly walked, unaided, to the long sleek black canoe and took her place on a small hand carved stool in the middle of the homemade craft. Grandma sat directly behind Ester and their going was much different than their coming. The women chatted incessantly and pointed wildly to the beauties of the river and rain forest. Paddles dipped into the water and the canoe disappeared around a bend in the river.

Sunday morning brought a beautiful day on the banks of the Kusu River as people began gathering for church. Canoes of every description glided into the port and soon our parking lot was full. Others came by trail, walking one half hour from the village of Chipe. By 9:00 a.m. we were climbing the three hundred and twenty-five steps to the top of the hill where the church was located.

Entering the church, we saw Ester and Grandma sitting in the front on a backless bench. They had come from the village, leaving early in the morning. Ester had to walk a long way to board a canoe and travel one-half hour to the mission station. She then climbed those painful 325 steps to the church. We were amazed to see them there. All through the service Ester sat with her arms outstretched as if to say she wanted more, more of the singing and preaching.

Every Sunday this process was repeated, and soon it was time for our furlough. We were gone for a year, and our first Sunday back was one of great excitement. Addie noticed that Ester and Grandma were not in their usual places on the front row, and, in fact, were nowhere to be seen. She started to ask someone about them, but people kept crowding around to greet her and ask questions about our year in the United States.

Time slipped away in each of the first two Sundays. On the third Sunday, Addie emphatically called a halt to the questioning and asked about Ester and Grandma. "Where are they? I notice that they have not been here for three Sundays. Are they sick? Do we need to send them medicine or have they moved to another village?"

The noisy chatter ceased for a long moment, then someone from the village spoke, "We forgot to tell you that when you were in your homeland last year, they both passed away. Ester developed epilepsy and while she was down at the river she had an attack, fell into the water, and drowned. Grandma died of old age." Those words landed like a ton of bricks. Addie was devastated at hearing the news of their demise. She had anticipated seeing them both upon returning to the jungle. For several days she was haunted by the reality that they both were gone, then one day the realization struck her that two people are now in Heaven because she finally had said, 'Yes,' to God's call on her life. What if she had not obeyed that call? Would someone else have gone to tell them of His love?

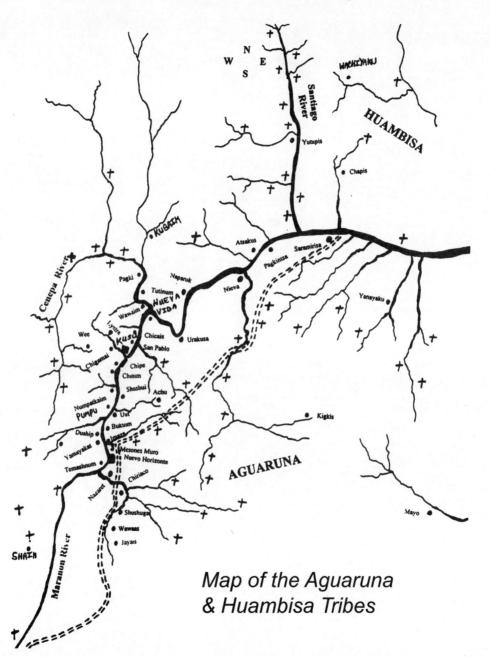

Map of the Aguaruna & Huambisa Tribes